MW01634361

Sister

TO THE

PROPHET

Sister
TO THE
PROPHET

THE LIFE OF
*Katharine Smith
Salisbury*

KYLE R. WALKER

Religious Studies Center
Brigham Young University

Published by the Religious Studies Center, Brigham Young University, Provo, Utah, in cooperation with Deseret Book Company, Salt Lake City, Utah. Visit rsc.byu.edu.

Cover and interior design by Carmen Durland Cole.

ISBN 978-1-9503-0457-8

Library of Congress Cataloging-in-Publication Data
Names: Walker, Kyle R. (Kyle Rex), author.
Title: Sister to the prophet : the life of Katharine Smith Salisbury / Kyle
  R. Walker.
Description: Provo, Utah : Religious Studies Center, Brigham Young
  University ; Salt Lake City, Utah : Deseret Book Company, [2024] |
  Includes bibliographical references and index. | Summary: "This is a
  biography of Katharine Smith Salisbury, the longest-surviving member of
  the Joseph Sr. and Lucy Mack Smith family. The book is based on a cache
  of letters, interviews, and recorded speeches. It records a life of
  challenges, including religious prejudice and ostracism. Three of
  Katharine's children died in infancy. Her husband was only
  intermittently available as a provider. The Salisburys were driven from
  Ohio and Missouri, and her husband died at forty-four. Through all these
  challenges Katharine remained loyal to her brother Joseph Smith Jr.,
  vouching for his prophetic appointment. The challenges she endured
  solidified her commitment to take up her cross for the cause of her
  faith"—Provided by publisher.
Identifiers: LCCN 2024007327 | ISBN 9781950304578 (hardcover)
Subjects: LCSH: Salisbury, Katharine Smith, 1813–1900. | Smith family. |
  Smith (Family : 1796– Smith, Joseph, Sr., 1771–1840) | Church of Jesus
  Christ of Latter-day Saints—History—19th century. | Reorganized Church
  of Jesus Christ of Latter Day Saints—History—19th century. | Latter
  Day Saint women—Biography. | Latter Day Saint churches—History—19th
  century. | LCGFT: Biographies.
Classification: LCC BX8695.S2 W35 2024 | DDC 289.3092
  [B]—dc23/eng/20240323
LC record available at https://lccn.loc.gov/2024007327

DEDICATED

*to three generations of women
who have had a profound influence
on my life:*

FOR MY MOM, Sharon Jensen Walker Haworth,
who shares the grit of our pioneer forebears
and ensured that both our home and
her children's intellect blossomed as the rose.

FOR MY WIFE, Daylene, whose generous heart
and vibrant faith have been a blessing
to all those who know her.

FOR MY DAUGHTER, Kelsie, whose sensitivity
and kindness have made her
a peacemaker wherever she goes.

Contents

Acknowledgments

SHORTLY AFTER THE RECONSTRUCTION of the Nauvoo Illinois Temple, I was busily engaged researching for a book that would explore the lives of each member of the Joseph Sr. and Lucy Mack Smith family. While researching in Carthage and Macomb, Illinois, I was thrilled to discover property records that helped establish where Lucy Mack Smith and the three Smith sisters lived in the decades after the deaths of Joseph, Hyrum, and Samuel Smith that fateful summer of 1844. I was able to locate, photograph and document those sites to include in several publications written about Katharine and her sisters.

An unexpected result of that research trip was locating and connecting with many of Katharine's descendants who still resided in western Illinois and southeastern Iowa. While in Nauvoo, I met Estel Neff, who owned a used bookstore on Mulholland Street. I was delighted to discover that he was direct descendant of Katharine Smith Salisbury through her eldest son, Solomon, and we quickly formed a fast friendship. Estel shared with me many stories of the Salisbury family who remained in the area after the main body of Saints migrated to Salt Lake City in 1846, and he directed me to other family members who still resided in the vicinity. One of those was Mary Dennis, who lived across the Mississippi River in Burlington, Iowa; was a descendant of Katharine's son Don Carlos; and had inherited most of Katharine's surviving family mementos. I vividly recall the day she brought out a photobook owned by Katharine with pictures of Emma Hale Smith, William B. Smith, George A. Smith, and a host of other Smith relatives. Mary also had in her possession a locket containing a photograph of her husband, Jenkins; an original letter sent to Katharine by Brigham Young; a cache of Civil War letters written by her son Don Carlos; several early family histories; and other treasured heirlooms. Mary was anxious to have those items conserved in a repository so they could be appreciated by future generations, and I was grateful that she trusted me and Brigham Young University librarian David Whittaker to help facilitate their transfer to the L. Tom Perry Special Collections in Provo, Utah. Mary ended up becoming a close family friend, and those materials she had carefully safeguarded for decades substantially contributed in telling Katharine's story. Now, some twenty years after that original research trip, a full-length biography of Katharine Smith Salisbury has finally come to fruition.

As with any book, many have labored behind the scenes to help make this manuscript a reality, and I want to express my appreciation for their contributions. Foremost among them is the Community of Christ Archives staff in Independence, Missouri, where most of Katharine's surviving documents, photographs, and letters are housed. Rachel Killebrew has been especially helpful in locating archival materials and has always been prompt in responding to my research requests. Lachlan Mackay, a historic sites director and apostle in the Community of Christ, has also aided with my research needs, including providing photographs of several quilts made by Katharine. Ronald Romig, former Community of Christ archivist, was also helpful in locating materials on Katharine when I first began my research on the Smith family several decades ago.

I would also like to acknowledge the assistance of Keith Bruns, research specialist at the Hancock County Historical Society in Carthage, Illinois, who helped in tracking down materials related to Katharine's descendants, including providing sources related to the murder of Alvin Salisbury. Katharine descendants Mary Dennis, Tom and Carla Duke, and Estel Neff were instrumental in locating and sharing Salisbury family materials, including letters and photographs in their possession that have been used in the book. Gracia N. Jones, a representative of the Smith family organization, has also been generous in sharing photographs and other historical items with me throughout the writing of this book. Elspeth C. Young generously allowed me to use a recent painting she did of Katharine and her son Solomon entitled *Shall We Not Go On* that depicts preparing for the migration from Ohio to Missouri.

I have appreciated the input of several colleagues in the Department of Religious Education at BYU–Idaho for their helpful suggestions, including Ryan Gardner, John Thomas, and Nathan Williams. Also, Phillip Allred and Dale Sturm, who both served as the department chair of Religious Education, and Reed Stoddard, my direct supervisor, were all supportive of my research efforts through the years. I want to acknowledge those at the Church History Library in Salt Lake City, who have been untiringly helpful. Mark L. Staker has been particularly supportive in locating materials at the Church History Library in Salt Lake City and has generously shared sources related to his own research on the Joseph Sr. and Lucy Mack Smith family. David Whittaker, John Murphy, and Cindy Brightenburg were effective in researching Smith family sources located at the L. Tom Perry Special Collections at Brigham Young University in Provo, Utah. Several private historians have been generous in sharing sources with me that have strengthened this biography. Bill Shepard has been very gracious in sharing numerous sources with me related to James J. Strang as I have gathered material on Katharine Salisbury and William B. Smith through the years. David and Sue August were supportive of a research trip to Voree, Wisconsin, and I appreciate their encouragement of my research interests over the course of this project. Brigham Young University faculty member Alexander L. Baugh kindly shared several early photographs that were used in this volume. Robert Cook has also been helpful in tracking down property records and locating historic sites related to the Salisbury family in Hancock and McDonough Counties.

I want to thank the staff at the Religious Studies Center, who collectively have lent their efforts in bringing this manuscript to publication. Jared Ludlow, Leigh Ann Copas, and Brent Nordgren have been supportive and interested in the manuscript from the beginning. Devan Jensen and Emma Eastman, who served as copy editors, were a pleasure to work with and helped improve the manuscript and contributed substantially to its publication. Carmen Cole has been most helpful in assisting with the photographs, cover design, and layout of the volume.

Finally, I appreciate the support of my family on the many research trips to notable historic sites, and to not-so-notable cemeteries on meandering country roads in Illinois. I appreciate the tried patience of my children—Joshua, Drake, Kelsie, Andrew, and Kyler—who have often grumbled, "Not another cemetery!" I hope that they will someday understand and appreciate my passion for church history. I also want to recognize the constant support of my spouse, Daylene. She has been wonderfully supportive of my research interests, and due to her talents and endearing personality, has become a contributor to many historical organizations. She is my best friend, and I love the life we have built together.

Introduction

Katharine was the longest-surviving member of the Joseph Sr. and Lucy Mack Smith family, passing away at the age of eighty-six, on February 2, 1900. Her longevity meant that she, unlike her two sisters, had ample opportunity to record her history, including a cache of letters, interviews, and recorded speeches that help document her remarkable life. She is one of a small cluster of first-generation female members of the Church of Jesus Christ of Latter-day Saints for whom a full-length biography can be written. One researcher has estimated that in the archives of the church, men's diaries and histories outnumber women's ten to one, making it difficult to document women's lives and experience.[1] The same, if not a greater disparity, holds true in the Community of Christ's Library-Archives. "Although limited education may have contributed to the scarcity of women's writings" among female Saints, explained Laurel Thatcher Ulrich, "a more important factor was the cultural assumption that their words—like their duties—were essentially private and therefore beyond the reach of history. Men, not women, routinely served missions, and diary keeping was a missionary duty."[2] Thus, Katharine's recollections, despite most coming later in life, contribute to our appreciation of women's lived experience and contributions in the early church, as well as enriching our understanding of the founding family of the Restoration.

Katharine was one of eleven family members who were present during the time her brother Joseph recounted his earliest visionary experiences. She was at home when her brother retrieved the Book of Mormon plates from a hiding place in the woods in late September 1827 and was active in protecting the plates during those few months while the plates were housed in the Smith home. She attended the meeting of church organization on April 6, 1830, and was baptized at the first church conference held a few months later, on June 9, 1830. Katharine also attended the dedication of the Kirtland Temple and contributed significant work efforts to the interior of the finished edifice. She migrated with the Saints from New York to Ohio, then to Missouri, and finally to Illinois. Before her family's move to Illinois, she was often present at major church events, as she frequently resided with her parents in Kirtland and in Missouri, even after her marriage to Jenkins Salisbury in 1831. Thus, Katharine's surviving recollections about early church history contribute to our understanding of these early Restoration events, particularly from a Smith family perspective. Her recitals about the First Vision, Moroni's visits, her company's migration to Kirtland, and the hostilities the Saints experienced in Missouri and Nauvoo contain details that are not mentioned in any other source.

Katharine's recollections are also critical in understanding the views of Smith family members as to why they did not follow Brigham Young's leadership after the year 1846. William Smith, the only surviving male member of the Smith family after the summer of 1844, had a profound influence on his sisters, including his advocating for lineal succession after his own clash with leaders at Nauvoo in the year 1845. Nowhere is William's teachings and influence on his siblings more evident than in the surviving writings of

Katharine and her posterity. However, unlike William's persisting hostility towards the Mountain Saints, Katharine's attitude towards those in the West softened during the final decades of her life. More so than any of her siblings, Katharine maintained positive exchanges with church leaders in Salt Lake Valley, as well as with her Smith nephews as they crisscrossed through Illinois during their missionary travels. Those documented interactions fill important gaps in the historical record, resulting in a more nuanced understanding of the relationship between surviving Smith family members in the Midwest and church leaders in the West during the second half of the nineteenth century.

During the decade of the 1870s, Katharine and her children linked themselves with the Reorganized Church of Jesus Christ of Latter Day Saints (RLDS, now Community of Christ). In her final years, she was viewed as a living link between the early church, which her brother Joseph had founded, and the Reorganization, led by her nephew Joseph Smith III. Because of the respect RLDS church members held for the Smith family, Katharine was afforded privileges that were denied other women of her day, including speaking at the Church's general conference and sitting on the stand at RLDS district meetings. In both the venue of RLDS conferences, and with the publication of her letters in the church-sponsored newspaper the *Saints' Herald*, Katharine found channels where she could express her views. Through these mediums she often recounted her recollections of early church history and perpetuated feminine ideals, much like her mother Lucy had done in Nauvoo in an earlier era.

Katharine's life was filled with hardships and challenges. Beginning in her teen years, her life was riddled with religious prejudice and the resulting ostracism she experienced from her peers. After her marriage, three of her children died in infancy. She experienced a challenging marriage to her husband, who was only intermittently available as a provider and vacillated in his loyalty to the faith she espoused. This led to a life of poverty and struggle, made more challenging when the Salisburys were driven from Ohio and Missouri in company with the Saints, and more especially after her husband passed away at forty-four. Raising four boys as a widow in rural Hancock County, Illinois, surrounded by neighbors who had earlier driven the Saints from town, she and her children continued to experience untold hardships as her connection to Joseph Smith became known to neighbors. Through all these challenges she remained loyal to her brother, vouching for his prophetic appointment for the remainder of her life. She successfully perpetuated that belief to her posterity. Her faith in Christ and in her brother's teachings helped her endure life's hardships.

Notes

1. Maureen Ursenbach Beecher, introduction, "The Life Writings of Ordinary Women," in *The Personal Writings of Eliza Roxey Snow*, ed. Maureen Ursenbach Beecher (Salt Lake City: University of Utah Press, 1995), xv, as cited in Laurel Thatcher Ulrich, *A House Full of Females: Plural Marriage and Women's Rights in Early Mormonism, 1835–1870* (New York: Alfred A. Knopf, 2017), xxi.
2. Ulrich, *A House Full of Females*, xxi. Ulrich notes as an example that out of the 114 missionary diaries digitized by Brigham Young University Library, only five were written by women (401–2n28).

CHAPTER ONE

Farm Work and Faith— Palmyra Childhood

*I saw two stout, bare-footed girls, each with a tin bucket of red raspber-
ries. . . . There was no lack of these, and if any left the table without a
really good supper, it was not the fault of the hostess.*
—Thomas Gregg

TIMES WERE CHALLENGING for the Joseph Sr. and Lucy
Mack Smith family as they entered the second decade of their marriage. Several failed business ventures left the growing family destitute, and poverty kept them on the move through the New England
countryside as they attempted to find a location where they could eke
out a living for their growing family. Katharine was born July 28,
1813, at Lebanon, Grafton County, New Hampshire, the seventh
surviving child and second daughter of Joseph Smith Sr. and Lucy
Mack Smith.[1] In the year preceding her birth, typhoid fever raged
through the upper Connecticut Valley, which escalated to epidemic
proportions, killing more than six thousand people in five months.[2]
The disease eventually infiltrated the Smith home. While pregnant

with Katharine, Lucy spent the better part of three months caring for her eldest daughter, Sophronia.

In time, all the Smith children eventually contracted typhoid fever. While ten-year-old Sophronia nearly died, and seven-year-old Joseph Jr.'s bout led to osteomyelitis that came close to causing the amputation of his leg, all the family eventually recovered. These experiences exhausted Lucy's strength to its limits and reduced the family's limited financial resources. After nearly a year of "sickness and distress," Lucy recounted, "health again returned to our family, and we most assuredly realized the blessing."[3] Katharine's birth corresponded with the family's improving health and was a welcome distraction from the challenges of the previous year.[4]

The Smiths' limited financial resources kept the family on the move, this time back across the New Hampshire border into Norwich, Vermont, before Katharine had even reached her first birthday. Here they attempted to farm, but three consecutive years of crop failures eventually led to the decision to leave the region for good. Katharine was only three when her parents decided to relocate in the winter of 1816–17, a move compelled by poverty and reports of plentiful crops of wheat raised in Western New York. Joseph Sr. went ahead of the others and decided to settle at Palmyra, New York, and soon afterward arranged for his family to follow.[5]

Lucy's resourcefulness was evident as she prepared for the journey, settling the family's debts in her husband's absence and finalizing arrangements with a teamster named Caleb Howard to transport their belongings. Lucy said she had barely eight cents in her pocket when they arrived in Palmyra, and even their eldest daughter Sophronia's precious earrings were sold to help defray expenses to pay for the trip.[6] If it wasn't for her resolve and quick thinking en route, the family might have arrived in New York more destitute than they already were. Howard attempted to take both the horses and wagon when the company had stopped in the town of Utica, New York, until Lucy fortuitously created a public scene, causing Howard to retreat from his plan. Now without Howard's services, Lucy led out in ensuring the family completed their journey to Palmyra, where

Eastern view in Main-street, Palmyra, engraving from John W. Barber and Henry Howe, *Historical Collections of the State of New York* (New York: Tuttle, 1841).

they arrived sometime in January 1817.[7] Katharine was too young to recognize her mother's resourcefulness and determination when the family relocated to New York, but in the ensuing years such qualities would have a marked influence on her developing personality.

This area of Western New York would be the only childhood home Katharine would recollect, as she grew to maturity in the area and was only a toddler when the family uprooted from Vermont. Now with eight children, the Smiths were starting all over again in New York. Despite the family's destitute circumstances, the prospects of the bustling community looked bright. Construction of the Erie Canal through the Palmyra village began just six months after the Smiths' arrival, and as a result businesses were springing up all over town. By the year 1823 there were thirteen dry good stores, several large warehouses, three drug stores, two inns, two tanneries, a post office, and a printing shop. The Erie Canal was completed on October 26, 1825.[8] Just before the Smiths' arrival, the population of

Palmyra and nearby Macedon was approximately 2,200, but by 1830 it had grown by more than 1,200 inhabitants, a testament to the impact that the Erie Canal had on the region's growth.[9]

Within two years of their arrival in Palmyra, the Smiths articled for a one-hundred-acre farm just two miles outside of town, and the family relocated sometime in the spring of 1819.[10] By that point, the Smiths had already built a small log home on their property, which had two rooms on the main floor and two more upstairs in a low garret, with another sleeping room added later.[11] With the arrival of baby Lucy in 1821, the log home made for cramped living quarters for a family of eleven. Up until the time of his death, the eldest son, Alvin, led out in constructing a much larger frame home for his family, where the Smiths would reside from 1825 to 1829.[12] During their twelve-year-stay on the property, the Smiths eventually cleared sixty acres for farming, built a cooper's shop, a barn, and other outbuildings, tapped approximately twelve to fifteen hundred trees to make sugar and maple syrup during the winter season, and had a thriving apple orchard of approximately two hundred trees.[13]

Joseph and Lucy Mack Smith One-Hundred Acre Farm, Manchester, New York, August 1907, photograph by George Edward Anderson. Courtesy of L. Tom Perry Special Collections, Harold B. Lee Library, Brigham Young University.

Domestic Labor

Once the Smiths settled on their new farm, work efforts began in earnest. Lucy recalled that the whole family "sat down, and counselled together relative to the course which was best for us to adopt in our destitute circumstances, and we came to the conclusion to unite our strength." Lucy focused her initial efforts in painting oil cloth coverings, which she sold and paid for replacing the household furniture.[14] While male members of the family focused their efforts on clearing and preparing the land to plant crops and hiring out to local neighbors for day labor, the Smith women's work efforts were focused closer to home. Female labors on the farm in the first half of the nineteenth century typically consisted of "tending the vegetable garden, processing and preserving the year's supply of vegetables and fruits, and preparing meals." Additionally, women oversaw "cleaning the house, tending the fires, and sewing, laundering, and mending the family's clothing and household textiles." Barnyard chores, however, were typically shared responsibilities by both men and women, with women usually leading out in milking the family cow and churning butter.[15]

Like most families in the rural countryside, farm life for the Smiths centered on basic survival tasks. Thus, Katharine began mastering these necessary skills from her youth. During early childhood, Katharine began by assisting her older sister, Sophronia, with some of her home responsibilities. Ten years her senior, Sophronia adopted a special role in mentoring Katharine, and their bond was strengthened as they labored together performing these common chores. While both sisters were above average height, that is where their resemblance ended. Sophronia was described as "delicate-looking" in her youth, with "soft brown hair and big dark-brown eyes." She was serious, introverted, and even shy in her interactions with others. As she matured, Katharine grew exceptionally tall and by contrast, had blonde hair with a light complexion and was described as a "sturdy child, with bright, expressive blue eyes." She was more outgoing than her older sister and unafraid of expressing her views.[16] Also unlike Sophronia, whose constitution was fragile and marred

The White Cow, engraving by Ch. De Billy, based on painting by Julien Dupre, ca. 1889.

by health difficulties throughout her life, Katharine's health was robust, and she was physically strong and capable of assisting her mother with many of the chores assumed by adult women of her day from her youth.

By the time Katharine was a preadolescent, Lucy appears to have divided at least some of her daughters' daily chores based on hardiness, with Sophronia primarily assisting her mother in keeping house, while Katharine led out in the barnyard. As she matured, Katharine chopped and hauled wood for the fireplace and oversaw the family's small flock of sheep, bringing them into a protective enclosure each night and releasing them to graze each morning. She also took charge of milking the family cow from a young age, a task she grew to appreciate and would continue throughout her entire life.[17]

Despite the partial division of labor in the home, Katharine still drew to her many household tasks typically adopted by young girls of her day. She learned how to operate a spinning wheel while in her teens and manufactured cloth that was turned into clothing or bedding.[18] Katharine's granddaughter Mary Salisbury Hancock recalled how Lucy ensured that her daughters spent considerable time "spinning, weaving, sewing and knitting." She further recounted how the Smith daughters, under their mother's tutelage, produced "warm, substantial linsey-woolsey dresses [that] were processed and completed by their own hands."[19]

> *Joseph Sr. and Lucy Mack Smith Family*
>
> Unnamed Son (ca. 1796–ca. 1796)
> Alvin (1798–1823)
> Hyrum (1800–1844)
> Sophronia (1803–76)
> Joseph Jr. (1805–44)
> Samuel Harrison (1808–44)
> Ephraim (1810–10)
> William B. (1811–93)
> Katharine (1813–1900)
> Don Carlos (1816–41)
> Lucy (1821–82)

Katharine also assisted in washing clothes and in meal preparation. In the nineteenth-century rural home, cooking required the ability to manage and regulate the fireplace, which Katharine grew to handle with "masterly skill." Additionally, she was instructed by her mother in baking bread and churning butter. [20] In time she probably assisted in preparing food goods for noteworthy town events such as July Fourth celebrations or during weeklong camp meetings that took place in the vicinity. One Palmyra historian recalled Joseph Sr. peddling "gingerbread, pies, boiled eggs, root-beer" and other transportable food goods during such events in a crude handmade cart. The "brisk sales" reported at these events support the Smith women's capability in producing large quantities of such delicacies.[21]

By the early 1820s, Katharine also took on the role of caring for her younger sister, Lucy, born in the summer of 1821 and the last of the Smith children. Katharine looked after her younger sister and tutored her in performing farm chores, much like Sophronia had earlier done for her. Visitors to the Smith household attested to the proficiency with which the girls and their mother prepared family meals. Stephen Harding, a well-to-do lawyer and later governor of Utah Territory, made an unexpected visit to the Smith home in the summer of 1829, providing a glimpse of a typical evening at the Smith home. He observed:

> I saw two stout, bare-footed girls [Katharine and Lucy], each with a tin bucket of red raspberries. Soon after, the old man [Joseph Sr.] announced that supper was ready. We went into the other part of the house, where supper was waiting, consisting of brown bread, milk, and an abundance of fine raspberries. . . . There was no lack of these, and if any left the table without a really good supper, it was not the fault of the hostess. I remarked . . . that the supper was good enough for a king, and the berries on the table were better than could be bought in any city in America.[22]

Though there was a significant age gap between the three Smith sisters, the connection Katharine forged with her two sisters in childhood created bonds that lasted the remainder of their lives.

Religious Upbringing

Besides her contributions to helping the family settle the farm, Katharine's upbringing included extensive religious instruction. She grew up in a home where the Bible was read consistently, religious themes were a regular topic of discussion, and spiritually themed dreams were important enough to be recorded.[23] Joseph Sr. and Lucy were both actively involved in reading and instructing their children about religious principles and rehearsing stories from the Bible. In the final decade of her life, Lucy spoke to a gathering of Saints in Nauvoo, where she emphasized the central role that religious instruction had played in her approach to child-rearing. "I raised them [my children] in the fear of God," she began. From the age of "two or three years old I told them I wanted them to love God with all their hearts. I told them to do good." She then recounted to the congregation gathered that day how she had successfully instilled moral values into the hearts of her own children by teaching them the stories of the Bible at a young age, "about Joseph in Egypt and such things." She underscored that if mothers listening to her that day would do the same, "when they [your children] are four years old they will love to read their Bible."[24]

While only three years old when the family arrived in New York, Katharine was old enough to begin listening to stories from the Bible. Corroborating that Lucy practiced what she preached during her Nauvoo sermon, one Palmyra neighbor remembered that Lucy used the Bible as the family's first primer.[25] In later life, Katharine recollected with fondness these evening gatherings around the fireplace, where her father also "read from the Bible, explaining and extolling its passages." This happened frequently enough, Katharine recalled, that all the Smith children "became quite proficient in their knowledge of its teachings."[26] Her experience was perhaps akin to another early Latter-day Saint convert, Eliza Dana Gibbs, born the same year as Katharine. Gibbs said she "had always been a great bible reader from a child" and related that by her twenties she had "read the New Testament through seven times by course and the Old Testament once."[27] Similarly, by the time she was an adult, her surviving letters were brimming with biblical themes and scriptural references, attesting to the influence of these youthful readings.[28]

Reading the Bible to Grandpa, engraving based on painting by E. W. Perry, *Harper's Weekly* 21, no. 1068 (June 16, 1877), 460. Both Joseph Sr. and Lucy read from the Bible with Katharine from a young age and utilized the Bible as their children's first primer.

Katharine witnessed the occasional tension between her parents regarding their attitudes surrounding formal religious affiliation. Lucy felt that finding and attending a church that coincided with her religious views was essential to her salvation. Joseph Sr., on the other hand, was critical of organized religion (a belief he inherited from his own father), and he kept himself distanced from joining or attending any denomination. These differences led to occasional conflicts in the marriage and by the 1820s also created a divide among the children.[29] Alvin, Joseph Jr., and William appear to have all adopted their father's skepticism of organized religion, while Hyrum, Sophronia, and Samuel all linked themselves with their mother in joining the Western Presbyterian Church at Palmyra.[30] While Katharine was probably too young to decide about formally uniting with a church, her subsequent attitudes regarding religion signal that she would have sided with her mother. She was drawn to the traditional values extolled by Palmyra preachers and, like her mother, was strict in her religious practice.

While there was intermittent tension around formal religious practice, the Smith parents were united in their private religious habits in their home. Family prayer was attended to twice daily and was a joint effort by the Smith parents to ensure their children adopted a religious course from their youth, with Joseph Sr. and Lucy taking turns acting as voice with prayer.[31] Her next closest sibling, William, two years older than Katharine, recalled: "We always had family prayer since I can remember. I well remember father used to carry his spectacles in his vest pocke[t], . . . and when us boys saw him feel for his specks, we knew that was A signal for prayer, and if we did not notice it mother would say, 'William,' or whoever was the negligent one, 'get ready for prayer.'"[32] The Smith children recalled how during family prayer, their parents "pourd out their Souls to God the doner of all blessings, to keep and gard their children . . . from sin and from all evil works."[33]

After evening prayer, the children recounted how they typically sang a hymn. William recalled how the family only sang one or two variations of hymns, a practice he found "irksome." Perhaps he was not the only sibling who found the repetitive routine monotonous, but if so, none of the other children ever mentioned it. The practice of hymn singing in the home was a pattern typical of many Protestant families and imbued the Smith children with a fondness for music.[34]

Katharine's childhood was filled with responsibility in improving the farm, mastering skills related to her domestic responsibilities, and being instructed in religious values. She was also imbued with an openness to accepting the supernatural as she listened to her father's spiritual dreams and heard stories recounted by her mother about how the Lord had spared her own life and the lives of family members through the efficacy of prayer.[35] Little could Katharine imagine how those religious themes would coalesce in the decade of the 1820s.

Notes

1. Although there have been variations in the spelling of her name, she consistently spelled it "Katharine" in her holograph letters (1865–99), copies of which are in the author's possession. In the earliest surviving records, Katharine's birth date is given as July 28, 1813. Joseph Smith, Manuscript History of the Church, Book A–1, 10, Joseph Smith Papers, Church History Library, Salt Lake City (hereafter cited as CHL); Katharine Salisbury Patriarchal Blessing, December 9, 1834, Patriarchal Blessing Book 1, 7, CHL. Katharine also maintained she was born July 28, 1813, indicating that the date of July 8, 1812, as recorded by her mother Lucy in her history, was incorrect. It is also the date that appears on her gravestone. Warren L. Van Dine, "Catharine Smith Salisbury," unpublished manuscript, 1972, 31, typescript copy located in the Community of Christ Library-Archives, Independence, Missouri. Katharine Smith Salisbury, Affidavit, April 15, 1881, holograph, Community of Christ Library-Archives; Lucy Mack Smith, Biographical Sketches of Joseph Smith the Prophet and his Progenitors for Many Generations (Liverpool: S. W. Richards, 1853), 41. The author made a thorough search through New Hampshire town records and was unable to locate a birth record.

2. Joseph A. Gallup, *Sketches of Epidemic Diseases in the State of Vermont, from Its Settlement to 1815* (Boston: T. B. Wait and Sons, 1815), 69–70, 75, as quoted in Richard L. Bushman, *Joseph Smith, Rough Stone Rolling* (New York: Alfred A. Knopf, 2005), 20.

3. Lucy Mack Smith, *Biographical Sketches of Joseph Smith the Prophet and His Progenitors for Many Generations* (Liverpool, S. W. Richards, 1853), 65–66.

4. Lucy Mack Smith, *Biographical Sketches*, 58–66.

5. Lucy Mack Smith, *Biographical Sketches*, 66–67.

6. Lavina Fielding Anderson, ed., *Lucy's Book: A Critical Edition of Lucy Mack Smith's Family Memoir* (Salt Lake City: Signature Books, 2001), 317, see also n69; Joseph Smith History, 1838–1856, volume A-1 [23 December 1805–30 August 1834], 132, in *The Joseph Smith Papers*.

7. Joseph Smith History, 1838–1856, volume A-1, 132; Lucy Mack Smith, *Biographical Sketches*, 69–70; Donald L. Enders and Mark L. Staker, *A Visionary House: The First Visions of Joseph Smith's Family in Context* (Provo, UT: Religious Studies Center, Brigham Young University, forthcoming).

8. Lionel D. Wyld, ed., *40' x 28' x 4': The Erie Canal—150 Years* (Rome, NY: Oneida County Erie Canal Commemoration Commission, 1967), 5, 8–14; Horatio Gates Spafford, *A Gazetteer of the State of New York* (Albany: B. D. Packard, 1824), 400–1, as cited in Larry C. Porter, *A Study of the Origins of The Church of Jesus Christ of Latter-day Saints in the States of New York and Pennsylvania* (Provo, UT: BYU Studies, 2000), 15.

9. George W. Cowles, ed., *Landmarks of Wayne County New York* (Syracuse, NY: D. Mason, 1895), 179; William Darby and Theodore Dwight Jr., *A New Gazetteer of the United States of America* (Hartford: Edward Hopkins, 1833), 392.

10. Enders and Staker, *Visionary House*.

11. Pomeroy Tucker, *Origin, Rise, and Progress of Mormonism* (New York: D. Appleton, 1867), 12–13. See also, Thomas L. Cook, *Palmyra and Vicinity* (Palmyra, NY: Palmyra Courier Journal, 1930), 219, who gives almost an identical description of the Smith's log home.

12. Porter, *Study of the Origins*, 27, 37.

13. William Smith, *William Smith on Mormonism* (Lamoni, IA: Herald Steam Book and Job Office, 1883), 12–13; Donald L. Enders, "The Joseph Smith, Sr., Family: Farmers of the Genesee," in *Joseph Smith: The Prophet, the Man*, ed. Susan Easton Black and Charles D. Tate Jr. (Provo, UT: Religious Studies Center, Brigham Young University, 1993), 213, 219.

14. Lucy Mack Smith, *Biographical Sketches*, 70.

15. Nancy Grey Osterud, *Bonds of Community: The Lives of Farm Women in Nineteenth-Century New York* (Ithaca, NY: Cornell University Press, 1991), 147–50.

16. Mary Salisbury Hancock, "The Three Sisters of the Prophet Joseph Smith, Part 1" *Saints' Herald* 101, no. 2 (January 11, 1954): 11; "Sister of a Prophet," *Saints' Herald* 40, no. 36 (September 9, 1893): 565.

17. Hancock, "Three Sisters of the Prophet Joseph Smith, Part 1," 11; Van Dine, "Catherine Smith Salisbury," 34.
18. Van Dine, "Catherine Smith Salisbury," 34.
19. Hancock, "Three Sisters of the Prophet Joseph Smith, Part 1," 10–11.
20. Van Dine, "Catherine Smith Salisbury," 34.
21. Tucker, *Origin, Rise, and Progress of Mormonism*, 12–14.
22. Thomas Gregg, *The Prophet of Palmyra* (New York: John B. Alden, 1890), 41–42.
23. Lucy Mack Smith, *Biographical Sketches*, 56–59, 73–74.
24. William Clayton and Thomas Bullock, "Conference Minutes," *Times and Seasons* 6, no. 16 (November 1, 1845): 1013–14; Jennifer Reeder and Kate Holbrook, eds., *At the Pulpit: 185 Years of Discourses by Latter-day Saint Women* (Salt Lake City: Church Historian's Press, 2017), 21–26.
25. John Stafford, interview, as quoted in William H. Kelley, "The Hill Cumorah, and the Book of Mormon," *Saints' Herald* 28, no. 11 (June 1, 1881): 167.
26. Hancock, "Three Sisters of the Prophet Joseph Smith, Part 1," 11.
27. Andrea Ventilla, "'Death Had Lost All Terrors': Eliza Dana Gibbs (1813–1900)," in *Women of Faith in the Latter Days*, vol. 1, *1775–1820*, ed. Richard E. Turley Jr. and Brittany A. Chapman (Salt Lake City: Deseret Book, 2011), 32–33.
28. See, for example, Katharine Salisbury (Fountain Green, IL) to Dear Sisters, March 10, 1886, *Saints' Herald* 33, no. 17 (May 1, 1886): 260; and Katherine Salisbury (n.p.) to Sister Frances, December 24, 1886, *Saints' Herald* 34, no. 6 (February 5, 1887): 84.
29. Richard L. Bushman, *Joseph Smith Rough Stone Rolling* (New York: Alfred A. Knopf, 2005), 25–26, 46; Kyle R. Walker, *The Joseph Sr. and Lucy Mack Smith Family: A Family Process Analysis of a Nineteenth-Century Household* (Provo, UT: BYU Studies, 2008), 65–68.
30. Karen Lynn Davidson et al., *Histories, Volume 1: Joseph Smith Histories, 1832–1844*, vol. 1 of the Histories series of *The Joseph Smith Papers*, ed. Dean C. Jessee, Ronald K. Esplin, and Richard Lyman Bushman (Salt Lake City: Church Historian's Press, 2012), 208–9; Milton V. Backman Jr. and James B. Allen, "Membership of Certain of Joseph Smith's Family in the Western Presbyterian Church of Palmyra," *BYU Studies* 1, no. 4 (Summer 1970): 482–84.
31. William Smith, "Notes Written on 'Chambers' Life of Joseph Smith," ca. 1875, 29, CHL.
32. John W. Peterson, "Wm. B. Smith's Last Statement," *Zion's Ensign* 5 (January 1894): 6.
33. William Smith, "Notes on 'Chambers,'" 29.
34. William Smith, "Notes on 'Chambers,'" 29; Michael Hicks, *Mormonism and Music: A History* (Urbana: University of Illinois Press, 1989), 4. Emma Smith later included at least three of the Smith family's oft-sung

hymns in the Church's first hymnal. Emma Smith, comp., *A Collection of Sacred Hymns for the Church of the Latter Day Saints* (Kirtland, OH: F. G. Williams, 1835), 55–63, see *Hymns of the Church of Jesus Christ of Latter-day Saints* (Salt Lake City: The Church of Jesus Christ of Latter-day Saints, 1985), nos. 42–43, 48.

35. Lucy later recounted several of these stories when she was preparing her history in the mid-1840s, including how the Lord healed her from a life-threatening illness, and how the Lord spared Sophronia's life after she and her husband pled with the Lord in prayer when she contracted typhoid fever. Lucy Mack Smith, *Biographical Sketches*, 47, 60–61.

CHAPTER TWO

Heavenly Messengers

*He told us later that a personage had appeared to him and told him
"Join none of them, for they are all wrong."*
—Katharine Smith Salisbury

BY THE 1820S Lucy led out in getting most of the family to
attend local church services and, whenever they were in the area,
the camp meetings, with their more emotional, intense, and con-
centrated religious experiences. The Second Great Awakening with
its accompanying revivals drew women like Lucy out of the home
and into the community sphere in ever increasing numbers. Female
converts outnumbered males in congregations all over the country
as women's church affiliation increasingly drew them into the public
arena.[1] Lucy and her daughters were part of this wave of revivalism
sweeping through America.

Lucy's motivation to unite with a church increased after the
unexpected death of her eldest son Alvin, which occurred late in the
evening on November 19, 1823. After only a few days of sickness,
with symptoms characteristic of appendicitis, Alvin succumbed to
the disease.[2] Just before he passed, he gathered each of his family

Alvin Smith gravestone, General John Swift Memorial Cemetery, Palmyra, New York. Photograph by Kyle R. Walker, 2019.

members around him to give them a final charge. Though Lucy didn't record what Alvin said to ten-year-old Katharine, both his life and his parting counsel had an impact on her. She looked up to Alvin and admired his work ethic and example, later naming a son after her steady older brother.[3] Alvin's death was a psychological and economic blow that had lasting consequences for the family.[4]

Following Alvin's death, Lucy indicated that the family "flocked to the meeting house to see if their [*sic*] was a word of comfort for us that might relieve our overcharged feelings." Lucy led out in those efforts, even attempting to persuade her husband to join the rest, but neither of her Josephs would attend with her for long.[5] Notwithstanding, her efforts were influential, and the children described their mother as "a very pious woman and much interested in the welfare of her children, [and] made use of every means which her parental love could suggest, to get us engaged in seeking for our souls' salvation, or . . . 'in getting religion.'"[6]

Sketch of Union Hall, Palmyra, New York, where members of the Smith Family attended the Western Presbyterian Church of Palmyra. Courtesy of Village Hall, Palmyra, New York.

Lucy was enacting a role that was increasingly pervasive among women in the first half of the nineteenth century, who were customarily "the chief transmitters of religious and moral values."[7] Mothers did not simply "conduct their religious lives as disconnected individuals; instead they drew other members of their families into the congregation." The religious literature of the day counseled women to "set a powerful example for their household [and] their influence might help bring all the members of the family to God."[8] Katharine watched as her mother led out in these efforts becoming Katharine's role model for what it meant to be a devout mother.

Katharine was also influenced by the Palmyra community in her developing spirituality because the population was saturated with religious fervor during her youth. Palmyra was at the center of the "burned-over district," a label given to this area of Western New York because of the way religion spread like wildfire throughout the region.[9] She doubtless attended camp meetings with the rest of the family and watched as Sophronia joined her mother and brothers Hyrum and Samuel as they linked themselves with the Presbyterian faith.[10] She attended with her mother and older siblings when the Presbyterian congregation met in the Union Church House on Church Street but was too young to be received as a formal member. In one reminiscence, her brother William mentioned that Katharine also joined the Presbyterian Church, though this was probably a mistake, as he omitted her name on other occasions.[11] His slip in memory might have resulted from his and Katharine's affiliation with the Presbyterian Church's Sunday school during their youth.[12] The Presbyterian minister Benjamin Stockton had successfully recruited most of the Smith family to join his local congregation, and by establishing a youth Sunday school, he hoped it would ensure the younger generation would adopt the same course. The local Sunday school stressed memorization of scriptural passages such as the Lord's Prayer, the Ten Commandments, and Christ's Sermon on the Mount.[13] Katharine rapidly increased in her knowledge of the Bible during these formative years.

While religious enthusiasm permeated the town, what transpired within the Smith home proved to be even more impactful. During Katharine's youth she not only listened to details of her father's religious dreams (significant enough to her parents that Lucy ensured

A
NARRAITVE

OF THE LIFE OF

SOLOMON MACK,

CONTAINING

AN ACCOUNT

OF THE MANY SEVERE ACCIDENTS HE MET
WITH DURING A LONG SERIES OF YEARS,

TOGETHER WITH

THE EXTRAORDINARY MANNER IN
WHICH HE WAS CONVERTED TO THE

CHRISTIAN FAITH.

TO WHICH IS ADDED,
A NUMBER HYMNS COMPOSED ON THE
DEATH OF SEVERAL OF HIS
RELATIONS.

WINDSOR.

PRINTED AT THE EXPENCE OF THE
AUTHOR.

Title page of *A Narraitve* [sic] *of the Life of Solomon Mack*, published in 1811 by Katharine's grandfather.

they were later recorded in her history), but she also undoubtedly heard of her grandfather Solomon Mack's late life conversion to Christianity. Solomon had gone so far as to publish a small tract containing an account of his newfound faith, a copy of which was surely available for reading in the Smith home.[14] Katharine also learned from her mother how the efficacy of prayer spared Sophronia's life during her bout with typhoid fever in the year 1812.[15] The family's full confidence in God's divine intervention in their lives was a part of the Smith family oral culture and shaped their united acceptance of the supernatural occurrences that transpired in the 1820s.

The First Vision

In the year 1820, when Katharine's elder brother Joseph was just fourteen, he said that God and Jesus Christ appeared to him. After months of struggle and deliberation, and perhaps at the instigation of a local Methodist preacher, Joseph sought seclusion in a wooded grove on the family's one-hundred-acre property to seek forgiveness and ask which church he should join. He not only received the mercy he was seeking, but was also answered that he was not to unite with any particular faith, but that in time the true gospel would be revealed to him.[16] Probably because of Lucy's efforts to help the children investigate and unite with a church and due to her personal religious leanings, Joseph first reported to his mother that he had learned for himself that Presbyterianism was not true.[17]

While he appears to have been reluctant to share all that he learned during his theophany, according to Katharine he did share some details about his experience with the family that went beyond that brief conversation with his mother. Though she was young at the time and her memories were recorded only late in life, Katharine's recollections may help to sort out which details Joseph shared with his family during the decade of the 1820s. In one account, recorded by Katharine's adult granddaughter, Mary Salisbury Hancock, Katharine recounted that it was "in the spring of 1820, [that] a great religious revival took place in a beautiful grove near by." She continued, it was "after one of these [camp] meetings and at a time of great indecision your Uncle Joseph read in the Bible, during a time of meditation, 'If any of you lack wisdom, let him ask of God.' Thinking of this he went to the woods to be alone and pray. He told us later that a personage had appeared to him and told him 'Join none of them, for they are all wrong.'"[18]

On another occasion, in an account recorded by Katharine's son Frederick, Katharine provided additional details about Joseph's First Vision and its impact on the family. "After Joseph had seen the heavenly messengers," recorded Frederick from his mother's report, "she [Katharine] said that he would teach the family." Katharine described one evening when the family gathered around the fireplace after their work was completed and listened to Joseph's "description of the heavenly messages which he had received from God and his Son."[19] While it is possible that the identity of the messengers came from later recitals or publications which Katharine had read by the time she recounted these events, she most often recalled that Joseph was visited by a heavenly messenger(s) who directed him not to join any of the existing churches. Consolidating Smith family members references to the First Vision, it appears that Joseph may have simply shared with his family that he was visited by messengers or angels (a more general reference to any otherworldly visitor) who had answered his prayer that he must join none of the existing churches. Joseph's parents, and even Joseph himself on one occasion, similarly referred to God and Jesus Christ as the "first angels" who visited him when rehearsing the story of his First Vision.[20]

Smith family recollections of the First Vision do not indicate that Joseph disclosed at that time that he had been told about his future role in establishing Christ's restored church on the earth. Thus, for the Smiths, Joseph's posture during those intervening years was not unlike his father's: he kept himself distanced from formal affiliation of the religions in his community but often dialogued with family members about religious topics.[21] Following his First Vision, Joseph stopped attending the Presbyterian meetings with other members of the family but told his mother he did not wish to prevent her or the rest of the family from going to their meetings. "But do not ask me to join them," Joseph said tellingly. "I can take my Bible and go into the woods, and learn more in two hours, than you can learn at [your] meeting[s] in two years."[22] It was an obvious allusion to his First Vision. Katharine remembered her brother's spiritual struggle and was aware of his religious stance in the intervening years.

One element of Joseph's First Vision that Katharine frequently recounted in later life was Joseph's sharing his experience with a local Methodist minister and of the latter's negative reaction. This detail undoubtedly stood out to her because of its immediate impact on the entire family. "The next time Joseph saw the [Methodist] preacher he told him of his [First Vision] experience," related Katharine, and "the minister was very angry and told other ministers of Joseph's experience, which they all said could not have happened since angels did not visit the earth in these days. This caused a great uproar, and Joseph was soon in disgrace." Katharine further remembered that the entire Smith family "were shunned and their good deeds quickly forgotten."[23]

While both Joseph and the family experienced the harsh treatment by community members after the minister spread word of Joseph's First Vision, Katharine recollected that it especially impacted her older sister, Sophronia. "The ill treatment of her friends" contributed to both an emotional and physical decline, where "she grew thin and pale until it was feared she was developing 'quick consumption.'" Katharine recounted that her sister's illness occurred in the wake of the Methodist minister disseminating Joseph's story when Sophronia was seventeen, which would have been in the years 1820–21.[24] Her affinity for her eldest sister etched the experience into her childhood memory and corroborates what Joseph Jr. said about the persecution for both himself and the family during that early period.[25] Katharine described how the "persecution started against [my] brother at the time of his first vision, and increased after he had received the plates."[26]

Right: *Sacred Grove*, by George Edward Anderson, August 1907. Courtesy of L. Tom Perry Special Collections, Harold B. Lee Library, Brigham Young University.

The Angel Moroni

Katharine always differentiated between Joseph's First Vision and his initial experience with Moroni, something other family members did not always clearly delineate. Joseph said it was during the night of September 21, 1823, and into the next morning, when he was visited four times by an angel who identified himself as Moroni, an ancient American prophet. He had come in response to Joseph's inquiry about his standing before God. Katharine remembered that just before Moroni's appearance, Joseph had been musing over his First Vision during a time of prayer and contemplation.[27] Besides instructing him about a number of biblical prophecies about the last days, the angel informed him about an ancient record that was buried in a nearby hill that Joseph would be instrumental in translating.[28]

While Joseph was initially reluctant to share all the details about his experience with the Father and Son following his First Vision, this time he was instructed by the angel to tell his father of his experience. Katharine remembered that Joseph initially told his father and two of his brothers about his experience, probably Alvin and William.[29] She recollected that the three of them "talked quite a spell," and it made her curious about what was so important to take that much time away from their work, "because I knowed [*sic*] they were so busy with their harvesting." Later that day, Joseph shared his experience with the rest of the family. Katharine recollected several details that were unique, including Joseph recounting that Moroni's white clothing included "a girdle about his waist," and that in addition to his clothing, that his hands and wrists were also "pure and white."[30]

"The whole family were melted to tears," recalled William of the family gathering at the time Joseph shared his experience, "and believed all he said. . . . [We] were convinced that he was totally incapable of arising before his aged parents, his brothers and sisters, and so solemnly giving utterance to anything but the truth."[31] Katharine wholeheartedly accepted his accounts of heavenly visitors from the first and looked forward with eager anticipation to her brother retrieving the sacred record.

Notes

1. Martha Sonntag Bradley, "'Seizing Sacred Space': Women's Engagement in Early Mormonism," *Dialogue: A Journal of Mormon Thought* 27, no. 2 (1994): 59; Nancy Woloch, *Women and the American Experience: A Concise History*, 2nd ed. (New York: McGraw, 1994), 121, as cited in Susan M. Cruea, "Changing Ideals of Womanhood During the Nineteenth-Century Woman Movement," *ATQ: 19th Century American Literature and Culture* 19, no. 3 (2005): 195.

2. Lucy Mack Smith, *Biographical Sketches of Joseph Smith the Prophet and His Progenitors for Many Generations* (Liverpool: S. W. Richards, 1853), 87–90; Richard L. Anderson, "Alvin Smith," in *United by Faith: The Joseph Sr. and Lucy Mack Smith Family*, ed. Kyle R. Walker (American Fork, UT: Covenant Communications Inc.; Provo, UT: BYU Studies, 2006), 91–93, 98–99.

3. Katharine named her second son Alvin, who was born June 7, 1838, when the Salisbury family was migrating from Ohio to Missouri. Lucy Mack Smith, *Biographical Sketches*, 43, 219–20. Joseph Jr. recorded a few lines in his journal about his trusted older brother: "In him there was no guile. He lived without spot from the time he was a child. From the time of his birth, he never knew mirth. He was candid and sober and never would play; and minded his father, and mother, in toiling all day." Andrew H. Hedges, Alex D. Smith, and Richard Lloyd Anderson, eds., *Journals, Volume 2: December 1841–April 1843*, vol. 2 of the Journals series of *The Joseph Smith Papers*, ed. Dean C. Jessee, Ronald K. Esplin, and Richard Lyman Bushman (Salt Lake City: Church Historian's Press, 2011), 117.

4. The most immediate economic consequence was the loss of the family's one-hundred-acre property just two years later. Alvin had been instrumental in making the annual one-hundred-dollar payment on the farm, a demand the family failed to fulfill in the ensuing years. Anderson, "Alvin Smith," 91–93; Lucy Mack Smith, *Biographical Sketches*, 71.

5. Lavina Fielding Anderson, ed., *Lucy's Book: A Critical Edition of Lucy Mack Smith's Family Memoir* (Salt Lake City: Signature Books, 2001), 357, quote crossed out in original; and Lucy Mack Smith, *Biographical Sketches*, 90.

6. William Smith, *William Smith on Mormonism: A True Account of the Origin of the Book of Mormon* (Lamoni, IA: Herald Steam Book and Job Office, 1883), 6.

7. Ruth R. Bloch, "American Feminine Ideals in Transition: The Rise of the Moral Mother, 1785–1815," *Feminist Studies* 4, no. 2 (June 1978): 100.

8. Nancy Grey Osterud, *Bonds of Community: The Lives of Farm Women in Nineteenth-Century New York* (Ithaca, NY: Cornell University Press, 1991), 262–64.

9. Spencer W. McBride and Jennifer Hill Dorsey, eds., *New York's Burned-Over District: A Documentary History* (Ithaca, NY: Cornell University Press, 2023); Whitney R. Cross, *The Burned-Over District: The Social and Intellectual History of Enthusiastic Religion in Western New York, 1800–1850* (Ithaca, NY: Cornell University Press, 1950).

10. Karen Lynn Davidson, David J. Whittaker, Mark Ashurst-McGee, and Richard L. Jensen, eds., *Histories: Volume 1: 1832–1844*, vol. 1 of the Histories series of *The Joseph Smith Papers* (Salt Lake City: Church Historian's Press, 2008), 208. Historians Milton Backman and James Allen offer corroborating evidence on at least three members of the Smith family joining the Western Presbyterian Church at Palmyra when they document that the Smiths were visited by Presbyterian church leaders in March 1830 due to inactivity during the previous eighteen months. These three were Mother Lucy, Hyrum, and Samuel. There is no mention of Sophronia, although she was still living in the area. Milton V. Backman Jr. and James B. Allen, "Membership of Certain of Joseph Smith's Family in the Western Presbyterian Church of Palmyra," *BYU Studies* 10, no. 4 (Summer 1970): 482–84.

11. "Sermon by Elder Wm. B. Smith," 2; "Wm. B. Smith's Last Statement," 6. William failed to mention Sophronia's affiliation in this latter account, so he may have mistakenly substituted Katharine's name for Sophronia's. In another account, William omitted Samuel's name from the list, and apparently could not remember which sister it was that joined. Said William, "My mother and brother Hyrum and a sister were members of the Presbyterian Church." "William B. Smith: Experience and Testimony," 388.

12. "Sermon by Elder Wm. B. Smith," 2. Lorenzo Saunders recollected that Joseph Smith Jr. also attended Stockton's Sabbath School "at the old Presbyterian Church." Lorenzo Saunders, interview by William H. Kelley, September 17, 1884, 1–18, E. L. Kelley Papers, Community of Christ Library Archives, Independence, MO.

13. T. Osgood, "Messrs. Editors," *Wayne Sentinel* 2 (December 15, 1824): 2; "Many are inquiring . . .," *Wayne Sentinel* 2 (December 15, 1824): 2. See also H. Michael Marquardt and Wesley P. Walters, *Inventing Mormonism: Tradition and the Historical Record* (Salt Lake City: Smith Research Associates, 1994), 20, for a discussion of Stockton's religious activities in Palmyra.

14. Lucy Mack Smith, *Biographical Sketches*, 47, 60–61. When preparing her history in the 1840s, Lucy indicated she had in her possession "a sketch of my father's life, written by himself," and then quoted from his

book. Lucy Mack Smith, *Biographical Sketches*, 15–20; Solomon Mack, *A Narraitve* [sic] *of the Life of Solomon Mack* (Windsor, VT: self-pub., 1811).

15. Lucy Mack Smith, *Biographical Sketches*, 20, 60–61, 73–74.

16. Joseph Smith, "Church History," *Times and Seasons* 3, no. 9 (March 1, 1842), 706–7; "Sermon by Elder Wm. B. Smith," *Zion's Ensign* 3, no. 35 (August 27, 1892): 2.

17. Joseph Smith, History, 1838–1856, volume A-1 [23 December 1805–30 August 1834], 132, CHL.

18. Mary Salisbury Hancock, "The Three Sisters of the Prophet Joseph Smith, Part 1," *Saints' Herald* 101, no. 2 (January 11, 1954): 11. Mary Salisbury Hancock was in her twenties during the last decade of her grandmother Katharine's life. She quotes her grandmother throughout this article, indicating that she had documented what Katharine told the family on this occasion.

19. Frederick V. Salisbury, "The Teachings and Testimonies of My Mother," unpublished typescript, ca. 1926–28, 2, Warren L. Van Dine Papers, Hancock County Historical Society, Carthage, IL.

20. For a discussion of Smith family member's use of the word "angel" or "heavenly messenger" when referring to the First Vision, see Kyle R. Walker, "Smith Family Recollections of Joseph Smith's First Vision," *Journal of Mormon History* 47, no. 2 (April 2021), 5–6.

21. Anderson, ed., *Lucy's Book*, 335.

22. Lucy Mack Smith, *Biographical Sketches*, 90.

23. Hancock, "Three Sisters," 11. William said something similar, when he recalled the dramatic shift in the family's reputation, stating, "We never knew we were bad folks until Joseph told his vision." "Wm. B. Smith's Last Statement," 6. Jeremy Talmage summarizes that the most likely reason the Methodist minister rejected Joseph Smith's experience was because Joseph insisted it had been an "objective experience." Evangelicals contended that visions were "permissible as long as they preserved the strict separation between the spiritual and the sensory, mind and matter. Smith's conviction about the reality of his vision, including his detailed physical description of Divinity, is the most likely reason for his rejection." Jeremy Talmage, "'Effusions of an Enthusiastic Brain': Joseph Smith's First Vision and the Limits of Experiential Religion," *BYU Studies* 59, no. 1 (2020): 29.

24. Hancock, "Three Sisters," 11. If prejudice against the Smith family did not really begin until after Joseph received the plates in the fall of 1827, as several historians have postulated, then Sophronia would have been age twenty-four, and likely engaged to be married to Calvin Stoddard. Sophronia married Calvin Stoddard on December 30, 1827, just three months after Joseph received the plates. Stoddard Family Bible, photocopy in author's possession. During the time of their courtship, Calvin "often visited the Smith home and was much interested in Joseph's visit

with the angel. . . . Stoddard became fond of Sophronia, which fondness grew into affection and love during his frequent visits." Hancock, "Three Sisters," 12. For references related to Joseph overstating the persecution during the 1820–23 period, see Richard L. Bushman, *Joseph Smith: Rough Stone Rolling* (New York: Alfred A. Knopf, 2005), 43; Steven C. Harper, *First Vision: Memory and Mormon Origins* (New York: Oxford University Press, 2019), 48–49.

25. Joseph Jr. said that "telling the story [of the First Vision] had excited a great deal of prejudice against me among professors of religion and was the cause of great persecution which continued to increase . . . though I was an obscure boy only between fourteen and fifteen years of age." *JSP*, H1:216.

26. Salisbury, "Teachings and Testimonies of My Mother," 4.

27. Kyle R. Walker, "Katharine Smith Salisbury's Recollections of Joseph's Meeting with Moroni," *BYU Studies* 41, no. 3 (2002): 114.

28. *JSP*, H1:224–27.

29. *William Smith on Mormonism*, 9.

30. Walker, "Katharine Smith Salisbury's Recollections," 11–13.

31. *William Smith on Mormonism*, 9–10.

CHAPTER THREE

The Sacred Record

[Katharine] said she hefted those plates and felt that they were separate metal plates and heard the tinkle of sound they made.
—Herbert S. Salisbury

KATHARINE WAS TEN YEARS OLD when Joseph reported his initial encounter with the angel Moroni, and she turned fourteen when Joseph brought the plates home in the fall of 1827, mature enough to be an active and eager participant in the foundational events leading to the organization of the Church of Christ. The circumstances that occurred during this seven-year period (1823–30) dominated the memories of her youth and provide a unique perspective into the earliest Restoration events viewed through the lens of a teenage girl. Besides describing how these events impacted her personally, Katharine often underscored the influence they had on the family and their reputation in the greater Palmyra community. The circumstances related to the coming forth of the Book of Mormon unquestionably left an indelible impression on her youthful mind during these critical developmental years.

After her brother Joseph had learned of the ancient record from the angel Moroni, Katharine was excited as she and her family eagerly anticipated his bringing home the plates. However, she was heartbroken to learn that the angel initially prevented Joseph from retrieving the plates in his annual visits to the Hill Cumorah during the years 1823–26. "I well remember the trials my brother had before he obtained the records," wrote Katharine of that period. After he had seen the angel Moroni, she remembered that Joseph "went frequently to the hill," and how he recounted to the family that he had "seen the records, also the brass plates and the sword of Laban with the breast plate and interpreters." She recalled Joseph's disappointment when he could not obtain the plates during these visits and that he would often counsel with his father about why he could not get them. Katharine said that her father played a role of comforting his namesake son, explaining to Joseph that the timing must not have been right.[1]

Like Smith family friend Joseph Knight Sr., Katharine recalled Joseph being told to bring Alvin, and after Alvin's death in November 19, 1823, Emma, with him to the Hill Cumorah to obtain the plates.[2] When the time finally arrived for Joseph to receive the plates, Katharine said her brother was "commanded to go on the 22d day of September 1827 at 2 o'clock [a.m.]."[3] Mother Lucy remembered Joseph and Emma borrowed Joseph Knight Sr.'s wagon, who was then staying with the family, and that the couple left for the hill shortly after midnight.[4] It was a sleepless night for Lucy, and perhaps Katharine as well, as they anxiously waited for Joseph and Emma's return. Katharine and her mother both recall that Joseph initially hid the plates in a hollow log the same night he received them from Moroni. Mother and daughter also recounted their apprehension that outsiders might potentially locate the plates in the woods before they could be secured in the Smith home.[5]

The next day, Katharine was at home when Joseph retrieved the plates from their hiding place in the woods on September 23, 1827.[6]

Hill Cumorah, by George Edward Anderson, August 1907. Courtesy of L. Tom Perry Special Collections, Harold B. Lee Library, Brigham Young University.

She described how Joseph eventually reclaimed them from a hollow log in the woods and how he scuffled with three different men who were intent on taking the plates as he brought the frock-covered plates to the house. Because of an injury to his right hand and arm during these scraps, Katharine saw him carrying the bundle "clasped to his left side with his left hand and arm" as he came running onto the Smith family property.[7] When he entered the house, he was completely out of breath and then "threw himself on the bed and fainted." Katharine was evidently the first in the family to handle the plates while covered, as she took the bundle from Joseph, set them on the family table, and assisted her mother in reviving Joseph until he was breathing properly. She saw that his right thumb was dislocated and that his right arm "was very lame" from his exchange with the assailants. After examining his hand, she "treated it for the bruises on his knuckles" while her father went in search of the men who had attacked him.[8]

Like others in the family, Katharine also expressed disappointment in not being able to see the plates while uncovered. "We had supposed that when he [Joseph] should bring them home, the whole family would be allowed to see them," she recounted, "but he [Joseph] said it was forbidden of the Lord. . . . We had therefore to be content until they were translated and we could have the book to read."[9] Yet her youthful curiosity meant that she occasionally had opportunities to examine the plates while covered. She frequently recounted to her descendants how she had lifted and felt the plates on multiple occasions. In one instance, she discovered the plates wrapped up and sitting on a table while she was dusting a room where Joseph was in the habit of studying. She described how she "hefted the plates and found them very heavy" and estimated that they weighed about sixty pounds. She then examined them more closely, rippling her "fingers up the edge of the plates and felt they were separate metal plates and heard the tinkle of the sound that they made," noting that they were held together at the back by three rings.[10]

Despite the family being ostracized by the greater Palmyra community, a trusted few were still permitted into their family circle. The Smith parents confided the news of the receipt of the plates to prominent Palmyra resident Martin Harris.[11] Katharine felt confident enough in one close friend, Caroline Rockwell, just one year older than Katharine, to confide in her some details about the plates. She showed Caroline the locked chest where the plates were hidden and a previous hiding spot under the bricks of the hearth where the family had kept them safe from treasure seekers.[12] It was comforting for Katharine to have at least one confidant who believed the family's story.

For the next three years, Joseph would be consumed with protecting and translating the plates, and his family viewed themselves in a similar, albeit supportive role in the process. At least part of that perception stemmed from what Joseph related to them about Moroni's instructions, in which he directed family involvement, including a strict charge to keep the Book of Mormon plates safe from outsiders. Joseph also shared Moroni's warning of the necessity for the entire family to keep the plates secret or their very lives would be in peril. When Joseph was initially unable to obtain the plates until he was more spiritually minded, Lucy recorded that it wasn't just Joseph that needed to be prepared, but that "we"—the whole family—"doubled our diligence in prayer and supplication to God."[13] The Smiths strove to be worthy of such an important assignment, and once the plates were finally in their home, they were vigilant in fulfilling the angel's charge to use all their efforts to preserve and protect them. Like her mother, Katharine viewed protecting the plates and assisting with the publication of the Book of Mormon as a family effort. On one occasion, when recounting early Restoration events to an RLDS congregation of Saints later in life, Katharine declared, "I stand before you a remnant of the family that brought forth the sacred record."[14]

Such warnings about the family's safety were impactful on a fourteen-year-old girl, as evidenced in her surviving recollections. It's no wonder that Katharine remembered this three-month period when the plates were in the Smith home as one in which the home environment became filled with watchfulness.[15] "We got a chest and locked the records up in the house," recalled Katharine. "From that time on our house was searched all around; and our field and our wheat stacks were searched. The mob was around our house nearly every night, and one night they went into father's cooper shop and tore up his floor and dug the earth up."[16] At times she described these groups as "crowds" who would search their property and in one instance, "trying with iron rods to find the plates."[17] William similarly recalled groups surrounding the house, where they would "throw stones, sticks and dirt against it, and insult us in all manner of ways."[18] Though there were a number of documented instances of groups trying to wrest the plates from Joseph during this time, perhaps she overstated that a mob was around the home every night. Yet the fact that Katharine remembered it that way reveals the impact these events had upon her youthful mind.

Smith frame home, Manchester, New York. Photograph by Alexander L. Baugh, 2005.

Katharine also recounted one memorable experience in which she played a central role in safeguarding the plates. She recalled an occasion where Joseph had the plates outside of the family home. Hearing a ruckus outside, Katharine opened the front door just as her brother Joseph "came rushing up, panting for breath, . . . and in a gasping voice whispered hoarsely, 'take these quickly and hide them.'" Katharine, obviously prepared for such a circumstance by this juncture, took the bundle from Joseph to her room, where she and Sophronia slept. Her exceptional strength assisted her in hefting the heavy plates. Sophronia pulled back the covers, Katharine placed the bundle on the bed, and then they replaced the covers pretending to be asleep. "The mob, failing to find Joseph outside, returned to the house to search," as Katharine later recounted the incident to her family, "but they did not disturb the girls since they appeared to be sleeping."[19]

Such circumstances created fear for Katharine, as the family grew increasingly clannish to protect their mission from outsiders. In December 1827 Joseph and Emma took the record and left for Pennsylvania to find more solitude than the Palmyra community afforded, and Katharine's older siblings Hyrum and Sophronia both married and moved out of the home near that same time.[20] The Smiths who remained on the family property bore the brunt of continued harassment. According to Smith family accounts, the Smiths were hassled by local ministers, neighbors who were denied a look at the plates, lawsuits, copyright infringements, and creditors who uncharacteristically demanded immediate payment.[21] Also, after Alvin's death in 1823, the family failed to make their hundred-dollar annual payment on the property the following year, which resulted in them losing the property by 1825. While they were still allowed to live on the farm, by the year 1830 they were forced to move, losing all the improvements they had made to the farm and the two homes they had built.[22] It was a devastating financial blow to the family, as Joseph Sr. and Lucy, nearing their sixties, were now too old to try to start all over again.

Such difficulties, combined with the family's limited living space and lack of financial means, led Katharine to leave the immediate Palmyra vicinity as early as the winter of 1828–29. She traveled to nearby Farmington Township and began teaching school.[23] Because family circumstances were more settled during Katharine's teen years, she had been able to attend school with the younger Smith children. One schoolmate of the Smith children recalled rather generally that most of the Smith children were "dull scholar[s]" except for "[Samuel] Harrison and Catherine."[24] These educational opportunities, frequently denied the older Smith siblings, prepared Katharine to launch out on her own as a schoolteacher.

Although it's possible she lived intermittently with the family in Palmyra-Manchester, Katharine does not appear to have returned home again permanently until early October 1830. Her return coincided with the family's final weeks in the area, and those became some of the most difficult. Just before Katharine returned home,

Joseph Sr. was jailed for failure to pay a debt, and Hyrum had left for Colesville, New York, leaving the family unprotected during a time when the threat of violence persisted.[25] During this time, when the men of the family were absent, the Smith women experienced perhaps their worst encounter with a mob up to that time. Katharine remembered:

> A few days after he [Hyrum] was gone, a number of men, came and searched our house for him. Mother, myself and younger sister [Lucy] were the only ones at home. When we insisted that he was not there, their anger turned upon us and they commenced to rob the house. While they were plundering us, my brother, William, came. . . . Upon coming in he asked mother, 'What were those men doing?' She told him they had come for Hyrum and were now plundering the house. Arming himself with a stout club, he soon drove them from the house. They had come in carriages with dark lanterns, and if they had found Hyrum it was their intention to have him put to death.[26]

Her brawny elder brothers, including nineteen-year-old William, afforded her some sense of security during such episodes of harassment from neighbors.

Katharine was also a recipient of slander sometime during the years 1830–31 and beyond. After the Book of Mormon was published, antagonists developed several theories to try and explain how Joseph Smith produced such a complex and lengthy book with his limited education. The foremost theory in the early 1830s was that the Smith family had known Sidney Rigdon before the book's publication and that the two men labored for years to manufacture the text. Rigdon, they theorized, must have been instrumental in the book's publication.[27] To strengthen their hypothesis, a rumor was circulated that Katharine was pregnant with Rigdon's child while still living in New York, which would confirm that Rigdon had known the Smith family before December 1830. It is unknown when the rumor first surfaced, but probably at least by the year 1831. Surviving recollections of Palmyra neighbors, as well as the story appearing in a book published by Palmyra historian Pomeroy Tucker, provide evidence of how extensively the story circulated through the community.[28]

While the rumors about Katharine and Rigdon's relationship were untrue (as well as Rigdon knowing the Smith family prior to the publication of the Book of Mormon), the account no doubt left its mark, and neighbors later repeated their negative impressions regarding Katharine's reputation. Though nothing has survived related to how she responded to these rumors besides denying the family knew Rigdon before 1830, they must have been emotionally taxing and embarrassing to her.[29]

The decade of the 1820s was foremost in Katharine's memories when she reflected on her childhood in later years, as she claimed to "recall the time of the wonderful vision as vividly as though it were but yesterday."[30] The anxiety and hypervigilance about safeguarding both the plates and the family made these years especially challenging, but it was also because it had been a time where she experienced her own spiritual awakening. There was no question in her mind that her brother possessed the plates and that it contained a sacred record of an ancient people. The ostracism and fear she experienced was tempered by an air of excitement and increased devotion as the family unitedly prepared to read the promised record and looked forward to formally organizing the Church of Christ. "Every room was filled with the Holy Ghost," Katharine recalled of that three-month period in 1827 when the record was in their home. "You could go into any room in the house and feel the presence of the spirit."[31] Her faith was also strengthened by reading the Book of Mormon once it came off Grandin's Press in Palmyra. "Many times when I have read its sacred pages, I have wept like a child," recalled Katharine of her conversion, "while the Spirit has borne witness with my spirit to its truth."[32]

With the publication of the Book of Mormon in 1830, Joseph was eager to formally organize the Church of Christ, and Katharine was among those early believers who gathered at the Peter Whitmer Sr. home on April 6, 1830, at Fayette, New York. "I was one of the number who met in the first conference held in these last days, when the church was first organized," she recalled of the historic occasion. "We only numbered thirty, but we were a happy little band. It was

THE

BOOK OF MORMON:

AN ACCOUNT WRITTEN BY THE HAND OF MOR- MON, UPON PLATES TAKEN FROM THE PLATES OF NEPHI.

Wherefore it is an abridgment of the Record of the People of Nephi; and also of the Lamanites; written to the Lamanites, which are a remnant of the House of Israel; and also to Jew and Gentile; written by way of commandment, and also by the spirit of Prophesy and of Revelation. Written, and sealed up, and hid up unto the LORD, that they might not be destroyed; to come forth by the gift and power of GOD unto the interpretation thereof; sealed by the hand of Moroni, and hid up unto the LORD, to come forth in due time by the way of Gentile; the interpretation thereof by the gift of GOD; an abridgment taken from the Book of Ether.

Also, which is a Record of the People of Jared, which were scattered at the time the LORD confounded the language of the people when they were building a tower to get to Heaven: which is to shew unto the remnant of the House of Israel how great things the LORD hath done for their fathers; and that they may know the covenants of the LORD, that they are not cast off forever; and also to the convincing of the Jew and Gentile that JESUS is the CHRIST, the ETERNAL GOD, manifesting Himself unto all nations. And now if there be fault, it be the mistake of men; wherefore condemn not the things of GOD, that ye may be found spotless at the judgment seat of CHRIST.

BY JOSEPH SMITH, JUNIOR,

AUTHOR AND PROPRIETOR.

PALMYRA:

PRINTED BY E. B. GRANDIN, FOR THE AUTHOR.

1830.

Title page of the first edition of the Book of Mormon, 1830. Courtesy of McKay Library, BYU–Idaho.

a great day of rejoicing for us."[33] Though her parents were baptized that day, Katharine, along with brothers William (age nineteen) and Don Carlos (age fourteen) and her close friend Caroline Rockwell, waited until the next church conference to be baptized on June 9, 1830. Katharine, who turned seventeen that same month, was baptized by David Whitmer in the crystal clear waters of Seneca Lake, and Oliver Cowdery performed her confirmation the following day.[34] She was elated to finally unite with the newly restored Church, but never could have imagined the trajectory that decision would bring to her life in the ensuing decades.

Notes

1. Katharine Salisbury (Hancock County, IL) to Dear Sisters, March 10, 1886, *Saints' Herald* 33, no. 17 (May 1, 1886): 260. Katharine's mother Lucy does not mention Joseph viewing these other items in the stone box in her history during this time or afterward, and never notes the Liahona or brass plates. She does recount handling both the interpreters (Urim and Thummim) and breastplate, describing these items in detail in her history. As with Katharine's recollections, Lucy recounted her husband's surprise when Joseph could not obtain the plates but does not mention him comforting his son Joseph and offering an explanation as to why he could not yet obtain the record. Lucy Mack Smith, *Biographical Sketches of Joseph Smith the Prophet and His Progenitors for Many Generations* (Liverpool: S. W. Richards, 1853), 86, 101, 106–7.
2. Kyle R. Walker, "Katharine Smith Salisbury's Recollections of Joseph's Meetings with Moroni," *BYU Studies* 41, no. 3 (2002): 13–15; Dean C. Jessee, "Joseph Knight's Recollection of Early Mormon History," *BYU Studies* 17, no. 1 (1976): 31.
3. Salisbury to Dear Sisters, 260.
4. Lucy Mack Smith, *Biographical Sketches*, 99–100.
5. Walker, "Katharine Smith Salisbury's Recollections," 15; Lucy Mack Smith, *Biographical Sketches*, 102–4.
6. Lucy Mack Smith, *Biographical Sketches*, 102–5.
7. Herbert S. Salisbury, "Things the Prophet's Sister Told Me," 1, San Rafael, CA, June 30, 1945, typescript, CHL.
8. Walker, "Katharine Smith Salisbury's Recollections," 15; Isaac Birkenhead Ball, "The Prophet's Sister Testifies She Lifted the B. of M. Plates," typescript interview with Herbert S. Salisbury, ca. 1954, 2, CHL. Lucy Mack Smith, who was also present on this occasion, failed to mention that Joseph fainted, but noted that when he arrived at the

house "he was . . . altogether speechless from fright and fatigue of running." Additionally, Lucy commented on Joseph's dislocated thumb but did not mention his lame arm or bruised knuckles. Lucy Mack Smith, *Biographical Sketches*, 105–6.

9. Salisbury to Dear Sisters, 260.

10. Ball, "The Prophet's Sister Testifies," 1; Frederick V. Salisbury, "The Teachings and Testimonies of My Mother," 1926–28, unpublished manuscript, 14, Hancock County Historical Society, Carthage, IL. This account parallels Emma Hale Smith's, who said, "The plates often lay on the table without any attempt at concealment, wrapped in a small linen table cloth, which I had given them to fold them in. I once felt of the plates, as they lay on the table, tracing their outline and shape. They seemed pliable like thick paper, and would rustle with a metallic sound when the edges were moved by the thumb, as one does sometimes thumb the edges of a book." Joseph Smith III, "Last Testimony of Sister Emma," *Saints' Herald* 26, no. 19 (October 1, 1879): 289–90.

11. Lucy Mack Smith, *Biographical Sketches*, 102.

12. Arthur B. Deming, "Mrs. M. C. R. Smith's Statement," *Naked Truths about Mormonism* 1 (April 1888): 1. Caroline Rockwell was the daughter of Orin and Sarah Witt Rockwell and a younger sister to Orrin Porter Rockwell. The family lived within a mile of the Smith home. Members of the Rockwell family were some of the first to unite with the Church of Christ after its organization in 1830 and were frequent visitors in the Smith home. Harold Schindler, *Orrin Porter Rockwell: Man of God Son of Thunder*, 2nd rev. ed. (Salt Lake City: University of Utah Press, 1983), 3–6; Karen Lynn Davidson et al.,*Histories, Volume 1: Joseph Smith Histories, 1832–1844*, vol. 1 of the Histories series of *The Joseph Smith Papers*, ed. Dean C. Jessee, Ronald K. Esplin, and Richard Lyman Bushman (Salt Lake City: Church Historian's Press, 2012), 390.

13. Lavina Fielding Anderson, ed., *Lucy's Book: A Critical Edition of Lucy Mack Smith's Family Memoir* (Salt Lake City: Signature Books, 2001), 343; Lucy Mack Smith, *Biographical Sketches*, 84, 86.

14. Walker, "Katharine Smith Salisbury's Recollections," 11.

15. Mary Salisbury Hancock, "The Three Sisters of the Prophet Joseph Smith, Part 1," *Saints' Herald* 101, no. 2 (January 11, 1954): 12.

16. Walker, "Katharine Smith Salisbury's Recollections," 15–16.

17. Salisbury, "The Teachings and Testimonies of My Mother," 4; Eric A. Eliason, "Seer Stones, Salamanders, and Early Mormon 'Folk Magic' in the Light of Folklore Studies and Bible Scholarship," *BYU Studies* 55, no. 1 (2016): 73–93.

18. William Smith, *William Smith on Mormonism* (Lamoni, IA: Herald Steam Book and Job Office, 1883), 13.

19. Hancock, "Three Sisters," 12.

20. Hyrum had married Jerusha Barden on November 2, 1826, and after his marriage they moved into the log home where the Smith family had earlier resided on the property. Hyrum Smith Family Bible; Lucy Mack Smith, *Biographical Sketches*, 40; *William Smith on Mormonism*, 14. Sophronia married Calvin Stoddard on December 3, 1827. Stoddard Family Bible, original in possession of Reid Moon, Provo, UT. The author wishes to acknowledge Reid Moon for sharing high resolution photographs of the Stoddard Family Bible.

21. Lucy Mack Smith, *Biographical Sketches*, 95–98, 111–12, 159–65; *William Smith on Mormonism*, 12–14.

22. The Smith family was forced to move from their larger frame home back into their log home, where Hyrum and his family were living, sometime in the Spring 1829. By the summer of 1829, Hyrum was married and had two children of his own, making living space cramped. Larry C. Porter, *A Study of the Origins of The Church of Jesus Christ of Latter-day Saints in the States of New York and Pennsylvania, 1816–1831* (Provo, UT: BYU Studies and Joseph Fielding Institute for Latter-day Saint History, 2000), 37, 43n193; "Records of Early Church Families," *Utah Genealogical Magazine* 26 (1935): 103.

23. Catharine Smith v. Trustees of Farmington School District No. 5, February–June 1829, Judgment Docket, Victor, Ontario County Historical Society, Canandaigua, NU. For a further discussion on this source, see Dan Vogel, ed., *Early Mormon Documents*, vol. 3 (Salt Lake City: Signature Books, 2000), 503.

24. Arthur B. Deming, "C. M. Stafford's Statement," *Naked Truths About Mormonism* 1 (April 1888): 1.

25. Hyrum departed on either September 29 or October 6, 1830, to preside over the Colesville Branch of the church. Lucy Mack Smith, *Biographical Sketches*, 191. For a discussion on the specific timing of Hyrum's journey, see Porter, *Study of Origins*, 38; *JSP*, D1:268n152.

26. Katharine Salisbury (Fountain Green, IL) to Dear Sisters of the "Home Column," May 16, 1886, *Saints' Herald* 33, no. 26 (July 3, 1886): 405. Lucy Mack Smith recounted the same incident in her history but described William driving the mob out with a "large handspike, . . . exclaiming 'Away from here, you cut-throats, instantly, or I will be the death of everyone one of you.'" Lucy Mack Smith, *Biographical Sketches*, 164.

27. See, for example, Eber D. Howe, *Mormonism Unvailed* (Painesville, OH: Eber D. Howe, 1834), 100.

28. Pomeroy Tucker, *Origin, Rise, and Progress of Mormonism* (New York: D. Appleton, 1867), 81–82. See statements made by Palmyra neighbors Lorenzo Saunders and C. M. Stafford, cited in Vogel, *Early Mormon Documents*, 2:127, 163, 195.

29. "Testimony of Katherine Salisbury," Sworn Affidavit, April 15, 1881, copy of holograph, Community of Christ Library-Archives, Independence, MO, also printed in *Saints' Herald* 28, no. 11 (June 1, 1881): 169.

30. Walker, "Katharine Smith Salisbury's Recollections," 10.

31. Oscar Case, Reminiscence, ca. 1894, Tom and Carla Duke Papers, Burlington, IA, typescript copy in author's possession.

32. Salisbury to Dear Sisters, 260.

33. Salisbury to Dear Sisters, 260. David Whitmer remembered that "about 50 members & the 6 elders were present." Journal of Edward Stevenson, January 2, 1887, CHL. Larry C. Porter documents a list of seventy-three individuals who likely attended that day. Larry C. Porter, "Organizational Origins of the Church of Jesus Christ, 6 April 1830," in *Regional Studies in Latter-day Saint History: New York and Pennsylvania*, ed. Larry C. Porter, Milton V. Backman Jr., and Susan Easton Black (Provo, UT: BYU Department of Church History and Doctrine, 1992), 154–55. Katharine also indicated that her brother Joseph designated six original members of the Church: "Joseph Smith Jr., Oliver Cowdery, Samuel H. Smith, Hyrum Smith, David Whitmer, and Peter Whitmer Jr." Salisbury, "Things the Prophet's Sister Told Me." Katharine's list is identical to the six men Richard L. Anderson identified after consolidating surviving sources. However, neither Anderson nor Michael Hubbard MacKay were apparently aware of Katharine's list. Richard L. Anderson, "Who Were the Six Who Organized the Church on 6 April 1830?" *Ensign* 10, no. 6 (June 1980): 44–45. See also Michael Hubbard MacKay, *Sacred Space: Exploring the Birthplace of Mormonism* (Provo, UT: Religious Studies Center, Brigham Young University; Salt Lake City: Deseret Book, 2016), 52–55.

34. Davidson et al., *JSP*, H1:390.

CHAPTER FOUR

Migrating to Ohio

[Mother's] faith was strong in the Lord, for she believed that he had commanded us to go and would carry us safely through.

—Katharine Salisbury

WHILE STILL LIVING IN NEW YORK, Katharine became acquainted with a recent convert named Wilkins Jenkins Salisbury, most likely when the Smiths were living near Waterloo, New York, not far from Fayette. The Smiths had moved to the area after being forced from their property in the fall of 1830. Jenkins, as he was known, was born January 6, 1809, on the family farm, which was located between the towns of Middlesex and Rushville, Ontario County, New York (both towns became part of Yates County in 1823).[1] Jenkins's father, Gideon Salisbury, was a Revolutionary War veteran who first enlisted in 1777. One of Gideon's most notable contributions came serving as a private under the command of brigadier general "Mad Anthony" Wayne not long after the latter's victory in the Battle of Stony Point. Gideon later participated in the Battle of Stone Arabia. In the last battle, which the Americans lost to a combined army of British and American Indian soldiers, Gideon was shot five times through his clothes and had his cartridge box shot off his belt but escaped without injury.[2] After the war, Gideon married Margaret Elizabeth Shields in Philadelphia, and they relocated their family to Rushville, New York, being some of the earliest settlers in the region.[3]

The religious fervor connected to the Second Great Awakening swept through the town of Rushville, New York, during the same time it reached Palmyra, twenty miles to the north. In the year 1816 alone, more than one hundred converts were made to the Presbyterian faith during a season of revivals, a trend that continued intermittently through the year 1831. It is unknown what influence the increasing religious fervor had on Jenkins or his family, but during that fifteen-year period hundreds of converts linked themselves to several competing churches in the sparsely populated region.[4] The Salisbury family possibly participated in these religious gatherings, but at the very least were witnesses to the religious enthusiasm which permeated their community.

Jenkins was the youngest of eleven children born to the Salisburys.[5] His next older sister Samantha recalled that Jenkins left the family home in his youth, probably in his early teens, to learn the blacksmith trade. Samantha remembered their childhood relationship with fondness, describing Jenkins as a kind and thoughtful brother, but also remembered that she did not see him much after he left home.[6] It might have also been during this apprenticeship that Jenkins had some sort of training in law, though that experience appears to have been only minimal, as Jenkins worked as a blacksmith for most of his adult life.[7] It was common for families to hire out children during adolescence to learn a trade, which typically ended once a youth reached adulthood, between the ages of eighteen to twenty. Jenkins appears to have followed that pattern. Perhaps he had apprenticed as a blacksmith in the Seneca Falls–Waterloo region because it was one of the largest communities close to Rushville, just twenty-three miles northeast of the Salisbury home. Jenkins's father Gideon had lived near Waterloo before settling his family at Rushville, conceivably coordinating his son's apprenticeship with one of his former neighbors.[8]

Jenkins turned twenty in 1829. The completion of his apprenticeship coincided with the organization of the Church of Christ held at Fayette, New York, April 6, 1830, as well as the launching of missionary efforts throughout Western New York in subsequent months.[9] "My brothers and the Whitmer brothers, held meetings, first at one house and then at the other, for preaching and prayer," Katharine recalled of their six-month stay near Waterloo, "and this continued until near spring [1831], first one preaching and then the other, wherever they could get a hearing."[10] Perhaps Jenkins was among those that attended one of these preaching meetings held by the Smiths and Whitmers. Though details of Jenkins's conversion have not survived, he became an enthusiastic convert the first year after the church's organization. Katharine and Jenkins met while both were living in the region. If he was indeed residing near Waterloo, perhaps he was also among those who regularly gathered at the Smith home in Kingdom, a town midway between Waterloo and Seneca Falls.[11] Lucy Mack Smith recalled that her home became a place of resort for several dozen people, who would join them for their evening devotionals.[12]

Jenkins developed a fast friendship with Katharine's older brother William during this same period. Only two years apart in age (William turned twenty in March 1831), the two were entering the same life stage of launching into adulthood and shared independent and impetuous personalities. Jenkins had been separated from his family since his early teens, and of necessity made his way in the world without the immediate support of his family during his developmental years. William was unique among the Smith family. Though he had believed his brother Joseph's visionary experiences, he was the only member of the Smith family to manifest periods of religious indifference. He later confessed that he was less spiritually inclined than the rest of his family due to his "wild and inconsiderate" personality, which, he said, led to "frequent lectures from my mother and my brother Joseph." However, he had reconciled his skepticism by the time he and Jenkins first became acquainted, demonstrating his commitment by being baptized and confirmed in the newfound religion the previous summer.[13] The two would remain lifelong friends, and the handsome and charismatic younger brother of the Prophet would have great influence on Jenkins during the next quarter of a century. Jenkins also developed a fondness for the Smiths' daughter Katharine, seventeen years old at the time

William B. Smith, ca. 1860.
Original in the L. Tom Perry
Special Collections, Harold B. Lee
Library, Brigham Young University.
Photograph by Kyle R. Walker.
Courtesy of Mary Dennis.

they first met and four years younger than Jenkins. Family tradition holds that their relationship began before migrating from the state.[14]

In December 1830, Joseph Smith received revelation that the church should move en masse from New York to northeastern Ohio, where early missionaries had enjoyed marked success in making converts to the newly organized faith. Joseph Sr., Joseph Jr. and Emma, and Hyrum and Jerusha all left between January and March 1831, while the three branches of the church hurriedly prepared for an anticipated migration west later that spring. For Katharine and her family, the call to relocate meant prompt action, and "therefore all preparations were made for emigrating to the West."[15] Some others were less enthusiastic about uprooting. John Whitmer indicated that following the revelation to gather to Ohio there were a few church members who felt Joseph "had invented it himself to deceive the people that in the end he might get gain."[16] Katharine's twenty-three-year-old brother Samuel was also away from home at the time serving as a missionary in Ohio with Orson Pratt, leaving William as the oldest Smith brother at home and allowing him to take on an unexpected leadership role.[17] In an attempt to strengthen loyalty to his prophet-brother and as part of their spiritual preparation for their journey, William Smith "visited the church calling on every family (as our custom is) . . . [and] prayed with them and did not leave the house until every member of the family prayed vocally that was over eight years old."[18] The approach was effective in reinvigorating their faith, and the group eagerly anticipated the spring thaw, which would afford passage by canal.

New York canals opened for travel by mid-April, and word disseminated among Saints in the region that they should gather at the Smith home on the weekend of April 29–May 1, 1831. Among the group of fifty were the eight remaining Smith family members: Mother Lucy, her three daughters (including Sophronia's husband, Calvin Stoddard, and their one-year-old daughter, Eunice), sons William and Don Carlos, and family friend Jenkins Salisbury.[19] Just before leaving the state, Jenkins certainly visited his family one more time at their home near Rushville. He would rarely see them again.[20]

At the time of departure, Lucy tried to get fifty-four-year-old Solomon Humphrey or thirty-year-old Hiram Page to lead the migration, but after Page nominated Lucy as a capable leader, the large contingent of Saints received the proposal enthusiastically. The fact that Lucy, fifty-six years old and already a grandmother, directed the migration not only was an unusual occurrence for a woman in the early history of the church but also reflected the high regard the Saints held for the Smith family.[21]

On Monday, May 2, 1831, the Fayette Branch left for Ohio, initially traveling east on the Cayuga–Seneca Canal until it connected with the Erie Canal, where they headed directly west.[22] Lucy's proficient leadership during the migration had a marked influence on Katharine, as she rehearsed details of the journey on several occasions throughout her life. Lucy had demonstrated an astute leadership ability in previous settings, such as when the Smiths had migrated to Palmyra, New York, from Vermont, but never on such a large scale. "My mother took charge of the company," remembered Katharine, "and with the aid of Bro. Humphr[e]y and my brother William, we accomplished the journey as far as Buffalo" by canal boat.[23] Lucy embraced her leadership role in earnest, linking their journey to migrations described in the Book of Mormon and insisting the group evince comparable faith to those earlier Saints. "I then called the brethren and sisters together, and reminded them that we were travelling by the commandment of the Lord, as much as father Lehi was, when he left Jerusalem," she declared. "If faithful," Lucy continued, "we had the same reason to expect the blessings of God. I then desired them to be solemn, and lift their hearts continually in prayer, that we might be prospered."[24] Lucy went to such lengths as to attempt to separate men and women during the journey, no doubt to curtail flirting and rivet the company's focus on their spiritual migration. Perhaps Jenkins and Katharine's newfound relationship was part of her motivation to keep the group separated by gender because Lucy may have been concerned about Katharine's age (only seventeen) and the mutual attraction she observed between the two. After counseling with Humphrey and Page, she mandated that the group pray together twice daily and engage in regular hymn singing.[25]

Frustrated about the way mothers in the group were failing to manage their children, Lucy grew anxious for the children's safety and took matters into her own hands. She called for the children to gather around her and committed them to respond promptly when she signaled by raising her hand during times when their passage became dangerous. Lucy reported that the children all strictly kept their promise during the entire journey.[26]

Lucy also led out in managing the group's limited resources during the journey, as she indicated that most of the church branch were without enough food. The first leg of the journey took five days, and they arrived in Buffalo on Saturday, May 7, only to find the harbor blocked with ice.[27] Lucy scrambled to find shelter for her large group amid a freezing rainstorm. William held an umbrella over

Lucy Mack Smith, 1853, engraving by Frederick Piercy, in *Route from Liverpool to Great Salt Lake Valley* (Liverpool, Franklin D. Richards, 1855).

his aging mother's head as she negotiated with proprietors at the harbor.[28] Katharine likely stayed with Sophronia and her daughter Eunice and assisted in caring for her younger sister Lucy, only nine years old at the time of the journey.

The difficult circumstances again turned Mother Smith to her faith. After visiting with other migrating contingents also delayed at the harbor, she learned that they were concealing their faith, thinking that doing so might help them get to their destination sooner and prevent persecution. Lucy rebuked leaders from both groups, declaring, "If you are ashamed of Christ, you must not expect to be prospered; and I shall wonder if we do not get to Kirtland before you." Her declaration proved to be prescient.[29]

After securing passage on the ship *Niagara* captained by a man named Blake (an acquaintance of Lucy's deceased brother Stephen Mack), Lucy secured lodging for her company in a room on shore for the night. The following day, May 8, Captain Blake allowed the company to stay on board his ship, but after measuring the ice he and the other boatmen were skeptical that the ice would not break up for another two weeks. The news must have been devastating to the group. With the harbor thronged with people and limited finances and food, Lucy and the other leaders could not imagine trying to obtain lodging for their large group for two more weeks. Realizing their plight, Lucy summoned the group together and declared, "Now brethren and sisters, if you will raise your desires to heaven, that the ice may be broken up, and we be set at liberty, as sure as the Lord lives, it will be done."[30] Katharine recounted that the group "held a prayer meeting" under Lucy's direction, "and prayed that the Lord would open the way for us to reach our destination." Following their prayer, Katharine indicated that Lucy then directed them to sing "praises to our God for the blessings he had bestowed upon us in restoring the gospel in these last days."[31]

While the group was still singing, Captain Blake came to Lucy and requested that they stop, as he noticed movement in the harbor and needed his deck hands to hear his orders and prepare the sail. "Shortly afterwards we heard a great noise and cracking in the ice," described Katharine, and "the captain called all hands and set them to work, for the crack had widened and a channel had opened in the ice wide enough for our boat to pass out."[32]

Although Lucy and Katharine's accounts sound like theirs was the only ship that made it through the ice that day, three others successfully passed through before the ice prevented passage once again. A Buffalo newspaper reported that "the schr. [schooner] *Gov. Cass*, Capt. Whitaker, left our harbor this morning of the of 8th inst. although large quantities of ice impeded her offing; she was soon followed by the Steamboat *Pioneer, Niagara,* and *Superior* in succession."[33] For the company of Saints, the opening of the passageway through the harbor was nothing short of a miracle.

The two-to-three-day journey on Lake Erie nevertheless proved difficult. Apparently, the thin passageway through the ice had damaged the *Niagara*'s waterwheel, and Katharine recalled that their company had to stop that evening on the Canadian side of Lake Erie

Buffalo Village from the Light-house, 1826, from H. Perry Smith, *History of the City of Buffalo and Erie County,* vol. 2 (Syracuse, NY: D. Mason, 1884).

to make repairs to the ship. The weather during their lake passage also contributed to a demanding voyage. Captain Blake, who had been navigating on Lake Erie for nearly thirty years, informed the company "that it was the roughest time he had ever had" navigating his ship on the lake.[34] Hence, Mother Smith nursed a number of her group who were seasick in route.[35] "After a long and tedious passage," confirmed William, "facing many storms, cold winds and rains, we at length arrived at Fairport [Harbor]" in Ohio.[36]

Katharine's faith was strengthened by the entire experience, but most especially because of her mother's example. The night they had stayed on shore in Buffalo's harbor, she watched as her mother stayed up until two in the morning expounding the basic tenets of the Church of Christ to her elderly female host. The following day,

Steamboat on Lake Erie near Cleveland, Ohio, ca. 1834, sketch by Karl Bodmer, in Maximilian, Prinz von Wied, *Voyage dans l'intérieur de l'Amérique du Nord* (Paris: A. Bertrand, 1840). Courtesy of New York Public Library.

after the company gathered on the ship, and as the group's religious affiliation became known, a man yelled from shore, "Is the Book of Mormon true?" At the top of her lungs so that all within the sound of her voice could hear, Lucy replied, "That book was brought forth by the power of God, and translated by the gift of the Holy Ghost; and, if I could make my voice sound as loud as the trumpet of Michael, the Archangel, I would declare the truth."[37] Katharine's faith was especially strengthened when the ice blocking Buffalo's harbor seemed to miraculously part, allowing for the ship's passage. The previous night she had witnessed her mother on her knees from dusk to dawn praying for the group's "deliverance" from their "pitiable surroundings." She felt that the experience was a direct result of her mother's faith and spiritual direction.[38] She astutely watched her mother organize, protect, feed, house, and successfully relocate a company of fifty Saints three hundred miles to the west. "Mother bore all their complainings patiently, and had great charity for and sympathy with them," recalled Katharine. "Her faith was strong in the Lord, for she believed that he had commanded us to go and would carry us safely through."[39]

When they finally arrived at Fairport Harbor on May 9 or 10,[40] William Smith and Jenkins Salisbury went on foot ahead of the rest of the group to locate the rest of the Smith family, who were living in Kirtland some fourteen miles away.[41] They would not get far, as Joseph Jr. and Samuel were anxiously watching and waiting for the company in the vicinity, fearing their delay meant an accident had occurred. Upon seeing her sons coming toward her, Lucy took Samuel by the right hand and Joseph by the left, and they all wept for joy at their safe arrival. The Smith brothers took them immediately to the home of Edward Partridge, a recent convert who lived nearby in Painesville, Ohio, where they enjoyed their first full meal since leaving two weeks earlier. "My brothers [then] took us to Kirtland where we met father," Katharine recalled with fondness. "I can tell you it was a day of rejoicing, and when memory brings these things afresh to my mind I can not help weeping. . . . We were a united, happy family."[42]

Notes

1. Gideon Salisbury Family Bible, photocopy of original in Gideon Salisbury Revolutionary War Pension File, US Revolutionary War Pension and Bounty-Land Warrant Application Files, 1800–1900, ancestry.com.

2. Gideon Salisbury Family Bible.

3. Lewis Cass Aldrich, ed., *History of Yates County, N. Y.* (Syracuse, NY: D. Mason, 1892), 473–74; Warren L. Van Dine, "Statement About His Salisbury Family" (unpublished typescript, ca. 1975), 7, Hancock County Historical Society, Carthage, IL.

4. Presbyterian reverend James H. Hotchkin documented that the converts made at Rushville, New York, was only surpassed by what was happening at Palmyra during that particular year. In September 1816 "a glorious work had commenced" at Palmyra, recounted Hotchkin, where "about 120 hopeful converts are stated on the minutes of the Synod, as the result of this effusion of the Holy Spirit." James H. Hotchkin, *A History of the Purchase and Settlement of Western New York, and of the Rise, Progress, and Present State of the Presbyterian Church in that Section* (New York: M. W. Dodd, 1848), 126, 130, 136, 146–47; Aldrich, *History of Yates County,* 464–66.

5. Gideon Salisbury Family Bible.

6. Samantha Arnold (n.p.) to Katharine Salisbury, January 1, 1853 [1854], copy of original in Katharine Smith Salisbury Correspondence, L. Tom Perry Special Collections, Harold B. Lee Library, Brigham Young University, Provo, UT.

7. Mary Salisbury Hancock, "The Three Sisters of the Prophet Joseph Smith, Part 1," *Saints' Herald* 101, no. 2 (January 11, 1954): 12; Emma M. Phillips, *Dedicated to Serve: Biographies of 31 Women of the Restoration* (Independence, MO: Herald House, 1970), 13.

8. Other possible nearby locations for his apprenticeship include Geneva, Penn Yan, Canandaigua, Lyons, or Palmyra. Gideon Salisbury Family Bible.

9. For a discussion on Fayette, New York, as the church's organizational location, see Michael Hubbard MacKay, *Sacred Space: Exploring the Birthplace of Mormonism* (Salt Lake City: Deseret Book, 2016).

10. Katharine Salisbury (Fountain Green, IL) to Dear Sisters of the "Home Column," May 16, 1886, *Saints' Herald* 33, no. 26 (July 3, 1886): 404–5.

11. Larry C. Porter, *A Study of the Origins of The Church of Jesus Christ of Latter-day Saints in the States of New York and Pennsylvania, 1816–1831* (Provo, UT: BYU Studies and Joseph Fielding Institute for Latter-day Saint History, 2000), 104–5.

12. Lucy Mack Smith, *Biographical Sketches,* 167–68.

13. William was baptized on June 9, 1830, on the same day as Katharine and their younger brother Don Carlos. William Smith, *William Smith on Mormonism* (Lamoni, IA: Herald Steam Book and Job Office, 1883), 6, 10, 15–16. For more information on William's lack of spirituality in his youth, see Kyle R. Walker, *William B. Smith: In the Shadow of a Prophet* (Salt Lake City: Greg Kofford Books, 2015), 66–69.

14. Van Dine, "Statement About His Salisbury Family," 9.

15. *William Smith on Mormonism*, 18.

16. John Whitmer, History, 1831–circa 1847, in Karen Lynn Davidson, Richard L. Jensen, and David J. Whittaker, eds., *Histories, Volume 2: Assigned Historical Writings, 1831–1847*, vol. 2 of the Histories series of *The Joseph Smith Papers*, ed. Dean C. Jessee, Ronald K. Esplin, and Richard Lyman Bushman (Salt Lake City: Church Historian's Press, 2012), 21.

17. Orson Pratt described that "on the 2d of January, 1831, I attended a conference at the house of Father Whitmer; and soon after Samuel H. Smith and myself commenced laboring for one of the Saints Joseph Coe, to assist him in making preparations to remove to Ohio. . . . And in a few weeks, Elder Samuel H. Smith and myself started on foot for Kirtland, Ohio, a distance of several hundred miles." The two missionaries arrived in Kirtland on February 27. Orson Pratt, "History of Orson Pratt," *Millennial Star* 27 (October 21, 1865), 55; Dean L. Jarman and Kyle R. Walker, "Samuel Harrison Smith," in *United by Faith: The Joseph Sr. and Lucy Mack Smith Family*, ed. Kyle R. Walker (American Fork, UT: Covenant Communications, 2006), 212–14.

18. Lavina Fielding Anderson, ed., *Lucy's Book: A Critical Edition of Lucy Mack Smith's Family Memoir* (Salt Lake City: Signature Books, 2001), 511.

19. Lucy Mack Smith, *Biographical Sketches*, 172–73. "I do not remember how many there were in our company," recalled Katharine of the journey, "but of our own family there were eight. Mother, my oldest sister, her husband [Calvin] and one child [Eunice], brother William and Don Carlos, myself and sister Lucy." Salisbury to Dear Sisters, May 16, 1886.

20. Writing to her sister-in-law Katharine Salisbury in 1854, Jenkins's sister, Samantha Arnold, indicated that she had not seen Jenkins for fourteen years. He likely visited them again during his mission to New York in the year 1831 (see chapter 5). Samantha Arnold to Katharine Salisbury, January 1, 1853 [1854].

21. Anderson, *Lucy's Book*, 512–13.

22. Larry C. Porter, "'Ye Shall Go to the Ohio': Exodus of the New York Saints to Ohio, 1831," in *Regional Studies in Latter-day Saints Church History: Ohio*, ed. Milton V. Backman Jr. (Provo, UT: Brigham Young University Department of Church History and Doctrine, 1990), 15.

23. Salisbury to Dear Sisters, May 16, 1886.

24. Lucy Mack Smith, *Biographical Sketches*, 173.

25. Lucy Mack Smith, *Biographical Sketches*, 173, 179–80; Anderson, *Lucy's Book*, 514.

26. Lucy Mack Smith, *Biographical Sketches*, 174–75.

27. Lucy Mack Smith, *Biographical Sketches*, 176–78.

28. Anderson, *Lucy's Book*, 523.

29. Lucy Mack Smith, *Biographical Sketches*, 176.

30. Lucy Mack Smith, *Biographical Sketches*, 181.

31. Salisbury to Dear Sisters, May 16, 1886.

32. Salisbury to Dear Sisters, May 16, 1886.

33. "Opening of Navigation," *Buffalo Journal & General Advertiser* XVI, no. 48 (May 11, 1831), 2, as cited in Fred E. Woods, "Mormon Migration on Lake Erie and Through Fairport Harbor," *Inland Seas* 60 (Winter 2004): 297.

34. Salisbury to Dear Sisters, May 16, 1886.

35. Lucy Mack Smith, *Biographical Sketches*, 181–82.

36. *William Smith on Mormonism*, 19.

37. Lucy Mack Smith, *Biographical Sketches*, 178–80.

38. "Awaiting a Revelation—Story of a Winter Journey," *Kansas City Daily Journal* 37, no. 304 (April 12, 1895): 3.

39. Salisbury to Dear Sisters, May 16, 1886.

40. Fred Woods documents that Lucy's group left Buffalo Harbor on May 8, 1831. Katharine indicated that they spent the night of the 8th on the Canadian side of Lake Erie making repairs to the ship, meaning that the earliest date they could have arrived in Kirtland would be May 9. Woods, "Mormon Migration on Lake Erie," 297–98.

41. *William Smith on Mormonism*, 19.

42. Lucy Mack Smith, *Biographical Sketches*, 183; Salisbury to Dear Sisters, May 16, 1886. The Smiths in Kirtland were apprehensive for the safety of the group in the days leading up to their arrival. Lucy indicated that Samuel "had been warned of God in a dream to meet the company from Waterloo, and feared that some disaster had befallen me." Lucy Mack Smith, *Biographical Sketches*, 183. Katharine remembered that her brothers were waiting in the vicinity because "word had reached them that we were all drowned." Salisbury to Dear Sisters, May 16, 1886.

CHAPTER FIVE

Building Up the Kingdom

While we lived in Kirtland, . . . my mother and myself spent our whole time in waiting upon the comers and goers in cooking and washing.
—Katharine Smith Salisbury

UPON HER ARRIVAL IN OHIO, Katharine resided with her parents at the home of forty-five-year-old Isaac Morley, a well-to-do farmer and recent convert who resided in Kirtland. Several weeks later, the Smiths removed to the farm of Frederick G. Williams.[1] Katharine remained with her parents on Williams's farm for less than a month. Family tradition holds that Jenkins and Katharine had discussed marriage before they left New York but was possibly not yet common knowledge among the Smith family.[2] Whether her parents knew or not, their bond deepened in the weeks after arriving in Ohio. Because she was a month shy of her eighteenth birthday, Katharine had to obtain permission from her father before she could marry. Ohio law stipulated that women between the ages of fourteen and eighteen, could be married only if they "first obtain the consent of their fathers, respectively; or in the case of the death or incapacity of their fathers, then of their mothers or guardians."[3] Jenkins accordingly spoke with Katharine's parents about their intention of marriage, and procured a statement signed by both Joseph Sr. and Lucy confirming their consent for their daughter's marriage. The couple presented this certificate to Geauga County clerk D. D. Aiken, from whom they obtained a marriage license in early June. They then sought out the celebrated reformed Baptist preacher and recent Ohio convert, Sidney Rigdon, who performed Katharine and Jenkins's wedding ceremony at Kirtland, on Wednesday, June 8, 1831.[4]

Sidney Rigdon, ca. 1873. Photograph of original by Fox & Symonds, Salt Lake City, ca. 1900. Courtesy of Church History Library.

The couple settled in Chardon, Ohio, ten miles southeast of Kirtland, to live near Katharine's eldest sister Sophronia. Jenkins presumably found work as a blacksmith in the area. The wedding celebration did not last long among the Smith clan, as just two weeks later Sophronia's one-year-old daughter Eunice passed away on June 24, 1831.[5] Katharine's brother Joseph and his wife Emma also lost twins earlier in March, just hours after they were born. Their grief was somewhat assuaged two weeks later when widower John Murdock asked Joseph and Emma to raise his twins as their own after Murdock's wife Julia died in childbirth.[6] Katharine played the role of comforter to both women during those early months in Kirtland, most especially to Sophronia due to her living so close.

THE STATE OF OHIO,
GEAUGA COUNTY, ss. PERSONALLY APPEARED
Jenkins Salisbury and made application for a MARRIAGE LICENSE,
for *himself* and *Catharine Smith* of
the township of *Kirtland* in said county, and made solemn oath
that *he* the said *Jenkins Salisbury* is of the age of twenty-one years,
and the said *Catharine Smith* is *under* the age of eighteen years;
& over the age of fourteen years
that they are both single, and not nearer of kin than first cousins; that
he knows of no legal impediment against their being joined in marriage.
that he saw the parents of Catharine Smith sign a certificate of their consent to said marriage

Sworn and subscribed, this *8th* day of *June* 183*1*
BEFORE ME,
J. D. Aiken CLERK.

Jenkins Salisbury and Katharine Smith Marriage License Application, June 8, 1831, Geauga County, Ohio, Probate Court, Marriage Records. The clerk D. D. Aiken recorded that "he saw the parents of Catherine Smith sign a certificate of their consent to said marriage."

Sophronia's health had always been fragile, having nearly died from typhoid fever during her youth.[7] On April 12, 1832, Calvin and Sophronia welcomed another baby girl to their home, their last and only surviving child, whom they named Mariah.[8] It appears that Sophronia continued in poor health in the months following Mariah's birth, requiring the assistance of both Katharine and their younger sister Lucy. Just eleven years old at the time, Lucy moved to Chardon sometime in the period of 1832–33 to assist her eldest sister during her prolonged illness in managing her home and in caring for her infant daughter.[9] Similar to her experience with typhoid fever in her youth, doctors attended Sophronia for a time but eventually declared that she was "beyond the reach of medicine." Both doctors and family members felt she had only days to live as she lay motionless on her bed. According to her mother, Lucy, divine intervention once again spared her life. After Jared Carter, Joseph Sr., and several Smith brothers jointly blessed her by the laying on of hands,

Katharine Smith Salisbury, ca. 1880. Photographer unknown. Courtesy of Community of Christ Library-Archives. Note Katharine's hair, "parted in the middle, combed back and done up in a coil and fastened with a comb" and "combed smooth behind the ears" just as she had instructed Saints.

Sophronia's health began to improve, and she was back on her feet again within days.[10]

In contrast to her older sister, Katharine's health was vigorous and surviving descriptions often noted her exceptional strength. A newspaper reporter who interviewed Katharine in later life thought she "resembled her noted brother [Joseph] very little save in stature." He thought that she instead looked most like her nephew, Joseph Smith III. Among her siblings, she most resembled her brother William, though he had brown hair and Katharine's hair was blonde. Both had deep-set blue eyes, thin lips, and a prominent broad nose, more characteristic of the Mack side of the family. Repeatedly noteworthy in surviving accounts was her uncommon height, a generational Smith family trait.[11] She was reportedly six inches taller than the average woman of her day, around five feet ten inches tall, and capable of performing the work of most men. One descendant thought that her large hands were also conspicuous, remembering Katharine as "unusually rugged and strong for a female."[12] Her stature would serve her well as the Saints located in frontier settlements in Ohio, Missouri, and Illinois.

Just three days before Sophronia gave birth to Mariah, Katharine and Jenkins welcomed their first child into their home on April 9, 1832, a baby girl they named Elizabeth. During pregnancy and in those first months after their girls were born, Sophronia and Katharine unitedly looked forward to the bond these cousins would share throughout their lives. Tragically, the Salisburys' daughter, Elizabeth, would not survive the summer, passing away just three months after she was born, on July 15.[13] Watching Sophronia raise Mariah in the latter part of 1832 may have initially brought painful reminders of the loss of her own daughter, but assisting with Mariah's care the following year during Sophronia's lengthy illness probably provided some purpose for her grief. The three Smith sisters bonded through these challenging times during those early years in Ohio.

Once Sophronia's health had fully recovered, Katharine turned her focus to building up the burgeoning church. Lucy Mack Smith had successfully transmitted traditional Christian virtues into the minds of her daughters. This included everything from attitudes about childrearing, their manner of worship, habits of Bible study and prayer, and even such everyday practices as frugality and their manner of dress. Katharine's surviving letters are filled with references to such values. One example that is repeated in her writings was her belief in dressing simple, and in later life she often remonstrated with those who were caught up in the ever-changing fashions she had witnessed during her lifetime, which spanned the entire nineteenth-century. Many of the religions of the day, including some that the Smith family had affiliated with during Katharine's youth, emphasized keeping dress and appearance simple. These denominations instructed that simplifying material needs demonstrated a willingness to sacrifice their means to spiritual purposes, such as missionary work, while others stressed that dressing plain indicated a preparedness to work and serve.[14] "In the old church we all dressed plain," described Katharine in a letter to her sister-Saints. "For my part I think it a shame to follow the fashions of the world. We all wore our hair plain in the old church, parted in the middle, combed back and done up in a coil and fastened with a comb," and "combed smooth behind the ears."[15] She stressed the importance of the "plain-ness" of bonnets and dresses, that she felt should be designed "for comfort and not for show." A bonnet, she instructed, should be no bigger than your hand, and felt it was excessive for women to "load their hats with ribbons, and artificial flowers, and feathers."[16] She held to these strict guidelines throughout her life, which reflected one aspect of her religious devotion.

Temple Construction and Work Efforts in Kirtland

Katharine also clung to the value of hard work, something she had also learned during her upbringing when the Smith family made their one-hundred-acre farm prosper during the decade of the 1820s. Her parents' home in Kirtland became a way station of sorts for missionaries and converts who were constantly moving in and out of the community. Though likely unconsciously assigned and certainly because of her connection to the church's founder, Mother Lucy embraced the role of housing, feeding, and mending clothes for the Saints who were coming and going during those early years in Kirtland. In her writings, Lucy often stressed the importance of building up the kingdom of God over personal comforts. "How often I have parted every bed in the house for the accommodation of the brethren," recalled Lucy of her time in Kirtland, "and then laid a single blanket on the floor for my husband and myself." More than a decade later, when dictating her biography to scribe Martha Jane Coray, Lucy mused, "I often wonder, when I hear brethren and sisters complain at the trifling inconveniences which they have to suffer in these days . . . [whether] salvation is worth as much now as it was in the commencement of the work."[17]

Katharine adopted her mother's mindset of sacrificing personal desires for the greater good of the community of Saints. It was one the primary reasons she felt that sisters should be modest in dress, so that the "money which all those needless trimmings cost could be saved to help spread the gospel."[18] Her writings evidence the value she placed on sacrifice. She often recounted the example of her brothers and other early missionaries during the Saints stay in

New York and Ohio, who often traveled with no money in their pocket and made great sacrifices to win new converts to the early church. Writing to members decades later, Katharine underscored these early missionaries' sacrifice and probed contemporary Saints as to "how many would respond to the call today if they had to go on foot without money?"[19] Her narrative of her efforts in Kirtland, and especially her extolling the value of sacrifice, precisely mirrored her mother's.

Katharine's efforts, though they did not include traveling abroad to spread the gospel message, differed in kind from the sacrifice made by her brothers. One summary of women's work efforts in the early church emphasized how their roles during that period were often connected to their husband's callings and missionary assignments. "Organized missionary work was a man's calling, except for contacts made by women among local family and friends. But the support— more often encouragement than cash—came from the women left at home. It was regarded as an act of faith to stay behind, maintain the home, and rear the children. It was also an act of sacrifice and love. . . . It appears that, for a woman, sending a man into the mission field was a vicarious religious experience."[20]

Yet sisters found practical ways to contribute their efforts in supporting missionary work while remaining at home. Katharine underscored her continual effort to clothe the traveling missionaries and care for the influx of converts who came to Kirtland. She recalled that "while we lived in Kirtland, my mother and myself spent our whole time in waiting upon the comers and goers in cooking and washing."[21] Women also worked behind the scenes to ensure meetings ran smoothly, such as baking bread for the sacrament or preparing food for feasts associated with sacred ceremonies leading up to the Kirtland Temple dedication.[22] While there was a noted distinction between male and female efforts to build up the kingdom, in Katharine's view they were all efforts to the same end.

Two years after settling in Ohio much of the focus of the Saints' work efforts shifted to the construction of the temple. While temple construction was first proposed in 1831, it wasn't until the Saints were rebuked through a revelation received by Joseph Smith on June 1, 1833, that enthusiasm increased. The latter revelation admonished the Saints for their failure to consider "the great commandment . . . that I have given unto you concerning the building of mine house."[23] Such a vast undertaking required the joint labors of the entire community of Saints. It also meant an increased workload for the greater Smith family. Hyrum, for one, felt impelled to get started on the construction immediately after the divine mandate was communicated to the Saints. After listening to Joseph describe his scope of the proposed structure, which he said had been shown to him in vision, Hyrum ran to his parents' home, grabbed a scythe, and began clearing weeds off the proposed temple site. Lucy remembered his eagerness at the time, recording that Hyrum told her that he was determined "that he would strike the first blow upon the house." He then grabbed a shovel and began digging a foundational trench for the walls of the temple. Such enthusiasm led to Hyrum being appointed one of three members who oversaw the temple's construction.[24] Because of the lack of financing and the difficulties the Saints

Interior of the Kirtland Temple, showing the curtains that were used to partition areas of the temple. Date and photographer unknown.

were experiencing in Missouri, temple plans in Kirtland took time to materialize.

Hyrum's initial excitement was representative of the entire Smith family. Lucy recalled, "There was but one mainspring to all our thoughts and actions, and that, was, the building of the Lord's house."[25] Joseph Sr., with Lucy's assistance, was appointed to oversee the sisters' work efforts. Once work efforts began in earnest on the construction of the Kirtland Temple, the Smith home became a hotbed of activity. While Jenkins and the Smith brothers began cutting and hauling stone for the temple's foundation and walls, Joseph Sr. supervised women's work contributions, including the making of carpets and curtains for the temple.[26] Katharine and Sophronia assisted in these tasks and produced clothing items for the men laboring on the temple. The Smith sisters accomplished this service by forming weaving clubs throughout the city wherever there were clusters of Saints, where looms were set up for weaving. Other groups of women were organized where they would gather to spin, knit, and card wool.[27] At one such gathering of sisters, Polly Angell, who was Katharine's age, remembered that while they were working on the veils of the temple, Joseph Smith and Sidney Rigdon stopped by the home while they were busily engaged. "Well sisters, you are always on hand," Joseph declared, "the sisters are always first and foremost in all good works. Mary was the first at the resurrection; and the sisters now are the first to work on the inside of the temple."[28]

Lucy grew frustrated at times with sisters who complained of what she considered trivial matters that prevented their work efforts during the time of the temple's construction.[29] Katharine noticed her mother's frustrations and similarly grew impatient with sisters who seemed more concerned with their appearance than in contributing their time and efforts. "Mother Smith, I would help you but I am afraid I will soil my dress," Katharine recalled of the sisters' complaints, "and this too when our tired limbs were about to fail us." Katharine had little patience for such excuses, recommending that when there was church work to be completed sisters should bring a calico dress with them so they could be fully engaged in such labor.[30]

The work was demanding and relentless, and Lucy enlisted the assistance of her daughters and other single or newlywed sisters to help her with the load. Twenty-four-year-old Mary Bailey and twenty-one-year-old Agnes Coolbrith, recent converts Samuel Smith baptized the previous summer in Boston, were two examples.[31] After they gathered with the Saints in Kirtland, the two lived with Joseph Sr. and Lucy during this period. Lucy remembered that Mary and Agnes "devoted their whole time to making and mending clothes for the men who were employed on the house."[32] Their closeness to the Smiths eventually led to romance, as Mary wed her missionary Samuel the following summer on August 13, 1834, and Agnes married the youngest Smith brother, Don Carlos, on July 30, 1835.[33]

Katharine bonded with her future sisters-in-law during this time, as she made the twenty-mile round trip from Chardon to Kirtland with regularity, likely remaining at her parents' home for days, perhaps even weeks or months when Jenkins was absent on his mission. She and Sophronia spent considerable time at their parent's home working alongside their mother, while they continued to be influenced by their mother's example and teachings. The greater Smith family excitedly anticipated the completion of the temple and the expansion of the church in the bustling community.

Notes

1.   Michael Hubbard MacKay et al., eds., *Documents, Volume 1: July 1828–June 1831*, vol. 1 of the Documents series of *The Joseph Smith Papers*, ed. Dean C. Jessee et al. (Salt Lake City: Church Historian's Press, 2013), 311; Lucy Mack Smith, *Biographical Sketches of Joseph Smith the Prophet and His Progenitors for Many Generations* (Liverpool: S. W. Richards, 1853), 184.

2.   Warren L. Van Dine, "Statement about His Salisbury Family," 1975, 9, typescript, Hancock County Historical Society, Carthage, IL.

3.   Act Regulating Marriages, January 6, 1824, in *Acts of a General Nature [. . .] of the State of Ohio*, vol. 29 (Columbus: Olmsted & Bailhache, 1831), 429.

4.   Ohio, United States, Geauga County Marriage Records, 1774–1993, Application for Marriage License, Jenkins Salisbury and Catharine

Smith, June 8, 1831; Marriage License for Jenkins Salisbury and Catharine Smith, June 8, 1831, Probate Court, Marriage Records, vol. B, 196, both available on Ancestry.com. Four years after he married Jenkins and Katharine, Sidney Rigdon was prosecuted in 1835 for illegally performing a marriage in the year 1834, because Judge Mathew Birchard determined he was not a "regularly ordained minister of the gospel." The charges were later dismissed. After examining Ohio law and the evidence in Rigdon's case, legal historian M. Scott Bradshaw concluded that the lawsuit appears to have been both politically and religiously motivated to curtail the Church of Christ's expanding influence in Geauga County, Ohio. M. Scott Bradshaw, "Joseph Smith's Performance of Marriages in Ohio," *BYU Studies* 39, no. 4 (2000): 23–69.

5. Stoddard Family Bible, photographs of original courtesy of Reid Moon, original in possession of Reid Moon, Provo, UT.

6. Karen Lynn Davidson, David J. Whittaker, Mark Ashurst-McGee, and Richard L. Jensen, eds., *The Joseph Smith Papers, Histories, Volume 1, Joseph Smith Histories, 1832–1844*, vol. 1 of the Histories series of *The Joseph Smith Papers*, ed. Dean C. Jessee, Ronald K. Esplin, and Richard Lyman Bushman (Salt Lake City: Church Historian's Press, 2012), 30; S. Reed Murdock, *Joseph and Emma's Julia: The Other Twin* (Salt Lake City: Eborn Books, 2004), 9–12.

7. Lucy Mack Smith, *Biographical Sketches*, 60–61.

8. Stoddard Family Bible.

9. Mary Salisbury Hancock, "The Three Sisters of the Prophet Joseph Smith, Part II," *Saints' Herald* 101, no. 3 (January 18, 1954): 10.

10. Lucy Mack Smith, *Biographical Sketches*, 204.

11. "Sister of a Prophet," *Saints' Herald* 40, no. 36 (September 9, 1893): 565; Interview with Catherine Salisbury, as reported in Gay Davidson, "Anniversary of Carthage," *Salt Lake Tribune* 44, no. 57 (June 24, 1894): 16.

12. Warren L. Van Dine, "Catherine Smith Salisbury, Sister of Joseph Smith," *Saints' Herald* 90, no. 32 (August 7, 1943): 24; Warren L. Van Dine, "Information on the Smith and Salisbury Families, 1966–1975," typescript of taped interview conducted by Norma Hiles, Burnside, IL, 1975, 27, CHL.

13. In the year 1865 Katharine sent genealogical information to her cousin George A. Smith in a letter per his request. Though her original letter has not been located, Smith recorded the information contained in the letter in his father's (John Smith) journal. George A. Smith (Salt Lake City) to Cousin Catherine [Salisbury], August 17, 1865, Historian's Office letterpress copybooks, 1854–79, vol. 2, 1859–69, CHL; John Smith Papers, 1833–54, Journal, 1846 February–1854 May, CHL. The author wishes to acknowledge Mark L. Staker for his assistance in locating this source. For further confirmation on Elizabeth's birth and death dates, see Lucy

Mack Smith, *Biographical Sketches*, 43; Dorothy D. Dean, handwritten family group sheet, copy of original in author's possession.

14. Mary Anne Caton, "The Aesthetics of Absence: Quaker Women's Plain Dress in the Delaware Valley, 1790–1900," in *Quaker Aesthetics: Reflections on a Quaker Ethic in American Design and Consumption*, ed. Emma Jones Lapsansky and Anne A. Verplanck (Philadelphia: University of Pennsylvania Press, 2003), 257–58; Matthew Simpson, *Cyclopedia of Methodism* (Philadelphia: Everts & Stewart, 1878), 311; William B. Sprague, *Annals of the American Pulpit* (New York: Robert Carter & Brothers, 1858), 139; Norman Fox, "George Fox and the Early Friends," *Baptist Quarterly* 11, no. 4 (October 1877): 437.

15. Katherine Salisbury (n.p.) to Sister Frances, December 24, 1886, *Saints' Herald* 34, no. 6 (February 5, 1887): 84.

16. Katharine Salisbury (n.p.) to Dear Sisters, July 2, 1895, *Saints' Herald* 42, no. 30 (July 24, 1895): 473. In another account, Katharine reiterated, "I think it is a sin to follow the fashions of the world. We are commanded to come out from the world, and be separate. Let us make our garments plain, as we are commanded to do, and not put two or three yards in a hump on the back. I think that needless expense could be put to better use." Katherine Salisbury (Fountain Green, IL) to Dear Sister Walker, December 29, 1888, *Saints' Herald* 36, no. 4 (January 26, 1889): 53.

17. Lucy Mack Smith, *Biographical Sketches*, 203–4.

18. Salisbury to Dear Sisters, July 2, 1895.

19. Katherine Salisbury (Fountain Green, IL) to Dear Sister Walker, February 27, 1888, *Saints' Herald* 35, no. 11 (March 17, 1888): 164.

20. Linda King Newell and Valeen Tippetts Avery, "Sweet Counsel and Seas of Tribulation: The Religious Life of the Women in Kirtland," *BYU Studies* 20, no. 2 (Winter 1980): 154.

21. Salisbury to Sister Frances, December 24, 1886.

22. Nancy A. Tracy reminiscences and diary, 1896 May–1899 July, typescript, 9, CHL. Kristine Wright, "'We Baked a Lot of Bread': Reconceptualizing Mormon Women and Ritual Objects," in *Women and Mormonism: Historical and Contemporary Perspectives*, ed. Kate Holbrook and Matthew Bowman (Salt Lake City: University of Utah Press, 2016), 84–85.

23. Gerrit J. Dirkmaat et al., eds., *Documents, Volume 3: February 1833–March 1834*, vol. 3 of the Documents series of *The Joseph Smith Papers*, ed. Ronald K. Esplin and Matthew C. Grow (Salt Lake City: Church Historian's Press, 2014), 105.

24. Lucy Mack Smith, *Biographical Sketches*, 203; Jeffrey S. O'Driscoll, *Hyrum Smith: A Life of Integrity* (Salt Lake City: Deseret Book, 2003), 86.

25. Lucy Mack Smith, *Biographical Sketches*, 203.

26. *Cleveland Herald* report reproduced in "General Conference," *Saints' Herald* 30, no. 16 (April 21, 1883): 242–43; Milton V. Backman Jr., *The Heavens Resound: A History of the Latter-day Saints in Ohio, 1830–1838* (Salt Lake City: Deseret Book, 1983), 158–59.

27. Hancock, "Three Sisters, Part II," 10.

28. Edward Tullidge, *The Women of Mormondom* (New York: Tullidge & Crandall, 1877), 76. Polly Angell was born at Riga, Monroe County, New York, on June 4, 1813, and was married to church architect Truman O. Angell.

29. Lucy Mack Smith, *Biographical Sketches*, 203.

30. Salisbury to Sister Frances, December 24, 1886.

31. Samuel Harrison Smith diary, 1832 February–1833 May, see entries for June 26, 1832, and July 30, 1832, CHL.

32. Lucy Mack Smith, *Biographical Sketches*, 203.

33. Sidney Rigdon also performed the marriage of Samuel Smith and Mary Bailey, while Seymour Brunson officiated at the wedding of Don Carlos Smith and Agnes Coolbrith. Ohio, United States, Geauga County Marriage Records, 1774–1993, vol. C, 60, 108, copy of originals available at Ancestry.com.

CHAPTER SIX

Family Life in Ohio

Jenkins, my son-in-law, my heart, as it were, bleeds for thee.
—Joseph Smith Sr.

ALL SEEMED TO BE FLOURISHING in the Church of Christ during those early years in Kirtland. Katharine relished the opportunity to be at the hub of church undertakings when she stayed with her parents in Kirtland. She enthusiastically wrote that the "church prospered greatly" in Ohio, "and members were added unto us daily."[1] Further to the west in Missouri, where Joseph Jr. had hoped to establish Zion, prospects were less encouraging. Katharine was distantly apprised of the Saints being driven from their homes in Jackson County.

At Kirtland, Katharine played an active role in assisting the dozens of missionary companionships sent in different directions throughout the country. That soon included her own husband. On Tuesday, March 12, 1833, during a meeting of high priests assembled on the top floor of Newel K. Whitney's store, Jenkins received his first proselytizing assignment. Joseph Smith appointed him to labor with Truman Waite, a convert of less than two months, on a mission "to the East." After accepting the call, Jenkins was ordained an elder by his brother-in-law Hyrum Smith during the same meeting.[2]

With little time to prepare, the missionaries left Kirtland just three days later, on March 15.[3] Katharine described the appearance and efforts of Jenkins and her brothers as they departed on their missions and left "on foot without purse or scrip." These early elders in the Church of Christ "only took their cane and their knapsack on their back, with a few books and one change of clothing," recalled Katharine. "When they were tired and footsore they would sit down by the way side or by a stream of water and bathe their blistered feet and call on the Lord for strength and then arise and travel on."[4] She obviously admired her brothers for the sacrifices they had made to make new converts and was thrilled that her husband was now willing to make a similar contribution.

Truman Waite summarized their missionary efforts in a report he wrote up after they returned, indicating they initially traveled northeast until they reached the town of Westfield, Chautauqua County, New York, where a branch of the church had already been established. After spending a few days preaching at Westfield, they continued further east to Warsaw and then southeast to Prattsburg, New York. Prattsburg was the furthest east the elders traveled, as they stopped and spent most of their mission laboring in the region.[5] Jenkins likely targeted that area of New York because it was only sixteen miles from where he grew up and most of his family was still in the area. The elders likely stayed with and attempted to proselytize Jenkins's family, but there is no evidence that any of his family ever joined.[6] However, the Salisbury family was warm and welcoming to traveling missionaries in subsequent years. In the summer of 1835, Jedediah Grant and Harvey Stanley were welcome guests at the Salisbury home during their mission several years later, evidence that the family was at least tacitly supportive of Jenkins's decision to join the Church of Christ.[7]

Prattsburg Presbyterian Church and Franklin Academy. Date and photographer unknown.

Jenkins was drawn to Prattsburg because he knew the town had long been a center of religious activity in the region, largely controlled by the Presbyterians since the early 1800s. A massive sixty-by-forty-foot Presbyterian church dominated the town's landscape, joined by a recently completed parsonage for the Presbyterian clergymen. A large academy stood adjacent to the church and parsonage, which was overseen by a local reverend and used by Presbyterian leaders for study and training.[8] As the elders entered the town seeking an audience, they were immediately met by several Presbyterian leaders who whisked them away into a room in the academy under the pretense of listening to the basic tenets of their faith.[9] Salisbury and Waite were ignorant of the religious tension that had pervaded the community since the Methodists and Baptists had made inroads in town during the previous decade, infiltrating the Presbyterians' stronghold. One example had been the Stephen and Clarissa Prentiss family, who had been staunch Presbyterians since they arrived in Prattsburg in 1805, but family members eventually broke with the faith over local leaders' strict attitudes about disciplining its members and the Temperance movement. Their daughter Narcissa Prentiss Whitman, who was born at Prattsburg and was just a year older than Jenkins, followed her father's lead in breaking with the church in the mid-1820s. She later gained notoriety for becoming a prominent missionary to the Indigenous population in Oregon country, being one of the first two women to cross the Rocky Mountains. Losing such a prominent and religiously committed family had agitated the presiding Presbyterian Reverend George Rudd and made him increasingly more protective of his adherents.[10]

Unaware of the tension existing in town, the elders naively thought the clergymen were interested in their message or that they were at least tolerant enough to allow them to preach in their spacious meetinghouse. After Reverend Rudd and several of his colleagues sat down with them in their academy room, the meeting quickly turned hostile. Waite recalled that two of the men "abused" them to such an extent that they were "obliged to leave the house." Reverend Rudd was known for his volatility while preaching with vigor and energy, even using "forcible gestures" during his sermons. Such tactics evidently frightened the much younger missionaries. Waite did not specify whether there was a physical altercation or if the "abuse" meant Rudd simply denigrated their teachings but recorded, "We were very ill treated by the Pharrisaical [Pharisaical] Presbyterians."[11] The clergymen likely felt justified in their treatment of the traveling missionaries, as they sought to protect their flock from the upstart religion. They had undoubtedly heard of Joseph Smith and the Book of Mormon by that juncture because Palmyra was only forty miles to the north.

We do not know if the two made any converts during their mission. Judging from the fact that Waite traveled a similar course during a second mission the following year, meant they likely had experienced at least some success, even if that simply meant plowing new ground. When Jedediah M. Grant and Harvey Stanley preached

Village blacksmith, ca. 1850s. Courtesy of Library of Congress.

in that same region of New York in the summer of 1835, locals remembered Salisbury and Waite's earlier mission, evidencing their influence.[12] After three months, the elders returned to Kirtland in mid-June, having traveled more than six hundred miles.[13]

In the ensuing years, Jenkins's skill as a blacksmith proved invaluable to the Saints. Construction on the temple had begun in earnest by that summer, and most Saints contributed substantial amounts of time in constructing the edifice. "When he [Jenkins] came home [from his mission] he found that he was greatly needed in the shops," remembered a granddaughter. "New wagons were being made and old ones mended. The wagons were needed to transfer material from the quarries to the temple site."[14] Jenkins must have been a skilled blacksmith if he worked on wagons and carriages in Kirtland. A novice blacksmith could shoe horses and manufacture typical farm implements such as shovels, hoops, pales, plows. A more skilled blacksmith had the additional expertise of "making machine parts, mill irons, and barouche (or carriage) irons as well as repairing equipment in steam mills and sawmills."[15] His extended apprenticeship in New York provided him with an indispensable trade in the frontier communities where the Salisburys lived. The exception would have been the communities of Kirtland and Chardon, which were well established by the time the Saints arrived, likely making it more difficult for Jenkins to launch his own business or to find work outside of the temple's construction. Moreover, despite the necessity of a blacksmith in bustling communities throughout the country, they were typically among the lower socioeconomic class in nineteenth-century America.[16]

Construction and repair on the wagons used for the temple's construction probably provided Jenkins a meager livelihood. The Saints' generous donations for the temple not only paid for materials but also provided much-needed income for those who otherwise would have been unemployed.[17] Considering the limited resources among the Saints during those early years in Kirtland, pay for his efforts constructing and repairing wagons was probably only minimal. He also lent his assistance in transporting stone and mortar for the temple's foundation and walls, working alongside his brother-in-law William Smith.[18] The Salisburys probably stayed with members of the Smith family for portions of the week, rather than make the daily twenty-mile round trip from Chardon to Kirtland. The Smith family also traveled to Chardon with regularity. Joseph visited his sisters at Chardon in late November 1832, recording in his journal that he "found them all well," and again on January 16, 1834, when Joseph spent the night at the Salisburys' home.[19]

Notwithstanding his work contributions on the temple, some members of the church began to have reservations about Jenkins's conduct. On December 27, 1833, a bishop's court convened to investigate unspecified complaints made against Jenkins. However, because the accusers did not show up in person to the trial, his case was dismissed. Judging from subsequent accounts of his behavior, the accusation was likely credible, but the specific complaint made against Jenkins that December was never reconsidered.[20] Those accusations regarding his standing in the church in December 1833 were a factor in his being summoned again by leaders the following year.

As early as the summer of 1831, Joseph Smith had received a revelation appointing Jackson County, Missouri, as a place of gathering, and began appointing Saints in Ohio to relocate eight hundred miles to the west to help settle the area. After establishing themselves in the region, the Saints almost immediately began to clash with the Missourians due to political, cultural, and religious differences, until locals forcibly drove them from the county. By the year 1834 the situation remained at an impasse, until Joseph received another revelation to organize a company (later designated Zion's Camp) to assist in reclaiming the Saints' properties in Jackson County.[21]

Whatever his difficulties had been that winter, Jenkins enlisted in Zion's Camp in the spring 1834, where more than two hundred volunteers marched to Missouri to redeem Saints properties in Jackson County, Missouri, after having been driven out the previous November. Jenkins joined his brothers-in-law Hyrum, Joseph, and William Smith, who were all part of the trek. Writing to his wife Emma from Indiana, Joseph Smith mentioned two of his cousins, Jesse and George A. Smith, along with Jenkins and William Smith, who were all "well and are humble [and] are detirmined to be faithful."[22] While Joseph spoke positively of Jenkins when he included a general report of his Smith relatives, others in the extended Smith family evidently did not share that same view. Sixteen-year-old George A. Smith felt that Jenkins's reputation on the expedition was not above reproach. Smith recalled:

> During the [day] being fatigued with carrying my musket, I put it into the baggage wagon. . . . When I arrived in the evening my gun could not be found, . . . and I was ridiculed for carelessness; Jenkins Salisbury took the most pleasure. I afterwards learned that my gun was pawned for whiskey by one of our company, and have always believed that Jenkins Salisbury was the culprit.[23]

George A.'s supposition was not without foundation because Jenkins later admitted to his penchant for drinking strong liquor. He appears to have struggled intermittently with excessive drinking during his marriage to Katharine, and it may explain his unpredictable and temperamental behavior.[24] His behavior was not entirely exceptional because heavy alcohol use was common in the early 1800s and nearly always present at any major event or town celebration. "During the first third of the nineteenth century the typical American annually drank more distilled liquor [up to 90 proof] than at any time in our history," summarized one historian, and such use led to an increase of reported family abuse, desertion and assaults.[25] Still, Jenkins's use of alcohol crossed those societal norms.

Wilkins Jenkins Salisbury, 1809–53. Photograph ca. 1850. Photographer unknown. Courtesy of Mary Dennis.

Growing up without his parents' example and discipline during his teen years apparently had its impact because Jenkins seemed to struggle with providing adequately for his family throughout his and Katharine's marriage, and he began to drink heavily in his early twenties. Though Jenkins's sister loved him and remembered his kindness in providing her with gifts when they were children, she pointed to a weakness evident in his personality that had earlier been a problem. Writing Katharine much later in life, Samantha Salisbury Arnold expressed her sympathy to her sister-in-law when she disclosed her view that her brother had likely "been unsteady throughout the better part of their marriage."[26] That perception could have been something that Samantha gleaned from Jenkins's correspondence with his family after his marriage, but neither Jenkins, nor Katharine for that matter, appear to have kept in close contact with the family after they left New York. More likely, her observation of his inconstancy was something she detected after he moved into adulthood after he had completed his apprenticeship and returned to the family. It appears she had become aware of his drinking habits before he left for Ohio in 1831 because Samantha was astute in her assessment of her brother.

Besides his three-month mission in the first half of 1833 and his journey with Zion's Camp in 1834, Jenkins appears to have remained at home with Katharine. However, his inconstant behavior gradually grew more disruptive in the home and, because of Katharine's prominent position in being a sister to the Church's Prophet, began to reflect negatively on the church. Jenkins's use of alcohol eventually led to periods of absence from the family, which made home life more trying for Katharine after the birth of their first surviving daughter, born on October 3, 1834. Appropriately enough, they named this daughter Lucy after Katharine's mother.[27] A son followed less than a year later, born on September 18, 1835, whom they named Solomon, after Katharine's grandfather Mack.[28]

All too often, Katharine found herself alone in raising her two young children. The emotional and financial strain on Katharine was challenging, and those closest to her noticed its impact. At a meeting on December 9, 1834, the greater Smith family gathered to receive their patriarchal blessings from their father, Joseph Smith Sr. Less than a year earlier, the Prophet Joseph had acted as voice in ordaining his father to the office of church patriarch, blessing him that he should predict whatsoever would befall his own posterity as well as the general membership of the Church. What should have been a joyous and spiritual occasion for the Salisburys was marred by Jenkins's recent behavior. In a handwritten note at the top of Jenkins's blessing it read, "This man, at the time of receiving his blessing, was not a member of the church, having been expelled for intemperance." Both Jenkins's and Katharine's blessings were replete with references to Jenkins's recent apostasy. "Jenkins, my son-in-law, my heart, as it were, bleeds for thee," Father Smith had started his blessing. "Thou hast turned thy back upon the cause of God: thou hast conducted thyself wickedly, and brought reproach upon the church, because thou art a member of my family." By the time of this meeting, just three years after the Salisburys' marriage, Joseph Sr. and Lucy were aware of Jenkins's inconstant behavior, and it had become public knowledge. Joseph Sr. was direct in calling Jenkins to repentance no less than eight times in his blessing but also held out hope that "if thou wilt turn and humble thyself, the Lord will yet bless thee, and thou shalt go forth in his name and do great good."[29]

Joseph Sr.'s sympathy for his daughter's predicament spilled out in Katharine's blessing. "My heart mourns for thee in consequence of the transgression of thy husband," her father began. "My soul is grieved that he should suffer himself to be lead away from his holy calling." Joseph Sr. commended Katharine for her conscientious concern for her parents' well-being and prophesied that she would play a future role in instructing female members of the church in "virtue and sobriety." But nearly half her blessing addressed the impropriety of her husband.[30]

The couple must have had mixed emotions leaving the meeting. Did Katharine find hope in what was proclaimed in their blessings, or did it only increase her fears about her husband's character? If nothing else, it clearly demonstrated the supportiveness of her immediate family in their expressions of compassion for her circumstances. The ensuing weeks brought at least some relief to Katharine because Jenkins appears to have responded favorably to his father-in-law's call to repentance. Jenkins's former missionary companion

Truman Waite also played a role in his reformation as he labored with Jenkins during those winter months to help restore his faith. Waite recorded that he "[re]baptized J. Salisbury in the course of the winter," probably in January or early February of 1835.[31]

Joseph Smith's role as president and prophet had expanded by the mid-1830s as he was viewed as the mouthpiece of the Lord, receiving more than one hundred revelations before the Kirtland Temple's dedication. Those divine instructions more firmly established church protocol and procedures and defined the structure of the church's leadership.

On February 14, Jenkins evidenced his faith by attending a meeting where the Quorum of the Twelve was organized, and he was among those who were commended for marching with Zion's Camp the previous summer. Several weeks later, on March 1, Jenkins was installed as a member of the First Quorum of the Seventy. He was reordained an elder during his blessing, in which his father-in-law likely acted as voice[32] and Joseph Sr. once again included items related to his family. After instructing him to "go into all the world to preach the gospel to every creature," the pronouncement included a charge that after his missionary service, "you . . . shall return to the embraces of your family, and they shall have much peace with you."[33] Including this counsel in his blessing was an indirect way of encouraging Jenkins to continue to take a more active role in home responsibilities, a concern Joseph Sr. had expressed a few months earlier in his patriarchal blessing.

While Jenkins expressed his willingness to fulfill a proselytizing assignment with other members of his quorum at the time of his ordination, there is no record of him serving a mission that year.[34] Perhaps he stayed close to home because Katharine was in the late stages of pregnancy that summer and their son Solomon was born in September.

In the fall of 1835, William Smith had several disagreements with his brother Joseph over church protocol, which ultimately led to a physical altercation where William assaulted his older brother, severely injuring Joseph's side.[35] During these months of struggle, both Joseph and William went to other members of the extended

Smith family to gain support and defend their side of the conflict. Joseph was upset that William had "prejudiced the mind" of their brother Samuel, as well as Sophronia's husband Calvin Stoddard.[36] Stoddard had experienced his own conflict with Joseph earlier that same year, going so far as to seek legal action against his prophet-brother-in-law. Joseph was acquitted of any wrongdoing in the case, but Stoddard continued to experience his own vacillating loyalty to the church and Joseph.[37] Due to his own recent conflict, Stoddard sympathized with William's perspective. William also appears to have gone to the Salisburys with his complaints, gaining a sympathetic ear. While the standoff dragged on for several months, Joseph noted in his journal how the conflict had also impacted his sisters. "The Devil has made a violent attack on Br. Wm [Smith] and Br Calvin [Stoddard] and the powers of darkness, seeme [to] lower over their minds, and not only theirs but [has] cast a gloomy shade over the minds of . . . some of my brothers and sisters, which prevents them from seeing things as they realy are."[38] Eventually the brothers came to a place where they would reconcile their differences. With their father acting as mediator, Joseph and William met on New Year's Day 1836, both apologizing for the role they had played in the conflict. That sentiment appears to have permeated the rest of the Smith family.[39]

Less than two weeks later, Jenkins was preaching to a Sunday-morning gathering of the Saints in Kirtland, along with his brothers-in-law Samuel and Don Carlos, both of whom preached later in the afternoon. "They all did well concidering their youth," Joseph Smith summarized of their collective sermons, "and bid fair to make useful men in the vineyard of the Lord."[40] Jenkins had turned twenty-seven the previous day and was only three years younger than Joseph. It is somewhat surprising that the Prophet noted the inexperience of both Jenkins and Samuel (also twenty-seven at the time), considering their age and tenure in the church. Joseph's comment would seem to have been more befitting of his brother Don Carlos, who was only nineteen. Yet Joseph's passing comment was less about age than it was about ability. After the two had served a lengthy mission

Kirtland Temple, 1870. Photograph by W. A. Faze. Courtesy of Church History Library.

together in the early 1830s, Orson Hyde described Samuel as being "slow of speech and unlearned," and Samuel often deferred to Hyde and other missionary companions to lead out in explaining the tenets of the gospel message.[41] If the same was true of Jenkins, it might explain why he was reluctant to accept another mission assignment with his colleagues in the Seventy in the year 1835. While both

Jenkins and Samuel were experienced missionaries, their eloquence appears to have lagged behind that of other church officers.

Though not specifically named, Jenkins was assumedly among members of the Seventy who received their anointings later that same month in the Kirtland Temple. The spiritual outpouring many Saints experienced in those months leading up to, and during the temple's dedication, were some of most spiritual experiences of their lives. Many recorded remarkable spiritual manifestations that helped anchor their faith in the Church of Christ.[42] Blessing meetings were also a common occurrence during the mid-1830s, where according to an earlier revelation, children were to be brought by their parents to be blessed by the elders of the Church.[43] Accordingly, Katharine brought her two children, Lucy and Solomon, where they were blessed by her brother Joseph. She found comfort in Joseph's declaration upon the head of her infant son Solomon, "that the child would live to preach the gospel."[44]

Katharine attended church meetings in the months leading up to the temple's dedication and likely participated in a choir organized in Kirtland that met together for practice twice a week.[45] Katharine inherited her love of music from both her parents and had grown up singing hymns as part of their evening routine.[46] Being a part of the choir was a way that women could gather and connect during a time when their husbands were participating in meetings almost nightly. Caroline Crosby, six years older than Katharine, recalled participating in the choir in the early part of 1836, made up of everyone from the "young adult[s] to the old gray heads." She also recounted how sisters would come at daylight on Sunday mornings to get a seat at church services held on the bottom floor of the printing office, which stood next to the temple.[47]

Katharine never mentioned her recollections of the Kirtland Temple dedication services later that spring but, like many Saints that memorable week, probably felt amply rewarded for her many sacrifices she had made in its construction. Katharine and her sisters, along with their mother Lucy, had contributed heavily to help prepare the interior of the temple, including working on the curtains and rugs that helped add beauty to the massive structure at the time of its dedication.[48]

Jenkins may have missed the meetings associated with the temple that memorable week. At the same time as the spiritual jubilation was occurring with the temple's dedication, Jenkins was again wrestling with his own faith. His reformation during those early months of 1836 was evidently short-lived. He abruptly left home the same week as the temple dedication, leaving his family in an impoverished condition without enough wood to heat their home. More than a foot of snow blanketed the community of Kirtland the week he left, and the unusually cold weather persisted for several more weeks.[49] Jenkins left Katharine and their two children—both still under the age of two—with little or no food. Katharine was uncertain as to where he had gone or when he would return, which uncertainty was grueling for her. Jenkins had begun drinking again.

The Smith family became aware of Katharine's circumstances and stepped in to offer support. They were growing increasingly concerned over Jenkins's intermittent abandonment of his family, and his neglect of his church assignment as a Seventy. An earlier revelation received by Joseph Smith had reiterated the biblical mandate that men who were physically capable were to provide for their families or they shall not have place in the church.[50] When Jenkins finally returned in early May, Oliver Cowdery led out in bringing an ecclesiastical charge of "unchristianlike conduct" against Jenkins at a high council meeting held in Kirtland on May 14, 1836. During his trial, both Joseph and Hyrum Smith were called upon to testify about what they knew of their brother-in-law. Joseph testified that Jenkins had "neglected his family [and] left them in a starving condition and without Wood . . . when he ought to have been home." Evidence that the brothers were aware of their sister's mindset and circumstances during Jenkins's absence also came from Hyrum's testimony. "He [Jenkins] left his family without sufficient wood to last more than two days," confirmed Hyrum, "and no provision of any consequence in the house." He further stated that when Jenkins left "he gave his family no intimation where he was going or when he should return," and from what Hyrum had learned from his sister Katharine, had no intention of returning. Other accusations against Salisbury included the use of liquor, being intimate with other women, and talebearing—defined as spreading malicious secrets with the intent to do harm. John Johnson, who kept a tavern on the Kirtland flats, testified that he had personally witnessed Salisbury drink strong liquor on several occasions.[51]

In his defense, Jenkins denied being unfaithful to Katharine but confessed his propensity in "drinking strong liquor" and "talebearing." He never addressed how he had abandoned his family during the previous month and a half, which was probably Joseph and Hyrum's foremost concern. Sidney Rigdon, who presided over Jenkins's church trial, recommended that he be stripped of his office of an elder and of his membership in the Church, "until there be a thorough reformation." The high council unanimously concurred.[52] It was the second time in less than a year that Jenkins had been expelled from the Church.

It wasn't just her brother Joseph's revelations that would have led community members to take exception to Jenkins's conduct. Societal expectations during this era mandated that a husband was obligated to support his wife and children, and some wives who filed for divorce cited their husband's failure to provide as the primary cause.[53] Still, divorce was rare in the first half of the nineteenth century and only when a partner had "flagrantly digressed" the laws of marriage. Women were economically and legally dependent on their husbands and had little recourse when they experienced neglect by their husband. Divorce was difficult to obtain, and in cases where it could be obtained it still often left women impoverished and stigmatized. Even in cases of abandonment, women rarely followed through with legal action that would formally end the marriage. That meant that separation was more common than divorce, and partial estrangement was more common than total separation.[54] There is no evidence that Katharine ever considered such a monumental step. Her dependency on Jenkins meant she often suffered in silence with very limited options.

Notes

1. Katharine Salisbury (Fountain Green, IL) to Dear Sisters of the "Home Column," May 16, 1886, *Saints' Herald* 33, no. 26 (July 3, 1886): 404–5.
2. Minute Book 1, [ca. 3 December 1832–30 November 1837], March 12, 1833, 11, CHL. Truman Waite was baptized by Hyrum Smith on January 20, 1833, and ordained a priest the following day. Truman Waite, report, 1833, 1, Missionary Reports, 1831–1900, CHL.
3. Waite, report, 1833, 1.
4. Katharine Salisbury (Fountain Green, IL) to Dear Sister Walker, February 27, 1888, *Saints' Herald* 35, no. 11 (March 17, 1888): 164.
5. Waite, report, 1833, 3.
6. Jenkins's sister Samantha Salisbury Arnold, who lived in Gorham, New York, near where she and Jenkins grew up, reported that visits from her brother were rare. In 1854 she indicated that it had been fourteen years since she had seen her brother last. Samantha Arnold (n.p.) to Katharine Salisbury, January 1, 1853 [1854], copy of original in Katharine Smith Salisbury Correspondence, L. Tom Perry Special Collections, Harold B. Lee Library, Brigham Young University, Provo, UT.
7. Harvey Stanley Journal, in Jedediah M. Grant, journal, 1836 April–1839 August, 9, CHL.
8. W. W. Clayton, *History of Steuben County, New York, with Illustrations and Biographical Sketches of Some of Its Prominent Men and Pioneers* (Philadelphia: Lewis, Peck, 1879), 359–62.
9. Waite, report, 1833, 4–5.
10. Both Narcissa and her father, Stephen, eventually rejoined the Presbyterian faith at Prattsburg. Julie Roy Jeffrey, *Converting the West: A Biography of Narcissa Whitman* (Norman: University of Oklahoma Press, 1991), 8, 27–30.
11. Waite, report, 1833, 4–5; and Jeffrey, *Converting the West*, 31.
12. Stanley, journal, 9.
13. Waite, report, 1833, 2–5. Truman Waite returned to the East on a mission in the fall of 1834, and again in the summer of 1835. In 1834, he again visited Westfield, and other towns in Chautauqua County, New York. In 1835, he traveled as far as Lyons, New York. Waite reported that he baptized seventeen into the church during his 1834 mission. Waite, report, August 18, 1835.
14. Mary Salisbury Hancock, "The Three Sisters of the Prophet Joseph Smith, Part II," *Saints' Herald* 101, no. 3 (January 18, 1954): 10.
15. Michele Gillespie, "Artisan Accommodation to the Slave South: The Case of William Talmage, a Blacksmith, 1834–1847," *Georgia Historical Quarterly* 81, no. 2 (Summer 1997): 273.

16. James C. Boyles, "'Under a Spreading Chestnut-Tree': The Blacksmith and His Forge in Nineteenth-Century American Art," *Journal of the Society for Industrial Archeology* 34, no. 1–2 (2008): 10.

17. *Saints: The Story of the Church of Jesus Christ in the Latter Days*, vol. 1, *The Standard of Truth, 1815–1846* (Salt Lake City: The Church of Jesus Christ of Latter-day Saints, 2018), 213.

18. *Cleveland Herald* report reproduced in "General Conference," *Saints' Herald* 30, no. 16 (April 21, 1883): 242.

19. Dean C. Jessee, Mark Ashurst-McGee, and Richard L. Jensen, eds., *Journals, Volume 1: 1832–1839*, vol. 1 of the Journals series of *The Joseph Smith Papers*, ed. Dean C. Jessee, Ronald K. Esplin, and Richard Lyman Bushman (Salt Lake City: Church Historian's Press, 2008), 9, 24.

20. Minute Book 1, 26.

21. *JSP*, D3:3–5; *JSP*, D4:xviii–xxi.

22. Joseph Smith to Emma Smith, May 18, 1834, reproduced in Matthew C. Godfrey et al., eds., *Documents, Volume 4: April 1834–September 1835*, vol. 4 of the Documents series of *The Joseph Smith Papers*, ed. Ronald K. Esplin and Matthew J. Grow (Salt Lake City: Church Historian's Press, 2016), 50.

23. George A. Smith, "History of George Albert Smith: Zion's Camp," May 16–May 22, 1844, typescript, L. Tom Perry Special Collections, Harold B. Lee Library, Brigham Young University, Provo, UT.

24. Kirtland high council, minutes, May 16, 1836, in Minute Book 1, 206. Salisbury descendants have also mentioned Jenkins's alcohol use in their family history. Warren Van Dine, a descendant through Katharine's son Frederick, wrote, "There have been whispers in the Salisbury family through the years to the effect he [Jenkins] didn't take religion quite as seriously as his Mormon in-laws. That he was known on occasion to drink a bottle of pop. Maybe with a little alcoholic content, but let's call it pop anyway." Warren L. Van Dine, "Statement about His Salisbury Family," 1975, 15, typescript, Hancock County Historical Society, Carthage, IL.

25. W. J. Rorabaugh, *The Alcoholic Republic: An American Tradition* (New York: Oxford Press, 1979), 7, 190, as cited in Patricia Lewis Noel, "Reviving His Work: Social Isolation, Religious Fervor and Reform in the Burned Over District of Western New York, 1790–1860," (master's thesis, Virginia Commonwealth University, 2006).

26. Arnold to Salisbury, January 1, 1853 [1854].

27. George A. Smith (Salt Lake City) to Cousin Catherine [Salisbury], August 17, 1865, Historian's Office letterpress copybooks, 1854–1879, vol. 2, 1859–1869, CHL; John Smith Papers, 1833–1854, journal, 1846 February–1854 May, CHL; Lucy Mack Smith, *Biographical Sketches of Joseph Smith the Prophet and His Progenitors for Many Generations*

(Liverpool: S. W. Richards, 1853), 43; Dorothy D. Dean, handwritten family group sheet, copy of original in author's possession.

28. Jenkins and Katharine named their first son Solomon J. Salisbury. The middle initial "J" presumably stood for Jenkins, after the middle name of his father, although there is no primary source to confirm that. Solomon J. Salisbury, *Reminiscences of an Octogenarian* (n.p.: Solomon J. Salisbury, 1922), 3; Smith to Cousin Catherine, August 17, 1865, John Smith Papers, 1833–1854; Lucy Mack Smith, *Biographical Sketches*, 43.

29. Patriarchal Blessing of Jenkins Salisbury, December 9, 1834, in H. Michael Marquardt, comp., *Early Patriarchal Blessings of The Church of Jesus Christ of Latter-Day Saints* (Salt Lake City: Smith-Pettit Foundation, 2007), 18.

30. Patriarchal Blessing of Katharine Salisbury, December 9, 1834, in Marquardt, *Early Patriarchal Blessings*, 18.

31. Waite returned to Kirtland from a mission on December 17, 1835. He said he remained at Kirtland "through the winter[,] went to school about two months and a half," and had baptized Jenkins during that time. Waite, report, August 18, 1835.

32. Others who pronounced blessings that day included Joseph Smith Jr., Oliver Cowdery, and Sidney Rigdon. *JSP*, D4:265n262.

33. *JSP*, D4:269.

34. Jenkins expressed his willingness to serve a mission at a meeting held on May 2, 1835. *JSP*, D4:301–4.

35. William and Joseph's conflict lasted for approximately two months, from October 29, 1835, through January 1, 1836. Kyle R. Walker, *William B. Smith: In the Shadow of a Prophet* (Salt Lake City: Greg Kofford Books, 2015), 107–24.

36. *JSP*, J1:80, 140.

37. "To the Editor," *Painesville Telegraph* 1 no. 25 (June 26, 1835): 3; and *JSP*, D4:347–49. Like Jenkins, Calvin Stoddard had experienced vacillating loyalty to Joseph Smith and the church. Hyrum Smith's journal entry for February 2, 1832, indicated that he had "labored in a conference meeting with Calvin Stoddard which was called in consequence of his open rebellion against the laws of God." Though Stoddard attempted reform that year, even serving a mission with Jared Carter, by December 1832 he gave up his preaching license, confessing that he had not magnified his priesthood office and transgressed. Hyrum Smith, diary, 18 November 1831–21 February 1835, 16–17, Joseph Smith Sr. Family Collection, L. Tom Perry Special Collections, Harold B. Lee Library, Brigham Young University, Provo, UT; Gracia N. Jones, "Sophronia Smith McCleary," in *United by Faith: The Joseph Sr. and Lucy Mack Smith Family*, ed. Kyle R. Walker (American Fork, UT: Covenant Communications; Provo, UT: BYU Studies, 2006), 172–77.

38. *JSP*, J1:140.

39. Walker, *In the Shadow of a Prophet*, 122–25.

40. *JSP*, J1:147.

41. Orson Hyde, "The History of Orson Hyde," *Millennial Star* 26, no. 49 (December 3, 1864): 774. Daniel Tyler listened to Samuel preach on one occasion and indicated that his preaching "was more like a narrative than a sermon." Daniel Tyler, "Incidents of Experience," in *Scraps of Biography* (Salt Lake City: Juvenile Instructor, 1883), 23, as cited in Richard Lloyd Anderson, "Joseph Smith's Brothers Nauvoo and After," *Ensign* 9, no. 9 (September 1979), 31; Dean L. Jarman and Kyle R. Walker, "Samuel Harrison Smith," in Walker, *United by Faith*, 217–20.

42. *JSP*, J1:174–75.

43. *JSP*, J1:125; see Doctrine and Covenants 20:70. For a discussion on these early blessing meetings, see Jonathan A. Stapley, *The Power of Godliness: Mormon Liturgy and Cosmology* (New York: Oxford University Press, 2018), 57–60.

44. Frederick V. Salisbury, "The Teachings and Testimonies of My Mother," 1926–1928, unpublished manuscript, 20, Hancock County Historical Society, Carthage, IL.

45. Edward Leo Lyman, Susan Ward Payne, and S. George Ellsworth, eds., *No Place to Call Home: The 1807–1857 Life Writings of Caroline Barnes Crosby, Chronicler of Outlying Mormon Communities* (Logan: Utah State University Press, 2005), 40.

46. William Smith, "Notes Written on 'Chambers' Life of Joseph Smith," ca. 1875, 28, CHL. Historian Michael Hicks presumes that Lucy may have been a part of the Palmyra Presbyterian choir, since the Mack family both sang and wrote hymns. Hicks further summarizes the Macks' fondness of music: "Lucy Smith's father, Solomon Mack, was enamored of Isaac Watts's enormously popular *Hymns and Psalms* and tried, rather feebly, to emulate Watts in a set of verses published in his 1811 *Narraitve* [*sic*]. Lucy's sisters Lovina and Lovisa, both of whom died young, composed several of their own hymn texts and sang duets on Watts's lyrics. Lucy recalled Lovina chanting Watts with her dying breath. And Lovisa, whose voice was 'high and clear,' sang Watts's 116th Psalm ('My God hath saved my soul from death') later in life with 'angelic harmony.'" Michael Hicks, *Mormonism and Music: A History* (Urbana: University of Illinois Press, 1989), 4, 15–16n17.

47. Lyman et al., *No Place to Call Home*, 42.

48. Hancock, "Three Sisters, Part II," 10; Backman, *The Heavens Resound*, 158–59.

49. *JSP*, J1:199.

50. See Doctrine and Covenants 75:28–29, and 1 Timothy 5:8.

51. Kirtland high council, minutes, May 16, 1836, as cited in Brent M. Rogers et al., eds., *Documents, Volume 5: October 1835–January 1838*, vol. 5 of the Documents series of *The Joseph Smith Papers*, ed. Ronald K.

Esplin and Matthew J. Grow, and Matthew C. Godfrey (Salt Lake City: Church Historian's Press, 2017), 243–46.

52. Kirtland high council, minutes, May 16, 1836, as cited in Rogers, *JSP*, D5:243–46.

53. Megan Owens, "Divorce and Family Life in Nineteenth-Century Vanderburgh County," *Grand Valley Journal of History* 7, no. 1 (October 2019): 3–4.

54. Nancy Grey Osterud, *Bonds of Community: The Lives of Farm Women in Nineteenth-Century New York* (Ithaca, NY: Cornell University Press, 1991), 130–31.

CHAPTER SEVEN

Migrating to the Frontier, 1838–39

We went from the frying pan into the fire.
—Katharine Smith Salisbury

THE SMITH CHILDREN were collectively moving into a new stage of life by the mid-1830s. Except for youngest sister Lucy, all of Katharine's siblings had married and were now raising families in Ohio. The Salisburys were now a family of four and managed to eke out a living in Chardon. Katharine continued to enjoy her close association with her elder sister, Sophronia, and the two lived close during their seven-year stay in Ohio. As their husbands wrestled with their loyalty to the church and its founder, the Smith sisters found solace in their common experience, intensified because of the publicity it created in being members of the founding family of their shared faith.

Tragedy struck Sophronia in the fall of 1836 when her husband Calvin contracted tuberculosis. Sensing that he would not recover, Sophronia brought him home to his family in Macedon, New York

Calvin Stoddard gravestone, Palmyra, New York. Photograph by Kyle R. Walker, 2019. The bottom of the inscription reads "Altho' he is dead, he is still speaking to you; His language is this, bid your follies adieu."

(six miles west of Palmyra), to be near his family during his final weeks. Calvin died on November 19 and was buried in a small plot on the family's property, and Sophronia and her only surviving daughter, Mariah, returned to Ohio after the funeral.[1] Over the next year Katharine assumedly played a supportive role in consoling and comforting her older sister as she grieved Calvin's death until Sophronia eventually met William McCleary the following summer, whom she married on February 11, 1838, in Kirtland.[2]

By that point, the church was being forced out of Ohio. The failure of the Kirtland Safety Society and other financial and ecclesiastical difficulties had led some leaders to denounce Joseph Smith's leadership. Forming their own Restoration offshoot—deemed the original Church of Christ, these dissidents threatened not only lawsuits but even the lives of Joseph Smith and other church leaders. Joseph Smith was warned in a revelation received in January 1838 that members of the First Presidency, their families, and loyal followers should leave Ohio for Zion "as soon as it is practicable."[3] With discord building in Kirtland, Joseph had decided to transfer church headquarters to Missouri, and because of increasing attacks, he, Hyrum, and Sidney Rigdon had fled Kirtland that same month ahead of the rest of the Smith family. The Salisburys experienced their own financial losses during the year 1838 because they had invested their small income in the Kirtland Bank. Both Katharine and Sophronia each bought twenty thousand shares, which amounted to about $107 and was all the savings the Salisbury family possessed.[4] The rest of their earnings was spent on property in Kirtland right next to where William Smith had built his home. Their dream of building a home next to his and finally settling in the city of the Saints never materialized.[5] Jenkins's inability to provide steady income prevented that project from ever getting launched.

Migration to Missouri and Alvin's Birth

Accompanied by a few close friends, the greater Smith family made the trek from Ohio to Missouri some two months before the main body, the latter dubbed the Kirtland Camp of Saints.[6] Brothers Hyrum, Joseph, and Samuel, with their families, had already relocated to Missouri.[7] The remainder of the Smith clan consisted of the families of Joseph Sr. and Lucy (which included their daughter Lucy, who turned seventeen that summer), William and Sophronia McCleary, William and Caroline Smith, Jenkins and Katharine Salisbury, and Don Carlos and Agnes Smith. The Smiths began their journey on May 7, 1838, with seven wagons, fifteen horses, two cows, and seventy-five dollars in cash, but the trip was fraught with challenges.[8] Leaving before the heat of summer arrived seemed like an ideal time to travel, but spring rains and unusually cold weather made the journey exceptionally difficult. Writing en route from Terre Haute, Indiana, Don Carlos described to his brother Joseph how the group had "camped out at night, notwithstanding the rain and cold," likely because they did not have money enough to secure lodging. "Father & Mother are not well," he further recounted, adding that

Shall We Not Go On, by Elspeth C. Young. An original oil painting depicting Katharine and her son, Solomon, preparing for the journey from Ohio to Missouri. Courtesy of Al Young Studios.

"we have had unaccountable bad roads, had our horses down in the mud, and broke of[f] one wagon tongue . . . and broke down the carriage twice."[9]

Lucy Smith's account of the journey spoke of the challenges of the journey as she indicated that her health declined to a point where she could no longer sit up in the wagon and had to reduce her travel to less than four miles a day. The journey was even more difficult for the Salisburys. Besides caring for three-year-old Lucy and two-year-old Solomon, Katharine was in the late stages of pregnancy. By the time the group reached the Mississippi River, these collective challenges were nearing a crisis. While waiting to cross the river, it rained for three days straight, and with no viable shelter they were unable to change out of wet clothing.[10]

After crossing the Mississippi, Katharine was on the verge of delivering her baby. The group hurriedly found a dilapidated and abandoned slave hut, as it provided the best shelter they could find for the expectant mother. Though Lucy was ill, she and her daughter

Sophronia assisted Katharine in delivering a healthy baby son on June 7, whom the Salisburys named for Katharine's respected elder brother Alvin. Joseph Sr. then went ahead of the group, securing more comfortable lodging for his daughter four miles further along the road. As evidence of Katharine's hardiness, she traveled four miles in a lumber wagon the same day she gave birth.[11]

At this juncture of their journey, the family decided it would be best to split into three companies. William, Don Carlos, and their families traveled on to Far West, Missouri, arriving sometime during the week of June 22–29.[12] Mother Lucy needed time to recuperate from her illness, and she and her husband found lodging at Huntsville, Missouri. William and Sophronia McCleary stayed behind with the Salisburys in the home that Joseph Sr. had procured, some forty miles east of Huntsville, to allow time for Katharine to recover from childbirth.[13]

Sophronia stayed especially close to Katharine in the days after Alvin's birth, caring for her and assisting in the care of her newborn son. Jenkins also did his best to care for Katharine during those intervening days of her recovery. Leaving Katharine in Sophronia's capable hands, he rode eighty miles round trip to Huntsville on horseback, where he reported to his in-laws on Katharine's improving condition and procured a wagon with which to transport his family. With only minimal time for recovery, Katharine was on the move again, traveling thirty miles just two days after delivering Alvin and another ten miles the next day to catch up with her parents in Huntsville. Mother Lucy was amazed at Katharine's remarkable recovery and her determination to travel so soon after giving birth. It rained continuously the day the Salisburys arrived in Huntsville, but Lucy remembered of her daughter's tenacity, "This did not stop [K]atharine." Despite suffering with chills and fever for a time, Katharine recovered quickly, and her delivery caused only minimal disruption on the journey.[14] This second contingent of the Smith family arrived in Far West, Missouri, sometime in mid-July.

Katharine and her descendants often recounted the trying circumstances surrounding Alvin's birth as evidence of the Salisburys' sacrifices made during their forced migrations in the years 1838–39. Family members recalled that the Salisburys lost most of their possessions during these two successive migrations, including all the furniture they owned.[15] The Salisburys' stay in Missouri lasted only seven months, and Katharine recalled that with their move to Missouri, "we jumped from the frying pan into the fire." In her assessment most of the conflict between the Saints and the Missourians centered on cultural and political differences, most especially stemming from the Saints opposition to slavery. She watched as the Missourians "began to raid the 'Mormon' settlements and towns, insulting the women, murdering the men, burning houses and carrying off cattle and other property." She recorded in her own history the familiar accounts circulated among the Saints related to the massacre at Hawn's Mill and the injustices they experienced in being driven from Missouri because of Governor Lilburn Boggs's Extermination Order.[16]

Migration to Illinois

Conflict between the Saints and the Missourians reached a crescendo that fall, and the Smith clan was once again on the move, this time in the dead of winter. Katharine's brothers Hyrum and Joseph were arrested on October 31 and remained imprisoned in Missouri for the next six months while Samuel fled from Missouri as a fugitive to avoid arrest. Her brother William also left a short time after the siege at Far West, leaving Don Carlos to relocate the remainder of the family.[17] "While my brother was detained in jail under false charges," recounted Katharine, "the rest of us were driven in a destitute condition through the winter snows to Quincy, Illinois."[18] Katharine and her son Solomon both said their family left the state in the fall of 1838, but that must have been just a general recollection because Lucy recorded that both Katharine and Sophronia, along with their families, were among their group that left Far West in mid-February, 1839.[19] This February departure date fits better with Katharine's depiction of "winter snows" during the exodus and Solomon's recollection that they traveled with "about one hundred and twenty-five families in the caravan, guarded by Missouri cavalry." Though Solomon was only four years old at the time, he remembered the difficulties associated with their journey east that fateful winter and crossing the frozen Mississippi River to Quincy, Illinois.[20] Like her sister-in-law Emma, Katharine carried her children in her arms as she crossed the ice-covered river.[21] Though her time in Missouri was brief, Katharine resented the way she and the Saints had been treated by the Missourians in being driven from the state. When recounting the details of these two migrations in later years, she was often overcome with emotion when she reflected on the suffering she experienced during that challenging winter of 1838–39.[22]

George Miller, 1794–1856 (n.d.), from H. W. Mills, "De Tal Palo Tal Astilla," *Historical Society of Southern California* 10, no. 3 (1917): 112–13.

Not long after landing at Quincy, Illinois, the Smith group who had migrated from Missouri all lived together in a house that Samuel had secured for them, but living in such cramped quarters with multiple families meant they were eager to find alternative housing. In what the Smith parents described as an answer to prayer, several of Katharine's brothers, along with Jenkins, were offered work and housing near Macomb, Illinois, some seventy miles northeast of Quincy. George Miller, a wealthy landowner and a faithful Presbyterian from nearby McDonough County, was eager to assist the beleaguered Saints. In addition to his eight-room home, Miller had some log houses that were in disrepair on his expansive three-hundred-acre property and offered living quarters and food in exchange for improving the homes. The Salisburys, along with the families of Samuel and Don Carlos Smith, enthusiastically took him up on the offer.[23] The Smith family had an immediate influence on Miller, and during those months they lived on his property they began teaching him about the church and gifted him a copy of the Book of Mormon. Miller was baptized that August, and shortly afterward he sold his property and moved closer to Nauvoo, where he was eventually appointed a bishop.[24] The Salisburys remained in McDonough County through the summer of 1839 but would be forced to search for a more permanent residence with Miller's departure.[25] The Salisburys would once again be drawn to live near Katharine's brother William.

Notes

1. Calvin's date of death is mentioned in the Stoddard Family Bible, photographs courtesy of Reid Moon, original in possession of Reid Moon, Provo, UT. For a discussion on the circumstances related to Calvin's death, see Gracia N. Jones, "Sophronia Smith Stoddard McCleary," in *United by Faith: The Joseph Sr. and Lucy Mack Smith Family*, ed. Kyle R. Walker (American Fork, UT: Covenant Communications; Provo, UT: BYU Studies, 2006), 77, 199n63.

2. In Sophronia's only known holograph letter, she said that she married William McCleary on Christmas Eve 1837. Sophronia McCleary (Nauvoo, IL) to Naomi Seaver, November 2, 1840, copy of original in author's possession, courtesy of Richard L. Anderson. However, in her family Bible she recorded the date as February 6, 1838. Stoddard Family Bible. Ohio marriage records indicate that she made application for marriage on February 6, but the couple was married on February 11, 1838. Geauga County, Ohio, Probate Court, Marriage Records, vol. C, 262, available at Ancestry.com.

3. Matthew C. Godfrey et al., eds., *Documents, Volume 4: April 1834–September 1835*, vol. 4 of the Documents series of *The Joseph Smith Papers*, ed. Ronald K. Esplin and Matthew J. Grow (Salt Lake City: Church Historian's Press, 2016), 441–42, 500–502.

4. Kirtland Safety Society Bank Stock Ledger, Kirtland Township, Geauga County, Ohio, October 18, 1836–June 12, 1837, 193–96, Chicago History Museum, https://www.josephsmithpapers.org/paper-summary/kirtland-safety-society-bank-stock-ledger-18-october-1836-12-june-1837/103.

5. Oliver Granger and William Smith, Bond, Kirtland Township, Geauga County, OH, to James Hall, assignee of Keeler, McNeil & Co., NY, January 20, 1843, Hiram Kimball Collection, CHL. The Salisbury

property was registered with the county clerk on March 7, 1838, but was likely purchased at an earlier date. Jenkins and Katharine officially registered the property with the county clerk in anticipation of leaving the state because they did not want to lose the property. The Salisburys had purchased the land from Sophia Stevens (the wife of Uzziel Stevens) and registered it in Katharine's name. She acquired a city lot on block 112 sub lots 19 and 20 that was 30/160 of an acre (four rods west of lot no. 10 on block 112, formerly owned by Hyrum Smith) and worth three hundred dollars. Witnessed Sybil Beall and W. D. Beall, JP October 15, 1839. Land transactions of Saints, Kirtland, Ohio 1830s & 1840s, August 5, 1893, CHL. Thanks to Mark L. Staker for sharing information on the Salisbury property.

6. The Kirtland Camp left Ohio for Missouri the first week of July 1838. Milton V. Backman Jr., *The Heavens Resound: A History of the Latter-day Saints in Ohio, 1830–1838* (Salt Lake City: Deseret Book, 1983), 354–55.

7. Brent M. Rogers et al., eds., *Documents, Volume 5: October 1835–January 1838*, vol. 5 of the Documents series of *The Joseph Smith Papers*, ed. Ronald K. Esplin, Matthew J. Grow, and Matthew C. Godfrey (Salt Lake City: Church Historian's Press, 2017), 441–42; Hyrum Smith to the Saints Scattered Abroad, in *Times and Seasons* 1, no. 2 (December 1839): 21; Dean L. Jarman and Kyle R. Walker, "Samuel Harrison Smith," in Walker, *United by Faith*, 224.

8. Lewis Robbins, Autobiographical Sketch, circa 1845, 4, MS 18637, CHL. Robbins was a close friend of the Smith family.

9. Don C[arlos] Smith (Terre Haute, IN) to Bro. Joseph [Smith], in Dean C. Jessee, Mark Ashurst-McGee, and Richard L. Jensen, eds., *Journals, Volume 1: 1832–1839*, vol. 1 of the Journals series of *The Joseph Smith Papers*, ed. Dean C. Jessee, Ronald K. Esplin, and Richard Lyman Bushman (Salt Lake City: Church Historian's Press, 2008), 280–81.

10. Lucy Mack Smith, *Biographical Sketches of Joseph Smith the Prophet and His Progenitors for Many Generations* (Liverpool: S. W. Richards, 1853), 219–20.

11. Smith, *Biographical Sketches*, 220–21; George A. Smith (Salt Lake City) to Cousin Catherine [Salisbury], August 17, 1865, Historian's Office letterpress copybooks, 1854–79, vol. 2, 1859–1869, CHL; John Smith Papers, 1833–1854, Journal, 1846 February–1854 May, CHL.

12. Lewis Robbins, Autobiographical Sketch, 4, said that he and the Smith clan started from Ohio on May 1, 1838, reaching Far West in "seven weeks and three days." Robbins had traveled with William and Don Carlos when the group split into three. However, May 1 appears to have been the date when Robbins started from Kirtland to Norton, Ohio, where he joined the Smith family. Don Carlos Smith to Bro. Joseph [Smith], dates their departure from Norton on May 7, making it difficult

to determine whether Robbins counted the opening date as their departure from Kirtland or Norton.

13. Lucy Mack Smith, *Biographical Sketches*, 219–20.

14. Lucy Mack Smith, *Biographical Sketches*, 219–20.

15. Warren Van Dine, "Biographical Sketch of Catherine Smith Salisbury," unpublished typescript, 1971, CHL.

16. "Reminiscences of Joseph Smith, as Told by His Sister, Catherine Smith-Salisbury, to Her Grandson, Herbert S. Salisbury," *Saints' Herald* 60 (October 8, 1913): 984. Herbert S. Salisbury quoted a lengthy history from his grandmother in this source, which is written in the first person. Herbert appears to have had a copy of a history written by his grandmother which has not been located.

17. Mark Ashurst-McGee et al., eds., *Documents, Volume 6: February 1838–August 1839*, vol. 6 of the Documents series of *The Joseph Smith Papers*, ed. Ronald K. Esplin, Matthew J. Grow, and Matthew C. Godfrey (Salt Lake City: Church Historian's Press, 217), 269–72; Dean L. Jarman and Kyle R. Walker, "Samuel Harrison Smith," in Walker, *United by Faith*, 226–27; Kyle R. Walker, *William B. Smith: In the Shadow of a Prophet* (Salt Lake City: Greg Kofford Books, 2015), 140–42.

18. "Reminiscences of Joseph Smith," 984.

19. Lucy Mack Smith, *Biographical Sketches*, 254; *JSP*, D6:331–32; William G. Hartley, "Missouri's 1838 Extermination Order and the Mormons' Forced Removal to Illinois," in *A City of Refuge: Quincy, Illinois*, ed. Susan E. Black and Richard E. Bennett (Salt Lake City: Millennial Press, 2000), 18.

20. Solomon J. Salisbury, *Reminiscences of an Octogenarian* (self-pub., ca. 1922), 3.

21. "Tells of Solomon Salisburys' Life," *Saints' Herald* 74, no. 5 (February 2, 1927): 136. Lucy Mack Smith indicated that she was ferried across the river. Lucy Mack Smith, *Biographical Sketches*, 324–25. It is possible that both accounts are accurate, as some who crossed the Mississippi River at this time indicated that they crossed "partly in a boat and partly on the ice." Scott H. Partridge, ed., *Eliza Maria Partridge Journal* (Provo, UT: Grandin Book, 2003), 7.

22. Mary Salisbury Hancock, "The Three Sisters of the Prophet Joseph Smith, Part II," *Saints' Herald* 101, no. 3 (January 18, 1954): 11.

23. Lucy Mack Smith, *Biographical Sketches*, 261; Richard E. Bennett, "'A Samaritan Had Passed By': George Miller—Mormon Bishop, Trailblazer, and Brigham Young Antagonist," *Journal of the Illinois State Historical Society* 82, no. 1 (Spring 1989): 3.

24. Bennett, "'A Samaritan Had Passed By,'" 4–5.

25. *JSP*, J1:341–42.

CHAPTER EIGHT

Plymouth, Illinois, 1840–44

Jenkins and I removed to Plymouth where he ran a blacksmith shop, and often received "coon" skins and maple sugar in exchange for work at the anvil.

—Katharine Smith Salisbury

KATHARINE'S BROTHER WILLIAM had left Missouri months earlier than most Saints, making little effort to assist his aged parents or sisters in their removal from the state. He had distanced himself from his faith and the Saints at that time, no doubt to protect himself and his family from the same legal difficulties his older brothers experienced. His erratic behavior was confusing to Katharine and the rest of the Smith family. As a member of the Quorum of the Twelve Apostles, he was called to account for his behavior the following spring, eventually reconciling with the church and the other members of the Twelve. Nevertheless, for more than a year after relocating to Illinois, William's focus was on improving his financial status more than attending to the needs of the Saints or fulfilling his calling. While other members of his quorum made great sacrifices to fulfill their appointed mission to England in the years 1839–41, William cited his family's poverty as his reason for remaining at home. It was an excuse that didn't sit well with his colleagues, and his decision no doubt impacted his reputation among the remainder of the Twelve.[1]

Plymouth, Illinois

By the time the Salisburys arrived in the state, William had already established himself at Plymouth, Illinois, located in the southeastern corner of Hancock County some thirty-five miles south of the Saints' eventual settlement at Nauvoo. He was drawn to the community because of its potential for growth as a railroad line that was to traverse the state was planned to run through the center of town.[2] After

This structure was built on the site of William Smith's "Mormon Hotel" in Plymouth, Illinois, 1869. An outbuilding, visible at the rear of the home, was likely part of William's original hotel property. Photograph courtesy of Virginia Metzgar.

engaging in some type of merchandising for five months, William purchased the largest building in the budding town from prominent business owner Sevier Tadlock, who had previously used the structure for the "triple purpose of dwelling, hotel, and store."[3] As evidence of his business acumen, in just two years William owned the hotel outright and expanded his property holdings to include five more town lots, a stable, and ten acres just outside of town. Locals eventually dubbed William's inn the "Mormon Hotel."[4]

Other Latter-day Saint immigrants followed William's lead. Local historian E. H. Young described the significant influx of Latter-day Saints to the area, estimating that half the town were members by the early 1840s.[5] The Salisburys were among those who were drawn to the area, no doubt at William's encouragement, because Jenkins ostensibly shared William's belief that it would be unwise for the Saints to gather en masse to a single location.[6] Though Jenkins was no longer an active participant in the church, he followed the greater Smith family in their migrations to Missouri and Illinois and maintained an amicable relationship with his in-laws, especially with William. He remained an interested observer of all that was transpiring with church developments in both Missouri and Illinois, albeit from a distance.

When the Salisburys first arrived in Plymouth in the fall of 1839, there were approximately fifteen families who had settled in the area, mostly hunters and trappers who lived in log cabins built along Crooked Creek and its tributaries. A post office was established two years earlier in 1837, and the only other business in town was Sevier Tadlock's grocery store and inn.[7] Katharine recalled that "Jenkins . . . and I removed to Plymouth, on the opposite side of Hancock County from Nauvoo, where he ran a blacksmith shop, and often received 'coon' skins and maple sugar in exchange for work at the anvil."[8] That probably meant that hard cash was difficult to come by in such a remote area, and residents used the barter system to meet their basic needs during those early years.

Economic Hardships

Several years of settlement had in fact done little to improve the family's economic status, because eldest son Solomon remembered how meager their living circumstances were by the year 1842, when he was seven years old. He described how the family had little beyond corn bread and bacon to eat and was grateful for the generosity of a kind neighbor who provided buttermilk for their evening meals.[9] Another son was born October 25, 1841, and named for Katharine's younger brother Don Carlos, who had passed away of pneumonia-like symptoms at Nauvoo a few months earlier, expanding the family to six during a time of limited resources.[10] Hunger and poverty were repeated themes in Solomon's recollections of his childhood:

> One night I went home with a boy and girl about my age. . . . After grating and sifting the meal [their mother] mixed it with lard and water, then, raking the coals out, placed the cake on the hearth and covered with ashes, after which they placed the coals back on the ashes. It was the next morning that the woman at this house was going through the same proceedings. We watched with hungry eyes. . . . For supper we had fruit, venison, buttermilk, and honey, and all the things that go with them. Since then I have eaten many wonderful dinners, but none of them do I remember like that one.[11]

It likely took a few years before Jenkins established his blacksmith shop in town, though he engaged in various jobs for neighbors laboring at his trade during those early years. He also appears to have been absent from the family for periods of time, evidence that he continued to struggle providing steady income for the family. When Joseph Smith and his entourage were returning from Springfield, Illinois, after being cleared from Missouri governor Thomas Reynolds' attempt at extradition, the group stopped in Plymouth on their way to Nauvoo.[12] Joseph and his secretary Willard Richards took the opportunity to visit the Salisbury home on the evening of January 9, 1843. Richards recorded, "While there my heart was pained to witness a lovely wife & sister of Joseph, almost barefoot, & four lovely children entirely so—in the middle of winter."[13] There was no mention made of Jenkins being present at home. His absence might explain the family's destitute circumstance. If true, that meant that Katharine continued to deal with the stress of intermittently caring for her family on her own, only this time far removed from the support of her family at Nauvoo.

Katharine possibly assisted William at his hotel to earn extra income and helped care for William's wife Caroline, whose chronic illness of dropsy (edema) would lead to her death a few years later in 1845.[14] She also attempted to sell clothing or rugs that she manufactured once the family could afford a loom, skills she had developed early in life.[15] Her efforts to supplement the family income would still have provided for only their most basic needs.

Willard Richards noted in his account of his and Joseph's visit to the Salisbury home in January 1843 that it was the first time Joseph had been to their home in Plymouth. Joseph and Katharine took time to reminisce about their upbringing, including sharing several anecdotal stories about their admired elder brother Alvin, who had died twenty years earlier. After commenting on Alvin's handsome appearance, Joseph recounted an incident of a fight between "2 Irishmen" and that when "one was about to gouge the others eyes, Alvin took him by his collar. & breeches & threw him over the ring which had been formed to witness the fight."[16] Reminiscing about these childhood events served the dual purpose of mourning for their admired elder brother while also strengthening sibling bonds.

Probably due to his hectic schedule, Joseph was rarely in the area, but his presence in the community created quite a stir in the small town. Local history recorded Joseph's occasional visits to the area, where he typically stayed at William's "Mormon Hotel" and "sometimes manifested his love of worldly enjoyments by the spending of night participating in the sports of a merry dancing party."[17] Katharine brought her family to the hotel on these occasions, where she also enjoyed an entertaining evening.

Due to the distance, Joseph also stayed in touch with the Salisburys through writing letters. On occasion he wrote specifically to Jenkins, expressing his friendship and undoubtedly

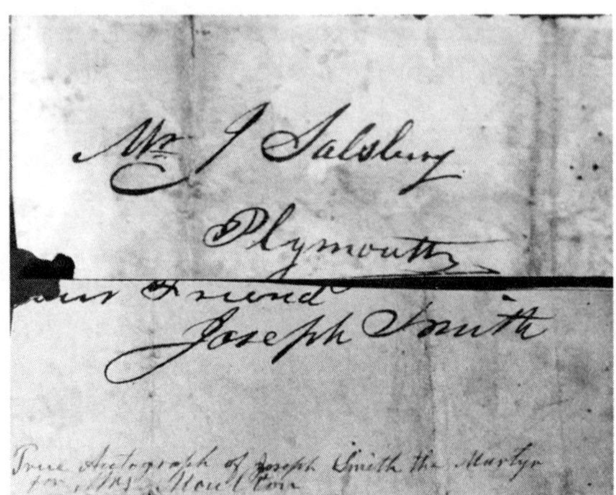

Fragments of letter from Joseph Smith to Jenkins Salisbury, ca. 1841–44. Courtesy of Greg T. Walker.

encouraging him in reconciling his faith and fulfilling his family roles.[18] Katharine was among those neighbors in the Plymouth community who thronged the post office when the mail was delivered twice each week, and she especially treasured these letters that kept her connected to her family.[19]

Katharine longed for more connection with her relatives at Nauvoo, especially her mother and sisters, and would make the seventy-mile round trip as often as feasible. She was likely present during a time of celebration when her brother Joseph married their younger sister Lucy to Arthur Millikin on June 4, 1840, and at the funeral for her younger brother Don Carlos when he died in the summer of 1841.[20]

On other occasions she missed important family gatherings due to distance. When Joseph Sr.'s health began to decline in fall of 1840, he sensed his time was short and sent for all his children and their families to gather at his bedside. He immediately sent son-in-law Arthur Millikin for Katharine, but with the time it took to deliver the news and make the return trip she arrived too late. Not only did she miss seeing her father before he passed and receiving an in-person final blessing from him as other family members did, but she also missed the funeral the following day. Mother Lucy recorded that Jenkins was ill with "ague" when Katharine received news of her father's declining health, which delayed her arrival until the following evening after the funeral. In her haste to arrive before his death, she speedily drove a wagon the thirty-five miles to Nauvoo with her husband sick on a makeshift bed in the back. Her mother recorded that Katharine remained at Nauvoo "for some length of time for we felt so desolate that we could not endure to be separated more than could possibly be avoided."[21] A granddaughter recounted that each time Katharine had to leave Nauvoo and return home to Plymouth, she experienced a deep sense of loneliness.[22]

Other trips to Nauvoo were filled with positive memories for Katharine and her children, especially during the holidays. Solomon recalled that each year the family lived at Plymouth, his uncle Joseph "sent for mother and the children to spend the holidays at Nauvoo. And mother and the children crossed the prairie every year from 1839 to 1843 from Plymouth to Carthage thence to Nauvoo."[23] Jenkins evidently did not join the family on these extended visits because he probably could not leave his blacksmithing trade for a prolonged period. Katharine similarly recalled these Christmas visits with fondness, describing how she and the children "often visited Nauvoo, where my brother, Joseph, entertained us royally and gave me silk dresses and other valuable presents." She described her brother's hospitality and kindness on such occasions and remembered how he and Emma always "kept [an] open house to friends and strangers alike."[24] When Katharine and the children eventually left for home after these memorable visits, Joseph and Emma sent her "laden with food,

Emma Hale Smith, 1845.
Courtesy of Community of Christ
Library-Archives.

money, and clothing."[25] Katharine had not experienced that sort of care or prosperity since her marriage, and she and the children relished those experiences.

Joseph obviously took a special interest in looking out for Katharine and her family because poverty had plagued them from their earliest years of marriage in Kirtland. In the summer of 1842, Katharine and the children stayed for an extended period at Nauvoo, perhaps for the entire summer. Joseph provided her with employment as she worked in his Red Brick Store, where she recorded purchases and transactions that summer.[26] Joseph continued to monitor the Salisburys' well-being while at Plymouth. When Joseph had visited at their home in January 1843 and when Willard Richards noted their poor living conditions, Joseph gave her all the cash and coins he had in his pocket to assist in meeting her immediate needs. Joseph inadvertently gave her his lucky penny, which was stamped 1830—the year the church was established.[27] It became a treasured family heirloom, along with a quilt Emma had made and gifted to the family, presumably during the early 1840s.[28] Katharine admired Emma, and the two would remain close friends for the remainder of their lives.

The Salisburys' visits to Nauvoo included major church or community events. Katharine recounted that anytime there were noteworthy gatherings in the city, such as general conference or July Fourth celebrations, her brothers would send for her.[29] She was present at a major gathering of the Saints and other local dignitaries on April 6, 1841, where somewhere between seven and ten thousand people were present. A procession of the Nauvoo Legion began marching early in the morning in sixteen companies and carried a "beautiful silk national flag." The day included trumpeters heralding the ceremonies, a full brass band on the temple grounds, the ceremonial laying of three cornerstones for the Nauvoo Temple, as well as speeches by several church leaders.[30] Of all the festivities that day, the splendor of the Nauvoo Legion is what stood out most to attendees.[31] Katharine's personal recollections of that memorable occasion included a depiction of her younger brother Don Carlos just before

"LIEUTENANT-GENERAL" JOSEPH SMITH REVIEWING THE NAUVOO LEGION.

"Lieutenant-General" Joseph Smith Reviewing the Nauvoo Legion, from J. H. Beadle, *Life in Utah*.

his death, who served as brigadier general in the military unit. Only Joseph Smith and John C. Bennett held superior offices to Don Carlos.[32] Katharine recounted that when Don Carlos was outfitted in his blue uniform, "as an officer of the Nauvoo Legion and riding his charger on parade," he was the most striking man she ever saw.[33] Emma Hale Smith, who was part of the procession that day, concurred with

Nauvoo House cornerstone, photograph by George Edward Anderson, 1907. Courtesy of L. Tom Perry Special Collections, Harold B. Lee Library, Brigham Young University.

Katharine's assessment. She recalled that her six-foot-four-inch, two-hundred-pound brother-in-law "was the handsomest man she ever saw—That when in uniform and on horse back . . . he was magnificent."[34] "It was inspiring to see the Legion in parade," Katharine further described of these occasions, "with my brothers and the other officers on their charges in command, accompanied by ladies in silks and satins, also mounted."[35]

The Salisburys were also present the following October for the church's general conference. Katharine recalled the cornerstone-laying ceremony for the Nauvoo House, then under construction, and remembered her brother Joseph including the original Book of Mormon manuscript inside the cornerstone, along with other notable items related to the church's brief history.[36]

These extended stays in Nauvoo tempered her feelings of isolation and loneliness, but it continued to be difficult for Katharine to live so far removed from family. It helped having William and Caroline Smith in town during those early years in Plymouth, and Katharine's brothers Samuel and Don Carlos also bought property in the area and assisted in managing the hotel for brief periods of time.[37] However, the Salisburys' decision to live far from Nauvoo and Jenkins's decision to remain outside the faith meant the family missed out on many of the key theological developments transpiring at Nauvoo. There is no evidence that Katharine understood or participated in vicarious work for the dead or in the endowment or understood the concept of eternal sealings. While her sister-in-law Emma, her mother, and her sister Lucy were actively involved in the Nauvoo's Female Relief Society, Katharine's name is absent from those records.[38] She also had no knowledge of plural marriage, something her brother Joseph only shared with his most trusted followers. Katharine would later state that the first time she heard of plural marriage being practiced at Nauvoo was more than a year after Joseph's death, further evidence of how little she understood about doctrinal developments occurring at Nauvoo.[39] Katharine not only missed her family during these years, she missed out on actively participating in the church.

Finances appear to have improved for the family by the latter part of 1843, perhaps due to Jenkins establishing his blacksmith shop more permanently in town. Besides William Smith's "Mormon Hotel," the only other Mormon business of note in the town's history was Jenkins's blacksmith shop. Local historian E. H. Young added that Jenkins's business was "short-lived," further evidence that his actual shop was not completed until the year 1843.[40] His business probably also benefited from the town's increasing population. On September 15, 1843, the Salisburys purchased multiple lots just a few blocks away from the town square and within a short walking distance from the "Mormon Hotel." Their property, approximately seven acres in total, butted up against the proposed railroad line that was to run through the town and stood adjacent to several lots that William Smith owned. Revealingly, all lots were purchased in Katharine's name only, with no mention of Jenkins.[41] The same had been true of their Kirtland property.[42] Perhaps she was protecting herself and the children from the financial instability of her husband because he would have been unable to sell the property without her consent. It is also possible that they were protecting their property from any creditors that Jenkins owed. Once again, the Salisburys were finally in a financial position to purchase property and contemplated building a more permanent home in Plymouth.

Notes

1. William Smith to D[on] C[arlos] Smith, December 1, 1840, in "Communications," *Times and Seasons* 2 (December 15, 1840): 252–53; Kyle R. Walker, *William B. Smith: In the Shadow of a Prophet* (Salt Lake City: Greg Kofford Books, 2015), 140–45.
2. The railroad was not completed until the mid-1850s. E. H. Young, *A History of Round Prairie and Plymouth, 1831–1875* (Chicago: Geo. J. Titus, Book and Job Printer, 1876), 105–6.
3. Young, *History of Round Prairie and Plymouth*, 41–42.
4. William Smith to Brother [Edmund L. Kelley], ca. 1893, Suplaiment [*sic*], Miscellaneous Letters, P19, folder 49, Community of Christ Library-Archives; Young, *History of Round Prairie and Plymouth*, 64–65. For more information on William's activities in Plymouth, see Walker, *William B. Smith*, 144–47.

5. Young, *History of Round Prairie and Plymouth*, 64–65.

6. Walker, *William B. Smith*, 144.

7. Solomon J. Salisbury, *Reminiscences of an Octogenarian* (self-pub., ca. 1926), 3; Young, *History of Round Prairie and Plymouth*, 41–42.

8. Herbert S. Salisbury, "Reminiscences of Joseph Smith, as Told by His Sister, Catherine Smith–Salisbury, to Her Grandson, Herbert S. Salisbury," *Saints' Herald* 60, no. 41 (October 8, 1913): 984.

9. Salisbury, *Reminiscences of an Octogenarian*, 3.

10. George A. Smith (Salt Lake City) to Cousin Catherine [Salisbury], August 17, 1865, Historian's Office letterpress copybooks, 1854–79, vol. 2, 1859–69, CHL; John Smith Papers, 1833–54, journal, 1846 February–1854 May, CHL; Lucy Mack Smith, *Biographical Sketches of Joseph Smith the Prophet and His Progenitors for Many Generations* (Liverpool: S. W. Richards, 1853), 43; Dorothy D. Dean, handwritten family group sheet, copy of original in author's possession. For Don Carlos Smith's death date and cause of death, see "Death of General Don Carlos Smith," *Times and Seasons* 2, no. 20 (August 16, 1841): 503; Roy B. Huff and Kyle R. Walker, "Don Carlos Smith," in *United by Faith: The Joseph Sr. and Lucy Mack Smith Family*, ed. Kyle R. Walker (American Fork, UT: Covenant Communications; Provo, UT: BYU Studies, 2006), 384.

11. Salisbury, *Reminiscences of an Octogenarian*, 3–4.

12. For more information on Missouri's attempt to extradite Joseph Smith over the attempted shooting of Lilburn W. Boggs, see Spencer W. McBride et al., eds., *Documents, Volume 11: September 1842–February 1843*, vol. 11 of the Documents series of *The Joseph Smith Papers*, ed. Matthew C. Godfrey et al. (Salt Lake City: Church Historian's Press, 2020), xix–xxiv.

13. Andrew H. Hedges, Alex D. Smith, and Richard Lloyd Anderson, eds., *Journals, Volume 2: December 1841–April 1843*, vol. 2 of the Journals series of *The Joseph Smith Papers*, ed. Dean C. Jessee, Ronald K. Esplin, and Richard Lyman Bushman (Salt Lake City: Church Historian's Press, 2011), 242–43.

14. Mary Salisbury Hancock, "The Three Sisters of the Prophet Joseph Smith, Part III," *Saints' Herald* 101, no. 4 (January 25, 1954): 82.

15. Katharine manufactured rugs and carpets that she sold later in life to earn extra income. Autobiography of Mary Salisbury Hancock, 1963, 2, L. Tom Perry Special Collections, Harold B. Lee Library, Brigham Young University, Provo, UT.

16. Among other things, Joseph also commented on Alvin's handsome appearance and superior strength during his visit with Katharine, declaring that his attractiveness was surpassed by none but "Adam & Seth." *JSP*, J2:242–43.

17. Young, *History of Round Prairie and Plymouth*, 65.

18. Joseph Smith (n.p.) to Jenkins Salisbury, ca. 1841–44, letter cut and most content removed, original in possession of Gregory T. Walker, Mesquite, NV.

19. Salisbury, *Reminiscences of an Octogenarian*, 3.

20. "Hymenial," *Times and Seasons* 1, no. 8 (June 1840): 127; Hancock, "Three Sisters, Part III," 82; "Death of General Don Carlos Smith," *Times and Seasons* 2, no. 20 (August 16, 1841): 503–4; Dean L. Jarman and Kyle R. Walker, "Don Carlos Smith," in Walker, *United by Faith*, 384.

21. Lavina Fielding Anderson, ed., *Lucy's Book: A Critical Edition of Lucy Mack Smith's Family Memoir* (Salt Lake City: Signature Books, 2001), 723–24. Joseph Sr. blessed Katharine absentia, recounting her many sorrows and troubles and commending her for her enduring patience. He promised her, as he had in her patriarchal blessing pronounced in 1834, that she would eventually be prospered with "horses and land, and things round her to make her heart glad." Lucy Mack Smith, *Biographical Sketches*, 269.

22. Hancock, "Three Sisters, Part III," 82.

23. Salisbury, *Reminiscences of an Octogenarian*, 15.

24. Salisbury, "Reminiscences of Joseph Smith," 984.

25. Herbert S. Salisbury, "Things the Prophet's Sister Told Me," 4, unpublished typescript, San Rafael, CA, June 30, 1945, CHL.

26. Joseph Smith's Store Daybook B, Entry for Joseph Smith, Nauvoo, Hancock County, Illinois, 18 July 1842—A, 34[b], note, www.joseph smithpapers.org.

27. Salisbury, "Things the Prophet's Sister Told Me," 5.

28. "Jubilee Notes," *Deseret Evening News* 30, no. 117 (April 10, 1897): 1.

29. "Anniversary of Carthage," *Salt Lake Tribune* 44, no. 57 (June 24, 1894): 16.

30. Brent M. Rogers et al., eds., *Documents, Volume 8: February–November 1841*, vol. 8 of the Documents series of *The Joseph Smith Papers*, ed. Ronald K. Esplin et al. (Salt Lake City: Church Historian's Press, 2019), 98–99; Richard E. Bennett, Susan Easton Black, and Donald Q. Cannon, *The Nauvoo Legion in Illinois: A History of the Mormon Militia, 1841–1846* (Norman, OK: Arthur H. Clark Company, 2010), 170–71.

31. Robert B. Thompson, "Laying the Cornerstone of the Temple," *Times and Seasons* 2, no. 12 (April 15, 1841): 380–82; "The Mormons," *Warsaw Signal* 2, no. 2 (May 19, 1841): 2.

32. Bennett et al., *Nauvoo Legion in Illinois*, 112–22.

33. Salisbury, "Things the Prophet's Sister Told Me," 1; Salisbury, "Reminiscences of Joseph Smith," 984.

34. Emma's statement is recorded by her niece, Mary Bailey Smith Norman, who added, "and Aunt Emma was not given to undue laudations." Mary

Bailey Smith Norman to Ina Coolbrith, Community of Christ Library-Archives, Independence, MO.

35. Salisbury, "Reminiscences of Joseph Smith," 984.

36. Salisbury, "Things the Prophet's Sister Told Me," 7. It was thought that sealing and encasing the Book of Mormon manuscript in the cornerstone would protect it for "ages." However, "the building was so close to the east bank of the Mississippi River . . . that the box in the cornerstone experienced flooding at high-water times, significantly damaging the paper items deposited therein." *JSP*, D8:295–97.

37. Young, *History of Round Prairie and Plymouth*, 64, 87. Young recounts how Samuel lived "on a farm in the extreme north part of the prairie, near Crooked Creek. He bore the reputation of being a good, respectable citizen." Don Carlos Smith bought property in Plymouth in December 1840, but due to his responsibilities of publishing the *Times and Seasons* newspaper at Nauvoo, he rarely, if ever, lived at Plymouth. Bonds & Mortgages, Book 1, 102, Hancock County Courthouse, Carthage, IL; Kyle R. Walker, "'As Fire Shut Up in My Bones': Ebenezer Robinson, Don Carlos Smith, and the 1840 Edition of the Book of Mormon," *Journal of Mormon History* 36, no. 1 (Winter 2010): 1–12.

38. Emma Hale Smith was appointed the first president, and both Lucy Mack Smith and her daughter Lucy Millikin were actively involved in Nauvoo's Female Relief Society. Like Katharine, her sister Sophronia lived outside Nauvoo, and thus her name does not appear in the minutes of the Relief Society. Jill Mulvay Derr, Carol Cornwall Madsen, Kate Holbrook, and Mathew J. Grow, eds., *The First Fifty Years of Relief Society: Key Documents in Latter-Day Saint History* (Salt Lake City: Church Historian's Press, 2016), 37–38, 44–45, 49–50, 52.

39. "Aunt Katharine Salisbury's Testimony," *Saints' Herald* 40, no. 18 (May 6, 1893): 275.

40. Young, *History of Round Prairie and Plymouth*, 90.

41. This land was purchased for two hundred dollars on September 15, 1843. It appears that the Salisburys rented the log home and land that they lived on before that time. Deed Book L, 457–58, Land and Records Office, Hancock County Courthouse, Carthage, IL.

42. The Salisburys had purchased their Kirtland land from Sophia Stevens (the wife of Uzziel Stevens) and registered it in Katharine's name. She acquired a city lot on block 112 sub lots 19 & 20 that was 30/160 of an acre (four rods west of lot no. 10 on block 112 formerly owned by Hyrum Smith) and worth three hundred dollars. Witnessed Sybil Beall and W. D. Beall, JP October 15, 1839. Land transactions of Saints, Kirtland, Ohio, 1830s & 1840s, August 5, 1893, CHL. Thanks to Mark L. Staker for sharing information on the Salisbury propherty.

CHAPTER NINE

"My Brothers
Are Dead"

*I shall never forget that Saturday, June 23 [22], when I last saw my
brothers alive. It was my farewell to them on this earth.*
— Katharine Smith Salisbury

THE YEAR 1844 found the Salisburys on the cusp of financial
stability. Jenkins's blacksmith business was expanding, and they had
firmly established themselves in the Plymouth community. Their
family also continued to grow by the mid-1840s, with the arrival of
a daughter they named for their esteemed sister-in-law Emma, born
on March 25, 1844.[1] As they became more settled, the older children began attending school in a log schoolhouse under the tutelage
of Bryant Peterson, who later became a lawyer at Carthage.[2] As it
turned out, the summer of 1843 to the spring of 1844 was the most
secure period of their lives since their marriage thirteen years earlier.

While the inhabitants of western Illinois had welcomed the
beleaguered Saints just a few years earlier, by 1842 the Mormon
influence on the political climate within Hancock County negatively

impacted locals' view of the Saints. As the decade progressed, the community of Saints at Nauvoo increasingly clashed with their neighbors. As the Saints' political power increased, those in small communities throughout the county attempted to quell their influence. Community leaders at Carthage and Warsaw were particularly influential, including Thomas C. Sharp, who publicized his brash anti-Mormon views in his *Warsaw Signal* newspaper. Eventually those difficulties began to expand to outlying communities where Saints had gathered in small clusters, including those Saints in Plymouth. In December 1843, a mob robbed and then burned the home of a Latter-day Saint named David Holman in nearby Ramus, Illinois, where Katharine's sister Sophronia and her family lived.[3] As the Salisburys learned of these developments, it increased their apprehension for their own safety.

While Samuel Smith's reputation had been impeccable during the time he lived near Plymouth, his brother William's example had been less than admirable, perhaps contributing to the animosity towards the Saints that developed at Plymouth. His hot temper and brash reactivity often led to conflict with locals. In one instance, William engaged in a verbal exchange with a longtime Plymouth resident who probably reflected the sentiments of the community at large when he asserted his disappointment that Joseph Smith had not yet been arrested by the state. The brief exchange quickly led to an all-out brawl, where William gave the man a "stinging blow" that nearly leveled him. Eventually several residents intervened to break up the fracas, but word of the fight and William's reputation immediately spread throughout the small community.[4] Though William eventually relocated to Nauvoo in early 1842, he continued to stir up trouble with his combative editorials in the *Wasp* newspaper that he oversaw at Nauvoo. His election as a county representative to the Illinois legislature the following year, where he vociferously defended the controversial Nauvoo Charter, probably served only to heighten Plymouth residents' concerns about the political influence of Latter-day Saints in the county.[5] There are no surviving accounts of Jenkins Salisbury's reputation in the community, but he was definitely linked

Robert Campbell, *General Joseph Smith Addressing the Nauvoo Legion* (ink and watercolor on paper, 1845). This scene depicts Joseph Smith's address in Nauvoo on June 18, 1844. Courtesy of Church History Museum.

to his brother-in-law in the minds of his neighbors, as he remained supportive and close to William. It was also well known among locals that Katharine was a sister to the church's prophet in Nauvoo.[6]

Amidst the turmoil in Nauvoo in the month of June 1844, Katharine headed to the city of the Saints to visit family. Perhaps she wanted to ascertain for herself her brother's safety after reading about developments at Nauvoo once Joseph, as city mayor, ordered the destruction of the press of the *Nauvoo Expositor*, and state officials ultimately sought his arrest for his role in the event. As things escalated in the ensuing weeks, the Saints' efforts to try and allay feelings with Governor Thomas Ford and in outlying communities throughout Hancock County proved unsuccessful. An editorial in the *Warsaw Signal* written by Thomas Sharp in mid-June called for "war and extermination" of the Mormons, indicating it was not a time for words but that comments should instead "BE MADE WITH POWDER AND BALL!!!"[7]

Katharine arrived in the city the week of June 16–22 amidst turmoil. She probably had little time to personally visit with her elder brothers for any length of time owing to the chaos that had engulfed Nauvoo, perhaps staying at the Mansion House where her mother was then living.[8] On Tuesday, June 18, she listened to Joseph preach from a makeshift stand across the street from the Mansion House, which would be his final sermon to the Saints. "I was in Nauvoo a few days before my brothers were brought to Carthage," Katharine recalled of that day, "where Joseph preached a sermon to the largest crowd I have ever seen." In retrospect, she was grateful to have been present for his final discourse, describing his remarks that day as "more in the nature of a prophecy than a sermon."[9] Dressed in his full Nauvoo Legion uniform, he declared martial law but encouraged the Saints to only take defensive measures to protect themselves. At one point during his sermon, Joseph unsheathed his sword, expressing his determination to defend the Saints and their legal rights, "or my blood shall be spilt on the ground like water." "You are a good people; therefore, I love you with all my heart," he continued. "You have stood by me in the hour of trouble, and I am willing to sacrifice my life for your preservation."[10] Katharine remembered that he also made reference to enemies among the Saints who were present on that occasion, declaring "that there are those among you who will betray me soon; in fact, you have plotted to deliver me up to the enemy to be slain."[11]

Katharine felt that the Saints' political influence was the primary reason they clashed with their neighbors in the county. "The vote at Nauvoo soon became so large that the church held the balance of power in western Illinois," she later summarized. "As that part of the state was mostly pro-slavery, the same acts and scenes of violence were soon enacted as before in Missouri. False accusations and false stories circulated," she recalled, describing how these rumors persisted in Hancock County some fifty years after that tumultuous summer of 1844. Katharine also conceded that religious differences contributed to escalating difficulties.[12]

On Saturday, June 22, Katharine had her final exchange with her two brothers. As she prepared to return to her home in Plymouth, Joseph and Hyrum both met briefly with their younger sister. "Joseph took my hands tenderly in his," Katharine recalled of that poignant exchange etched in her memory, "saying: 'Goodbye, sister [K]ath[a]rine. When this trouble blows over I shall come down to Plymouth and make you a visit.'" She also recounted how Hyrum bid her a simple "goodbye," but thought that the tone of his voice "had a deeper feeling than I had ever known him to entertain." Katharine sensed the apprehensiveness her brothers were experiencing in contemplating being arrested and taken to Carthage, and those final exchanges became more poignant in her mind in light of the trauma that happened next. The Smiths turned themselves over to authorities two days later, and just five days after their exchange with Katharine, they were murdered by a mob while being held in Carthage Jail. "I shall never forget that Saturday, June 23 [22], when I last saw my brothers alive," she wrote. "It was my farewell to them on this earth."[13] Years later, she kept a picture of her brothers on her mantle that reminded her of the way her brothers were dressed the last time she saw them.[14]

Katharine was uneasy as she returned home on the evening of June 22. She learned of her brothers being arrested that next week and of various town militias gathering at Carthage. It was in the morning of June 28, the day after her brothers were murdered, that she received news from a courier of what had transpired.[15] Perhaps her brother Samuel had sent the messenger and buggy to transport her to Carthage. He had hurriedly ridden from Plymouth to Carthage the previous evening upon learning that his brothers were in danger, arriving in town just after the murders had occurred. Instead of helping defend his brothers, he performed the morbid task of removing his brother's lifeless bodies from the jail, and cleaning and preparing to transport them to Nauvoo the next day.[16]

Copy of lithograph of Joseph and Hyrum Smith, original created in 1847. Courtesy of Church History Library. Katharine kept this photo in her house and said that her brothers were dressed in these outfits when she last saw them.

In the weeks before the murder of Hyrum and Joseph, Jenkins had gone south to St. Louis to obtain work, promising to send money back to help support the family. As animosity increased towards the Saints, locals avoided going to him to do their blacksmith work because of the family's connection to the church's founder, something that would be a recurring theme in the ensuing years. Katharine was once again alone in raising their five children during a most difficult time. Probably to help generate income, but possibly for protection as well, the Salisburys had the John and Phebe Husbands family (also Latter-day Saints) move in with them after Jenkins left.[17]

After receiving the news from Carthage, Katharine left her children in the care of this family living in her home and immediately left for Carthage in a buggy.[18] Many Carthage residents had fled town, fearing the Saints would retaliate. When Katharine arrived in the deserted town, she located her brother Samuel at the Hamilton House, where she viewed the mangled bodies of her brothers and saw John Taylor, who had been wounded but had survived. Later that day, Artois Hamilton, the proprietor of the Hamilton House, along with his son William, drove a wagon carrying Hyrum's body back to Nauvoo, while Samuel Smith drove a second wagon with

Hamilton House, Carthage, Illinois, where the bodies of Joseph and Hyrum Smith were taken after they were shot at Carthage Jail. Courtesy of Church History Library.

Joseph's body.[19] Katharine had arrived in time to accompany Samuel and the cortege back to Nauvoo.[20]

"Every heart is filled with sorrow," Vilate Kimball wrote to her husband Heber, who was then in the East laboring as a missionary, "and the very streets of Nauvoo seem to mourn."[21] While the entire community of Nauvoo would remain in a state of mourning throughout the summer, for the Smith family, the deaths of Hyrum and Joseph meant an added measure of loss. They were not only heads of the church they espoused but also leaders of the greater Smith family and left a void that would never be filled. As Mother Lucy steeled herself to view her sons later that same day, she was overcome with emotion as she entered the room and saw the lifeless bodies and listened to the "sobs and groans . . . of their wives, children, brother, and sisters," who had all gathered at the Mansion House in Nauvoo.[22] Twenty-five-year-old Sarah Kimball was present at the Mansion House that day and also recounted listening to the "smothered sobs" throughout the room, describing how Lucy sat in an armchair in the corner of the room next to her namesake daughter. Sarah tenderly held Mother Lucy's hand, attempting to offer some consolation as Lucy sobbed in silence for more than three minutes. She finally spoke, expressing to Sarah her disbelief as to why anyone would want to kill her sons. Turning to her daughter Lucy, Mother Smith queried as if seeking confirmation, "Don't you know Lucy how mild Hyrum always was?"[23] She vocalized the shock her family was experiencing.

Ultimately Lucy said she found comfort through the lens of her faith and in an answer that she described as a "voice" reassuring her that her sons had been taken home to be with God and were now out of reach of their enemies.[24] She shared those impressions with her surviving children who were present. Katharine, who was dealing with her own grief, shared little about her feelings at the time. Much like her mother had described in her history, later accounts reveal she experienced mixed emotions of grief and indignation.[25] She heard rumors that Joseph had uttered the Masonic cry for help during the attack and that there were Masons among the mob who shot her

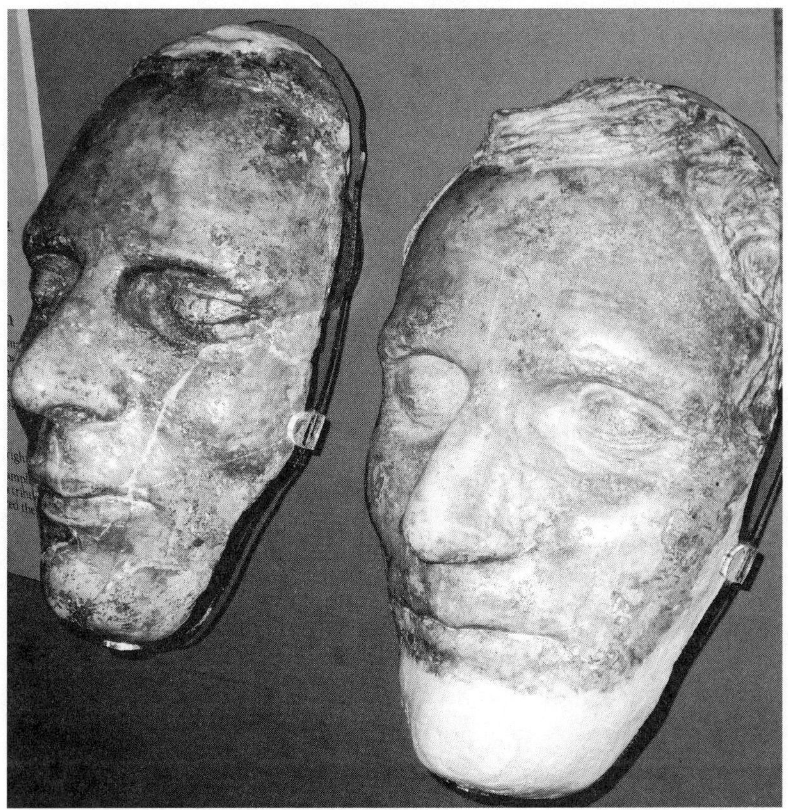

Death masks of Joseph and Hyrum Smith. Photograph by Kyle R. Walker, 2020.

brothers. Later, when her children and grandchildren affiliated with Masonry in the state of Illinois, she was incensed and would not support their decision because of the duplicity she perceived among its members related to the murder of her brothers.[26]

Katharine stayed in town long enough to participate in the funeral services held on Saturday evening, June 29. She was also one of a few trusted family members and friends who knew of the secret burial of her brothers in the basement of the unfinished Nauvoo House. "There was a price set on Joseph's head," she recalled of that chaotic time, "and we concealed the bodies for a day and a night."[27]

The bodies remained in that location until fall, when Emma had them secretly reinterred in unmarked graves across the street, in the yard of her and Joseph's original Homestead residence. Emma must have communicated that information to Katharine as well, as Katharine recalled that "we then buried them near the old home."[28]

When Katharine finally returned home after that haunting weekend, she was in for an additional shock. She had hurriedly left on Friday morning the previous week and thought her children would be safe when she left them with the Husbands family at her home in Plymouth. However, her son Solomon recounted that the Husbands family became fearful for their own safety in the aftermath of what had transpired at Carthage and decided to leave Plymouth immediately. Sometime during the night after Katharine had left, "they packed what clothing they could carry on their backs and left on foot for Nauvoo."[29] They left in secret, not even informing the Salisbury children of their intended departure, and the children awoke to find themselves alone.

Eldest daughter Lucy, nearing her tenth birthday, and Solomon, just a year younger, led out in trying to care for the younger children, which included four-month-old Emma. After two days on their own, the frightened and hungry children mustered up the courage to go across the street to the home of Dr. Henry P. and Lucy Griswold for food. Upon learning of their plight, Lucy took them in, fed them, and allowed them to sleep on their floor that night. Henry was among those who had gone to Carthage as part of a military contingent from Plymouth,[30] and when he returned home later that night and saw the Salisbury children in his home, he asked Lucy who the children were. Lucy, who had already learned of the murder of the Smiths at Carthage, informed him that "they are the little Mormon children from across the street; their mother has gone to Carthage where her brothers have been murdered and she has not returned." Indignantly, Henry replied, "sure, and we will all be murdered if we keep them here." "Certainly no one could blame us for feeding these hungry little children," Lucy protested, but Henry stood firm. The Griswolds reluctantly housed them that night and fed them the next morning, when they abruptly sent them back home, telling them,

"Your mother will surely be back today."[31] Katharine most likely arrived home on Monday, July 1. Reeling from the events of the previous few days, she must have felt additionally devastated after learning what had transpired at home in her absence.

She returned to Nauvoo just a month later, upon learning of Samuel's unexpected death on July 30, 1844.[32] Samuel had been involved in a high-speed horse chase at the time he was attempting to aid his brothers on June 27, from which he received an injury to his side. After arriving in Nauvoo with the bodies of his brothers, he confided to his mother about a severe, internal pain that he was experiencing. He was eventually diagnosed with "bilious fever," which caused his death only a few weeks later.[33] His death added to the overwhelming grief the Smith family experienced that fateful summer. Writing to her only surviving son William a few months after these events, Lucy Mack Smith reflected on the "deep affliction" the family was experiencing. "Wiliam I once had 5 noble and manly sons[,] a compa[n]ion who was the delight of my heart[,] besides 3 dutiful and affectionate Daughters whose affections . . . made me as happy as it was possible for a mother to be. 4[34] of those sons with their Father are in the cold and silent mansion of the tomb."[35] Lucy's "dutiful and affectionate" daughters would continue to fulfill that role in the years that followed.

In the ensuing weeks, life became increasingly dangerous for Saints who lived outside Nauvoo, and Plymouth was no exception. Animosity had increased during the previous year, but now it became more personal and progressively more threatening. As tensions reached a crescendo by the summer of 1844, the Salisburys became special targets of their neighbors' animosity for their connection to the divisive religion. Solomon described how the "mob spirit seemed to run riot" that summer. He recalled that on multiple occasions "when we got up in the morning we would find written notices giving us twenty-four hours to leave the country, or they would burn or kill the outfit." He further recalled that even before the death of his uncles at Carthage, his father had left for St. Louis, at least in part, because he felt fearful for his life. Jenkins returned at some point that summer, probably after learning of the murder of his brothers-in-law. The family stubbornly held on throughout most of the summer, but by August they felt it was too dangerous to remain in Plymouth.[36] For the third time in a decade, the Salisburys were forced to uproot and start again; only this time it was a financial blow from which they never recovered.

Notes

1. George A. Smith (Salt Lake City) to Cousin Catherine [Salisbury], August 17, 1865, Historian's Office letterpress copybooks, 1854–1879, vol. 2, 1859–1869, CHL; John Smith Papers, 1833–1854, journal, 1846 February–1854 May, CHL; Lucy Mack Smith, *Biographical Sketches of Joseph Smith the Prophet and His Progenitors for Many Generations* (Liverpool: S. W. Richards, 1853), 43; Dorothy D. Dean, Salisbury Family Group Sheet, n.d., copy of original in author's possession; Orville F. Berry, "The Mormon Settlement in Illinois," *Transactions of the Illinois State Historical Society for the Year 1906*, no. 11 (1906): 94.
2. Solomon J. Salisbury, *Reminiscences of an Octogenarian* (self-pub., ca. 1926), 3.
3. Andrew H. Hedges, Alex D. Smith, and Brent M. Rogers, eds., *Journals, Volume 3: May 1843–June 1844*, vol. 3 of the Journals series of *The Joseph Smith Papers*, ed. Ronald K. Esplin and Matthew J. Grow (Salt Lake City: Church Historian's Press, 2015), 150; Andrew H. Hedges, Alex D. Smith, and Richard Lloyd Anderson, eds., *Journals, Volume 2: December 1841–April 1843*, vol. 2 of the Journals series of *The Joseph Smith Papers*, ed. Ronald K. Esplin and Matthew J. Grow (Salt Lake City: Church Historian's Press, 2011), 323–24.
4. E. H. Young, *A History of Round Prairie and Plymouth, 1831–1875* (Chicago: Geo. J. Titus Book and Job Printer, 1876), 70–71.
5. Kyle R. Walker, *William B. Smith: In the Shadow of a Prophet* (Salt Lake City: Greg Kofford Books, 2015), 158–69.
6. Young, *A History of Round Prairie and Plymouth*, 64.
7. "Unparalleled Outrage at Nauvoo," *Warsaw Signal*, no. 18 (June 12, 1844): 2.
8. Sarah M. Kimball (Nauvoo, IL) to Mrs. Serepta Heywood, in *Joseph L. Heywood Letters*, 1841–47, CHL. Sarah indicated that Lucy Mack Smith had a room in the Mansion House during the summer of 1844.
9. "Anniversary at Carthage," *Salt Lake Tribune* 44, no. 57 (June 24, 1894): 16.
10. Joseph Smith History, 1838–1856, vol. F-1 [1 May 1844–August 1844, June 18, 1844], CHL. For a discussion on this sermon, see Brett D.

Dowdle et al. eds., *Documents, Volume 15: 16 May–28 June 1844*, vol. 15 of the Documents series of *The Joseph Smith Papers*, ed. Matthew C. Godfrey, R. Eric Smith, and Ronald K. Esplin (Salt Lake City: Church Historian's Press, 2023), 317–22.

11. "Anniversary at Carthage," 16. Because of later interpretations regarding succession, which stemmed from her brother William's narrative of events, Katharine later identified Brigham Young and other apostles as some of those conspirators who were present that her brother Joseph referred to during his speech. Young and most of the other apostles were laboring as political missionaries in the eastern United States during the time of this speech, so they would not have been present in the audience. George Laub, who was also present on this occasion, similarly remembered that Joseph spoke about his enemies seeking his life during his remarks. However, the only person Laub remembered Joseph specifically naming was Joseph Jackson, a noted enemy of the Saints by this juncture, and Laub did not record Joseph stating that there were enemies among the Saints that day when he spoke. George Laub, reminiscences and journal, 1845–46, 49–52, CHL.

12. "Reminiscences of Joseph Smith, as Told by His Sister, Catherine Smith-Salisbury, to Her Grandson, Herbert S. Salisbury," *Saints' Herald* 60 (October 8, 1913): 984.

13. "Anniversary at Carthage," 16.

14. "Anniversary at Carthage," 16.

15. Mary Salisbury Hancock, "The Three Sisters of the Prophet Joseph Smith, Part III," *Saints' Herald* 101, no. 4 (January 25, 1954): 82

16. Mary Bailey Smith Norman, "Samuel Harrison Smith," reminiscence, typescript, June 24, 1914, CHL; J. Winter Smith, taped interview by Dean Jacobs, transcription by Tom Duke, Smith Family Reunion, August 18–19, 1972, Nauvoo, IL; Dean L. Jarman and Kyle R. Walker, "Samuel Harrison Smith," in Kyle R. Walker, ed., *United by Faith: The Joseph Sr. and Lucy Mack Smith Family* (American Fork, UT: Covenant Communications; Provo, UT: BYU Studies, 2006), 230–31.

17. Solomon remembered that the Husbands family had "two girls and a boy whose ages ranged from 16 to 21." Salisbury, *Reminiscences of an Octogenarian*, 14; John and Phebe Husbands were endowed in the Nauvoo Temple on February 7, 1846. Nauvoo Temple Endowment Register, 1845–46, CHL.

18. Hancock, "Three Sisters, Part III," 82–83.

19. Statement of William R. Hamilton, in Orville F. Berry, "The Mormon Settlement in Illinois," *Transactions of the Illinois State Historical Society for the Year 1906*, no. 11 (1906): 99; Leonard, *Nauvoo: A Place of Peace, A People of Promise*, 400–401; Norman, "Samuel Harrison Smith"; J. Winter Smith, taped interview.

20. Hancock, "Three Sisters," 83.

21. Vilate Kimball (Nauvoo, IL) to Heber C. Kimball, June 30, 1844, CHL.

22. Lucy Mack Smith, *Biographical Sketches*, 279.

23. Sarah M. Kimball to Mrs. Serepta Heywood.

24. Lucy Mack Smith, *Biographical Sketches*, 279.

25. Lucy Mack Smith, *Biographical Sketches*, 278.

26. Herbert S. Salisbury, "Things the Prophet's Sister Told Me," 6, San Rafael, CA, June 30, 1945, typescript, CHL.

27. "Anniversary at Carthage," 16.

28. "Anniversary at Carthage," 16; Barbara Hands Bernauer, "Still 'Side by Side': The Final Burial of Joseph and Hyrum Smith," *John Whitmer Historical Association Journal* 11 (1991): 18–20; Leonard, *Nauvoo: A Place of Peace, A People of Promise*, 403–4.

29. Salisbury, *Reminiscences of an Octogenarian*, 14.

30. Statement of Solomon J. Salisbury, in Berry, "The Mormon Settlement in Illinois," 95.

31. Hancock, "Three Sisters, Part III," 83; Berry, "The Mormon Settlement in Illinois," 95. For information on the Griswolds, see Young, *A History of Round Prairie and Plymouth*, 45–46; 1850 United States Federal Census, Hancock County, IL, Henry P. Griswold. The Griswolds bought all the Salisburys' property in September 1844 after the Salisburys were forced from the community.

32. "Died," *Times and Seasons* 5, no. 14 (August 1, 1844): 606–7.

33. Norman, "Samuel Harrison Smith"; J. Winter Smith, taped interview; Lucy Mack Smith, *Biographical Sketches*, 280. For more information on the circumstances surrounding Samuel's death, see Jarman and Walker, "Samuel Harrison Smith," 230–34.

34. She was likely referring to the recent losses of Don Carlos (1841), Hyrum, Joseph, and Samuel. The number would have been five if Alvin was included.

35. Lucy Mack Smith (Nauvoo, IL) to Wiliam Smith, January 23, 1845, CHL.

36. Salisbury, *Reminiscences of an Octogenarian*, 4.

CHAPTER TEN

Succession

*Brigham Young assumed leadership and took many members to Utah.
. . . Joseph's family and all the rest of us stayed in Illinois, although
Brigham tried hard to get us to go with him.*
—Katharine Smith Salisbury

THE SALISBURYS HAD A DIFFICULT TIME deciding to leave
Plymouth, Illinois. They now owned substantial land in the area and
had built a blacksmith shop near their log home. Jenkins's blacksmith business had started to produce a steady income. That tem-
porary prosperity was fleeting as the Latter-day Saints' reputation
deteriorated at Plymouth, and residents refused to allow Jenkins to
cater to their needs for work at the anvil. That had forced Jenkins to
seek work in St. Louis by the spring of 1844. As threats increased
and income vanished, Katharine and Jenkins felt they had no other
option but to leave the community where they had resided for nearly
five years.

They immediately put their property up for sale, which sold a month later, on September 16, 1844, for just a hundred dollars. It was half of what they had paid several years earlier, despite improvements they had made, including construction of Jenkins's blacksmith shop.[1] The buyer was Dr. Henry P. Griswold, the neighbor who had refused to keep the Salisbury children at his home while Katharine was attending her brothers' funeral at Nauvoo. The purchase allowed him to expand his vast property holdings, and by 1850 he was among the wealthiest residents at Plymouth.[2]

Most of the Saints that had once swelled the population of the small community also left Plymouth that summer. E. H. Young's history of Plymouth recorded that most of the Mormon population in town moved after Joseph and Hyrum were murdered, some within days of the event. "They disappeared quietly and almost without observation," Young unsympathetically recorded, failing to mention the threats and intimidation by locals that led to their hasty departure. "A few, occupying farms near by, abandoned their crops, taking with them a few of their most portable goods." Young reflected the community sentiment that "Plymouth was thus relieved of its

Ferry crossing at Peru, Maine. Date and photographer unknown. Note the cables and poles to assist in crossing, similar to what Solomon described when his family crossed the Illinois River.

Mormon population in 1844" and proudly recounted how "a number of the citizens of Plymouth participated in the closing scenes of the so-called Mormon War" two years later, "which resulted in the expulsion of the Mormons from the state." The only vestige of Latter-day Saint occupation at Plymouth after the year 1846 was a signpost that still hung on the outside of William Smith's "Mormon Hotel," which William had sold several years earlier. Young described it as an "obnoxious remembrancer of the past." In a final act to permanently stamp out the influence of the church on their community, a "vigilance committee" was formed and tore down the sign, notwithstanding protests of the current owner of the hotel.[3] It marked the end of the church in Plymouth.

Beardstown, Illinois

The Salisburys headed forty miles southeast of Plymouth, landing in the town of Beardstown, located in Cass County, Illinois, where they crossed the Illinois River. Solomon recalled how their several wagons were "ferried across [the Illinois River] on a flatboat, one team at a time. They had a cable fastened on each side of the river, and pulled the boat across, assisted by a man on either side of the boat, using poles." The Salisburys settled about eight miles from Beardstown, initially staying with an older resident by the last name of Wagener while Jenkins hastily built a log cabin for his family. He advertised his work as a blacksmith and began making and repairing wagons, harnesses, and tools for the local farmers and businesses in town.[4]

Beardstown was a thriving manufacturing and shipping community, whose most prominent business was pork packing. During the peak season from November to February, anywhere from forty thousand to seventy-five thousand hogs were slaughtered in town and then shipped on the Illinois River. The town's production of pork rivaled any western city in the country, even that of Cincinnati, whose population was more than forty-four thousand than that of Beardstown.[5] The numerous local businesses in town provided Jenkins with the necessary blacksmithing work to provide for his family, much more so than in the remote town of Plymouth.

While the Salisburys thought removing themselves several counties away from the difficulties at Plymouth would allow them to earn a living in peace, someone soon learned of their identity. Hostilities toward Latter-day Saints had reached across county lines to Beardstown. "We soon found that we could not rest here in peace," recalled Solomon, "in a short time it was noised abroad that my mother . . . was a sister to the Mormon prophet."[6] After only five months at Beardstown, the Salisburys were already contemplating another move. In January 1845, Katharine wrote to her mother Lucy at Nauvoo, indicating that the family was managing well but that they were contemplating relocating to Nauvoo.[7] Evidently, things grew worse by spring, when residents warned them to leave town and gradually increased pressure by avoiding doing business with Jenkins. "They starved us out," recalled Solomon of the family's brief stay in Beardstown. "We were very poor, and all depended on father's work."[8]

Nauvoo, Illinois

During another precarious living situation, Jenkins left for St. Louis to try and obtain work. He returned after only working for a few months, and the family was again on the move by late May.[9] With hostilities still at a fever pitch in western Illinois, the Salisburys decided that it would be safer to move to Nauvoo, where they had the support of the greater Smith family. They traveled west on a back trail and then north through Carthage, arriving in Nauvoo in early June, 1845.[10] With no money or property to their name, the Salisburys moved in with William Smith, who had only recently moved into the William Marks home on Water Street.[11] Marks was now managing the Mansion House with Emma Hale Smith, and the church rented the home from Marks allowing William and the Smith family to live there rent-free.[12] Mother Smith, along with her daughter Lucy and her family, also resided in the home that summer. Though the home was a commodious brick residence, the arrival of the Salisbury family swelled the number living there to sixteen, making living space cramped.[13]

William Marks Home, Nauvoo, Illinois. Photograph by Kyle R. Walker, 2019.

Settling at Nauvoo

It was the first time Jenkins and Katharine lived in Nauvoo, though they had made regular visits. Due to their living in Plymouth from 1839 to 1844 and their one-year stay in Beardstown the following year, they had been absent during a critical transitional period for the church. The Salisburys missed Sidney Rigdon's attempt to move the church to Pennsylvania in a role as self-appointed guardian the previous summer. They also missed the Quorum of the Twelve's return to Nauvoo during that same period and the pivotal meeting held on August 8, 1844, where an overwhelming majority of Saints accepted Brigham Young's leadership.[14]

One would have initially thought Jenkins would have emerged as a natural leader at some point in the upstart religion, especially with his background in the law, but such was never the case. His brother-in-law Joseph had valued loyalty above all other traits when appointing individuals to leadership roles, and Jenkins's bouts of drinking and vacillating allegiance to the church prevented him from ever being a serious candidate in the church's hierarchy of leaders. By the mid-1840s, it had been more than a decade since he was actively involved with the church, and Brigham Young knew of Jenkins's long-standing position of agnosticism. This fact, combined with the family's decision to live distanced from Nauvoo, meant that the Salisburys remained on the periphery of meaningful church developments during the Nauvoo period, such as the introduction of temple ordinances and the covert practice of plural marriage.

Yet there was a spiritual resurgence that corresponded with Jenkins return to Nauvoo that summer. Perhaps the deaths of his brothers-in-law, who had remained supportive and encouraging of Jenkins, spurred him to reevaluate his religious position. He published a letter in the *Nauvoo Neighbor* that June indicating that he had reconciled aspects of his skepticism, "which have been the main pillars of my unbelief in Christianity the last ten years."[15] He also wrote several letters to Brigham Young, whom he addressed as "President"—an indication of his acceptance of his leadership of the church. "Of late there is a great many ideas runing through my weak head," Jenkins began one letter to Young, "but when I come in contact with any that I think is good I sometimes communicate them to others." Jenkins included items of information about prosecuting those he felt were responsible for murdering Joseph and Hyrum, as well his ideas about the church relocating to California. He was obviously informed on the current political climate of the United States and correctly anticipated a potential war with Mexico. Jenkins shared his view that the timing of a western migration was ideal, suggesting to Young that the Saints should immediately remove to California, make land claims, and then align themselves with the Mexican government in defending those claims against "this D——m government."[16] Like other Saints during this time period, the Salisburys were distrustful of the government to protect the rights of a religious minority, as they anticipated being driven from their homes once again.[17] Jenkins's few surviving holograph letters reveal his bright intellect, sense of humor, his expansive vocabulary, and how he drew upon his limited legal training in an attempt to secure justice for the Saints. He was obviously acting as an advocate for the church that summer and was fully supportive of Brigham Young's leadership. That dramatic shift must have been thrilling for Katharine and the children to witness.

William Smith and Succession

During the years 1843–45, Katharine's brother William had been absent from Nauvoo and Plymouth while serving as a missionary and overseeing the eastern branches of the Church. This meant that William had also been absent during this critical transitional period, in part because of the chronic illness of his first wife, Caroline, which had delayed his return to Nauvoo until May 4, 1845.[18] William had been introduced to plural marriage by his brother Joseph before the latter's death and had been sealed to a second wife, Mary Ann Covington, by Brigham Young in May 1843.[19] His leadership had been divisive during his time in the East, where he had introduced a loose version of plural marriage among the eastern branches of the Church and had taken excessive liberties in bestowing the sealing power on several cohorts in the area without authorization from leaders at Nauvoo.[20] Two of his colleagues in the Twelve, Wilford Woodruff and Parley P. Pratt, both wrote to Brigham Young expressing their reservations about William's leadership in the East when they traveled through the area in the years 1844–45.[21] As a result, Brigham Young eventually sent Parley P. Pratt to replace William as leader in the East, which did not sit well with William.[22]

The Salisburys return to Nauvoo coincided with the completion of William Smith's two-year mission. William had initially been supportive of Brigham Young's leadership after the death of his brother Joseph, writing to Young and indicating that "you are the President of the Corum, [as] Peater was head after Christ & had the Keys a[nd] right to get revelations."[23] The Salisburys shared that view, as evidenced in Jenkins's letters to Young in 1845. Throughout the first half of 1845, William appears to have increasingly desired a more expansive role in the church's leadership circle, lobbying for something akin to the positions his brother Hyrum held at the time of his death. This was especially true once he was replaced by Parley P. Pratt as the de facto leader of the eastern branches and felt his authority was being increasingly restricted after his return to Nauvoo. After Young and his colleagues of the Twelve ordained him to the office of presiding patriarch on May 24, 1845, William almost immediately began to try and expand the authority of that office. After some back-and-forth editorials between William and the Twelve published in the *Times and Seasons*, things finally reached a climax at a meeting held on June 25, 1845, at the Masonic Hall in Nauvoo.

During this critical meeting, William shared his evolving view that the priesthood came through his family, even threatening church leaders that if they continued to attempt to restrict his authority, he would take the entire Smith family and leave Nauvoo. "We received our priesthood from God through Joseph Smith and not through William," Young countered during the tense meeting, and "furthermore that where the Smith family goes the Church will not go, nor the priesthood either!"[24] John Taylor, William's colleague in the Twelve, recorded that William "seemed humbled under the influence of what Brother Brigham had said." William then retracted his declaration, responding that "he did not mean that he would take the priesthood away with him; but that he would take his family away." After several hours of

William B. Smith, ca. 1870. Photograph by H. P. Brown. Courtesy of Community of Christ Library Archives.

deliberation, Young and other church leaders felt they had allayed William's concerns, but inwardly he was seething.[25]

William fumed to his family who were present at home the next day about what had transpired at the meeting, venting about his perception that the whole Smith family was being undermined and how his rights as a leader in the church were being restricted. William had become skillful at playing the victim and successfully convinced his family that he had been wronged. He also expressed his concern about his personal safety, fearing that he might be harmed or murdered by either those inside or outside the church. That very night, Lucy Mack Smith had a dream where she "saw William in a room full of armed men and he having no weapons. They would have crushed him down, if it had not been for the power of God." The dream closely paralleled William's version of the meeting. Lucy was also told by an unnamed "messenger" during the dream that her family "were the first founders, fathers, and heads of this Church" and that William, as patriarch, was to be "President over all the church," where he would "regulate the affairs of the Church."[26] The timing of the dream was not coincidental, and it evidences William's influence in persuading his mother and sisters that he and the family were being treated unfairly. The Smiths relished their role in being the founding family of the Restoration, and William had convinced them that he should hold a more prominent place within the post-Joseph church.

News of Lucy's dream quickly reached church leaders. William ensured the dream was written down, but at least one church leader felt that it had been "corrected and altered by William Smith so as to suit his wishes by representing him as the legal successor of Joseph."[27] Several days later, on June 30, a majority of the Twelve met with Lucy and her daughters, explaining their concerns about William's ambition and views on leadership, and Lucy responded by retracting what was being construed from her dream. Lucy felt that the contents of her dream were not written down correctly and indicated that she never intended the dream to be read publicly and that she had only intended to share it with her "own children and not for the Priesthood or the church." She thought that "William did not want it [the presidency]," further explaining "that she wanted peace, union, and harmony" with the authorities. Katharine and her younger sister Lucy, along with Lucy's husband Arthur, were present on this occasion, and all expressed their "satisfaction" with acknowledging the leadership of the Twelve. The meeting was closed with prayer, "and the family manifested good feelings." Tellingly, neither William nor Jenkins were present at this meeting of reconciliation, though they had been invited.[28]

Members of the Twelve worked diligently in the ensuing months to assuage those feelings William had produced in the family, which included deeding property and a brick home in Nauvoo to family members, hosting a grand dinner celebration to honor the greater Smith family, and continuing to provide housing and money for William to meet his needs.[29] Still, William continued to feel like his authority in the church was being limited, and it certainly was. As the summer progressed, leaders at Nauvoo grew increasingly apprehensive about William's shifting ideas about leadership even as he began to distance himself from meetings with the Twelve. "Wm. . . . considers he is not accountable to Brigham nor the Twelve nor any one else," William Clayton recorded in his diary in summarizing the feelings of the Twelve, adding, "I fear his course will bring us much trouble."[30] The more William Smith felt reined in by other members of the Twelve, the more outspoken he became in promoting Smith family rights. It became a vicious cycle that ended up influencing the feelings of the entire Smith family. After several more clashes with his colleagues in the Twelve that summer and with little consultation with his mother or sisters, William fled Nauvoo in the middle of the night in mid-September 1845.[31]

During those final months in Nauvoo, he continued to experience anxiety about his personal safety at Nauvoo and not without cause. After he beat up Nauvoo policeman Elbridge Tufts for ignoring his directives in late June, William lost the support and protection of the police, and ever afterward he experienced concerns about his safety within the city.[32] Jenkins remained a close confidant to

William during this time and continued to adopt William's view that the Smith family had been wronged and that William should have a more prominent leadership role. As the two distanced themselves from the main body of leadership at Nauvoo, they felt increasingly ostracized. By September William's anxiety bordered on paranoia and was a factor in his leaving Nauvoo so impulsively. It was a decision he would later regret, but neither he nor Jenkins ever fully reconciled with Brigham Young and other members of the Twelve.

William's anxiety about his safety also impacted the family. At one point, in late summer, Katharine felt apprehensive about even stepping outside the home for fear that she would be mistaken for her husband or William due to her height.[33] Jenkins also felt fearful for his safety due to William repeatedly recounting how he felt like his life was threatened. It was Jenkins and Hiram Stratton[34] who came to William in a panic the night he fled Nauvoo, urgently warning him he needed to leave the city that very night as there was a "secret plot" to take his life.[35] Jenkins escaped the city a few weeks after William, after a close friend in Nauvoo "warned me not to stay in the county through the summer on peril of my life."[36] William later acknowledged that he, and by extension Jenkins, overreacted when they fled Nauvoo. He described how Stratton and Jenkins's "account of things in a tone of earnest zeal threw me into a dreadful state of excitement" and how this report, combined with other stresses at the time, "almost deranged my senses."[37] On the heels of the murder of her brothers, combined with the perception that the lives of William and Jenkins were threatened, Katharine and the children were overwhelmed with trepidation for their own safety.

Never one to react mildly to perceived injustices, William eventually published his grievances in a pamphlet he deemed *A Proclamation*, which denounced the Twelve and led to his excommunication from the church in October 1845. Foremost among places he sent copies of his pamphlets was to Thomas Sharp and his *Warsaw Signal*.[38] Sharp was an individual whom William previously clashed with in their respective newspapers a few years earlier, and who would be tried for the murder of his brothers.[39] Yet William knew it was one of the few outlets where his voice could reach the Saints after fleeing Nauvoo, and it was an avenue to gather Saints to support his views and potential leadership. Jenkins also voiced his endorsement of William's leadership, similarly publishing an editorial in Sharp's *Warsaw Signal* in which he defended William and the rights of the Smith family.[40]

In his "Proclamation," William had transformed his account of events that had transpired at Nauvoo into a narrative that bolstered his claims to leadership. Two rumors he generated at the time stuck in the minds of the Salisbury family: first, that Brigham Young had invented polygamy after Joseph's death and second, that his brother Samuel's death had resulted from being poisoned by Brigham Young at Nauvoo.[41] Neither was true, and William knew it. William had been sealed to Mary Ann Covington as a plural wife at Nauvoo before Joseph's death and with his brother's approval and assistance. Further undermining William's claims was that Brigham Young had been the one to perform this union to Mary Ann Covington in May 1843, as well as sealing several wives to William during the summer of 1845.[42] Similarly, contemporary accounts of Samuel's death note his cause of death as "bilious fever," and no Smith family member ever suspected foul play in the year 1844. William was absent on his mission during the time Samuel died, as was Brigham Young, whom William later implicated as orchestrating the poisoning. Any report of poisoning would have had to be secondhand at best.[43] Nevertheless, William succeeded in heightening animosity toward Brigham Young within the Smith family, and these rumors influenced Katharine and her posterity for generations.[44]

The winter of 1845–46 was a difficult period for the Salisbury family. There must have been mixed feelings for the family as they watched their fellow Saints eagerly receive temple ordinances and then depart on their epic journey to the Salt Lake Valley. For the first time since the 1820s, there appears to have been a division within the Smith family regarding their religious views. Mother Lucy and Sophronia and Sophronia's husband, William McCleary, all received their endowments in the Nauvoo Temple that winter.[45]

Daguerreotype of Nauvoo, with temple in the background. Photograph ca. 1846. Courtesy of Church History Library.

Jenkins and Katharine, along with Katharine's sister Lucy and her husband, Arthur Millkin, chose not to receive the ordinances of the temple. That decision resulted from their support of William Smith.

Both before and after the main body of the Saints left Nauvoo, Brigham Young had labored diligently to get the Smith family to join them on their journey, but to no avail.[46] Lucy Mack Smith had initially expressed a desire to join the Saints in the migration, but at age seventy she understandably decided to remain with her daughters and under their care. She also desired to be buried by the side of her husband in Nauvoo.[47] Katharine later recalled that "Brigham

Young assumed leadership and took many members to Utah, among them Hyrum Smith's family. Joseph's family and all the rest of us stayed in Illinois, although Brigham tried hard to get us to go with him."[48] The only member of the immediate Smith family who had leanings toward going West was Sophronia. Her husband, William McCleary, went ahead of her to Winter Quarters sometime in the year 1846, and when he returned in the spring of 1847 to bring Sophronia and his stepdaughter Mariah with him, Sophronia appears to have changed her mind about migrating West.[49] Perhaps like her mother, Sophronia decided to live near her remaining family members. The two ostensibly decided to separate for a time, as William returned alone to Winter Quarters, where he eventually migrated to Utah in October 1849 without Sophronia and Mariah.[50]

Katharine and the children remained interested observers of all that was transpiring in the ensuing months. As the main body of the church prepared to leave the city, the children remembered there were thousands of Saints who "had been picking corn all fall to secure money to go west."[51] Ten-year-old Solomon had a fond recollection of being taken by his mother on a tour inside of the Nauvoo Temple that fall as workers were hurriedly finishing the temple, and he was in awe at the cost and labor required to build the enormous structure.[52] He remembered that year was a particularly cold winter in which "the ice [on the Mississippi River] was three and a half or four feet thick in February." He described how the family watched as "most of the church [members] in Nauvoo, with Brigham Young, crossed over on the ice." Solomon added how "the winter of 1845 and 1846 was a hard winter on us," with "no work to be had."[53] With the departure of the Saints and with little or no regular income coming in, things were about to go from bad to worse.

Notes

1. Deed Book N, pp. 484–85, Land and Records Office, Hancock County Courthouse, Carthage, IL.
2. The Griswolds were one of the wealthiest families living at Plymouth, with approximately five thousand dollars in property holdings by the year 1850. 1850 United States Federal Census, Hancock County, Henry P.

Griswold. Griswold practiced medicine for thirteen years at Plymouth, retiring in the year 1850. "In removing to Hamilton [IL]," wrote his biographer, "Dr. G[riswold] retired from practice, preferring to live at his ease in the enjoyment of a moderate fortune." Thomas Gregg, *History of Hancock County, Illinois* (Chicago: Chas. C. Chapman, 1880), 806. See also E. H. Young, *A History of Round Prairie and Plymouth, 1831–1875* (Chicago: Geo. J. Titus Book and Job Printer, 1876), 45–46.

3. Young, *A History of Round Prairie and Plymouth*, 87–88, 92. William had sold his prosperous business to his brother-in-law, George D. Grant, for $1500 on November 10, 1840, who in turn sold the property to Don Carlos Smith the following month. The business appears to have become a family operation, as the property changed hands several times over the next few years, at one point being purchased in the names of William's daughters, Mary Jane and Caroline Louisa. Book H, Deeds and Mortgages, November 10, 1840, 638–39; Bonds and Mortgages, Book 1, 102; Bonds and Mortgages, Book K, 8; all in Hancock County Courthouse, Carthage, IL. E. H. Young noted the last Mormon ties to the hotel ended when it was sold to David Higby in the year 1847. Young, *A History of Round Prairie and Plymouth*, 91.

4. Solomon J. Salisbury, *Reminiscences of an Octogenarian* (self-pub., ca. 1926), 4. There are multiple families with the last name of Wagener that lived in Beardstown, IL.

5. William Henry Parrin, ed., *History of Cass County, Illinois* (Chicago: O. L. Baskin, 1882), 114.

6. Salisbury, *Reminiscences of an Octogenarian*, 4.

7. Lucy Mack Smith (Nauvoo, IL) to William Smith, January 23, 1845, CHL.

8. Salisbury, *Reminiscences of an Octogenarian*, 4.

9. W[ilkins] J[enkins] Salisbury (St. Louis, MO) to Brigham Young, May 9, 1845, Brigham Young Office Files 1832–78, General Correspondence, Incoming, 1844–77, box 20, folder 15, CHL.

10. Salisbury, *Reminiscences of an Octogenarian*, 4. The Salisburys appear to have arrived in Nauvoo in early June, as Jenkins had a letter published in the June 18 issue of the *Nauvoo Neighbor*. W. J. Salisbury to Mr. Editor, *Nauvoo Neighbor* 3, no. 7 (June 18, 1845): 3.

11. William said that he moved into the William Marks home "soon after" his wife Caroline's death, which occurred on May 22, 1845. William Smith to Joshua Grant Jr., August 12, 1845, *Nauvoo Neighbor* 3, no. 16 (August 20, 1845): 3. The Salisbury family appear to be living in the Marks home by the end of June 1845. See Dean C. Jessee, ed., *John Taylor Nauvoo Journal* (Provo, UT: Grandin Book, 1996), 79.

12. Brigham Young, in "Conference Minutes," *Times and Seasons* 6, no. 16 (November 1, 1845): 1014.

13. William had recently remarried Mary Jane Rollins on June 22, 1845, and he lived in the home with his new bride and two daughters. William Smith to Joshua Grant Jr.; "Married," *Nauvoo Neighbor* 3, no. 9 (July 2, 1845): 3. There were seven in the Salisbury family (including Jenkins, who remained in Nauvoo through June), three in the Millikin family, plus Lucy Mack Smith and her caregiver/granddaughter Mary Bailey Smith (Samuel's daughter).

14. Matthew J. Grow et al., eds., *Administrative Records, Council of Fifty Minutes, March 1844–January 1846*, vol. 1 of the Administrative Records series of *The Joseph Smith Papers*, ed. Ronald K. Esplin, Matthew J. Grow, and Matthew C. Godfrey (Salt Lake City: Church Historian's Press, 2016), 206–8.

15. W. J. Salisbury to Mr. Editor.

16. Salisbury to Brigham Young, May 9, 1845; W[ilkins] J[enkins] Salisbury (City of Joseph [Nauvoo, IL]), to Brigham Young, July 28, 1845, Brigham Young Office Files 1832–78, General Correspondence, Incoming, 1844–77, box 20, folder 15, CHL.

17. *JSP*, A1:6, xxv–xliii.

18. William Smith (Nauvoo, IL) to Dear Brethren, May 10, 1845, *Nauvoo Neighbor* 3, no. 2 (May 14, 1845): 2–3.

19. Mary Ann [Covington Sheffield] West, Testimony, in United States Testimony 1892, Court of Appeals (Eighth Circuit), 495–96, MS 1160, CHL; Kyle R. Walker, *William B. Smith: In the Shadow of a Prophet* (Salt Lake City: Greg Kofford Books, 2015), 179–80.

20. For more information on William's activities as president of the eastern branches of the church, see Walker, *William B. Smith*, 180–207.

21. Wilford Woodruff (Boston) to Brigham Young, October 9, 1844; Wilford Woodruff (Scarborough, ME) to Brigham Young, November 16, 1844; P. P. Pratt (New York City) to Brigham Young, May 7, 1845, all in Brigham Young Office Files 1832–78, Letters from Church Leaders and Others, 1840–77, CHL.

22. Walker, *William B. Smith*, 202–6.

23. William Smith (Bordentown, NJ) to Brigham Young, August 24, 1844, CHL.

24. William Smith, "A Proclamation," *Warsaw Signal* 2, no. 32 (October 29, 1845): 1.

25. Jessee, *John Taylor Nauvoo Journal*, 73–75. For further context on William Smith's views and behavior that led up to this meeting, see Walker, *William B. Smith*, 261–65.

26. Jessee, *John Taylor Nauvoo Journal*, 73–74.

27. George D. Smith, ed., *An Intimate Chronicle: The Journals of William Clayton* (Salt Lake City: Signature Books, 1995), 169–70.

28. Jessee, *John Taylor Nauvoo Journal*, 79. Taylor wrote a letter to William following the meeting with Lucy and her daughters, indicating that "we

expected to have had your company [at the meeting] but were disappointed." Jessee, *John Taylor Nauvoo Journal*, 79.

29. Kyle R. Walker, "Looking After the First Family of Mormonism: LDS Church Leaders' Support of the Smiths after the Murders of Joseph and Hyrum," *John Whitmer Historical Association Journal* 32, no. 1 (Spring/Summer 2012): 17–32.

30. Smith, *An Intimate Chronicle*, 166.

31. For a discussion on the timing of William's departure from Nauvoo, see Walker, *William B. Smith*, 299n68.

32. The conflict between William and the Nauvoo police was a central theme addressed during the June 25, 1845, meeting with other church leaders at the Masonic Hall. Jessee, *John Taylor Nauvoo Journal*, 69–73; Walker, *William B. Smith*, 261–66.

33. Mary Bailey Smith Norman (Idaho Falls, ID) to Ina Coolbrith, April 24, 1908, typescript, Community of Christ Library-Archives.

34. Hiram Stratton was a Zion's Camp veteran and would be disfellowshipped several months later, on January 18, 1846, for "unchristianlike conduct." "Notice," *Times and Seasons* 6, no. 21 (January 15, 1846): 1096.

35. William Smith, "A Proclamation," 1.

36. W. J. Salisbury (Nauvoo, IL) to Mr. [Thomas] Sharp for the *Warsaw Signal*, *Warsaw Signal* 3, no. 2 (April 8, 1846): 2. Jenkins was in St. Louis with William Smith by at least October 21, 1845. William Smith (St. Louis) to Emma Smith, October 21, 1845, CHL; see also William Smith (St. Louis) to Orson Hyde, November 12, 1845, in *Warsaw Signal* 2, no. 36 (November 26, 1845): 2.

37. William Smith (Springfield, IL) to Brigham Young, May 7, 1855, Brigham Young Office Files, 1832–78, Letters from Church Leaders and Others, 1840–77, CHL.

38. William Smith, "A Proclamation," 1.

39. William Smith Testimony, Temple Lot Case Testimonies, 186, US Eighth Circuit Court, 1892, MS 1160, CHL; Walker, *William B. Smith*, 158–62; Thomas Gregg, *History of Hancock County, Illinois, Together with an Outline History of the State, and a Digest of State Laws* (Chicago: Charles C. Chapman, 1880), 752–56.

40. Salisbury to Sharp, *Warsaw Signal* 3, no. 2 (April 8, 1846): 2.

41. William Smith, "A Proclamation," 1; William Smith to the editor, *New York Tribune* 17, no. 5025 (May 28, 1857): 5.

42. Mary Ann [Covington Sheffield] West, Testimony, in United States Testimony 1892, Court of Appeals Eighth Circuit, 495–96, MS 1160, CHL. William was sealed to Mary Elizabeth Jones by Brigham Young during the summer of 1845. Mary Ann [Covington Sheffield] West, Testimony, 497, 509. Under the date of August 8, 1845, Brigham Young recorded in his journal, "In the evening went to Wm. Smiths and sealed [him] to Miss [Henriette] Rice." Brigham Young Office Files, 1832–78,

Brigham Young Journals, 1832–46, CHL. For more details on these sealings, see Walker, *William B. Smith*, 573–81.

43. Lucy Mack Smith, *Biographical Sketches of Joseph Smith the Prophet and His Progenitors for Many Generations* (Liverpool: S.W. Richards, 1853), 280; Mary Bailey Smith Norman, "Samuel Harrison Smith" (reminiscence), typescript, June 24, 1914, CHL; J. Winter Smith, taped interview by Dean Jacobs, transcription by Tom Duke, Smith Family Reunion, August 18–19, 1972, Nauvoo, IL; Dean L. Jarman and Kyle R. Walker, "Samuel Harrison Smith," in Kyle R. Walker, ed., *United by Faith: The Joseph Sr. and Lucy Mack Smith Family* (American Fork, UT: Covenant Communications; Provo, UT: BYU Studies, 2006), 230–34.

44. For evidence of how William's narrative influenced Katharine and other members of the surviving Smith family, see Herbert S. Salisbury, "Reminiscences of Joseph Smith as Told by His Sister, Catherine Smith-Salisbury to Her Grandson, Herbert S. Salisbury," *Saints' Herald* 60, no. 41 (October 8, 1913): 983; Mary Bailey Smith Norman (Idaho Falls, ID) to My dear Ina (Coolbrith), n.d., Community of Christ Library-Archives, Independence, MO.

45. Nauvoo Temple Endowment Register, December 23, 1845, 50; Richard L. Anderson, "What Were Joseph Smith's Sisters Like, and What Happened to Them after the Martyrdom?," *Ensign* 9 (March 1979): 43.

46. Lucy Mack Smith, in general conference, October 8, 1845, Nauvoo, IL, Historian's Office, General Church Minutes, 1839–77, October 6–8, 1845, 7–13, CHL; Walker, "Looking After the First Family of Mormonism," 27–28.

47. Lucy Mack Smith, in general conference, October 8, 1845.

48. Salisbury, "Reminiscences of Joseph Smith," 984.

49. W. W. Phelps wrote to Reuben Miller on May 30, 1847, that "Bro McCleary came with me to take his wife, and mother Smith if she wishes, on to the camp." W. W. Phelps (Nauvoo, IL) to Reuben Miller, May 30, 1847, CHL.

50. William McCleary appears to have returned to Winter Quarters and migrated to the Salt Lake Valley as part of the Silas Richards company. The wagon company left Kanesville, Iowa, on July 10, 1849, and arrived in the Salt Lake Valley the last week of October. William McCleary, Silas Richards company, Church History Biographical Database, available at ChurchofJesusChrist.org. I have been unable to locate a death date for William McCleary, but he appears to have either died in Utah in the early 1850s or while on a return trip on the pioneer trail from Salt Lake City to Illinois.

51. Salisbury, *Reminiscences of an Octogenarian*, 4.

52. "Tells of Solomon Salisbury's Life," *Saints' Herald* 74, no. 5 (February 2, 1927): 136.

53. Salisbury, *Reminiscences of an Octogenarian*, 4–5.

CHAPTER ELEVEN

Tossed on the Waves of Affliction

When he found out how destitute we were, he cried [in pity].
—Solomon J. Salisbury

AS WILLIAM SMITH BEGAN PREACHING against the Twelve at St. Louis, in November 1845, Jenkins became his most ardent advocate. The only surviving Smith brother championed his family rights in his lectures to large audiences in the area and began promoting Joseph Smith III as the rightful successor to his father.[1] The intervening years revealed how William was less of an advocate for Joseph III's leadership than he was for himself, but it was a postulation that strengthened his own position. He contended that it was his own right to hold the office of president until the youthful Joseph III matured, and William later transposed this lineal argument into his own right to lead the Saints.[2]

William knew firsthand what issues resonated among scattered Saints who had not followed Brigham Young and the Saints who migrated west, and he used that to his advantage. He preached on an antipolygamy platform, attempting to expose the Twelve's private acceptance of the practice at Nauvoo. His duplicity was risky, but he recognized it as the best course to rally Saints to support his leadership. While his sensational disclosures wowed crowded audiences at St. Louis, and he successfully disrupted the local branch that had been loyal to the Twelve, his actual adherents were only about twenty. By the end of November, William decided to move further east to Cincinnati, leaving Jenkins in charge of his small branch of followers at St. Louis.[3]

In the meantime, Katharine and the children experienced a difficult winter at Nauvoo where they received little money from Jenkins's labors in St. Louis. That probably meant that Jenkins's efforts at preaching and retaining William's smattering of followers consumed his time more than securing steady work. Katharine found solace in her family relationships, including remaining close to her sister-in-law Emma Hale Smith. During that previous summer, Emma and William Smith had discussed their views on succession. Emma had experienced her own frustrations with the Twelve at Nauvoo, primarily over differentiating which properties and publications belonged to her family and which belonged to the church. It was an issue that was never fully sorted out and created animosity on both sides.[4] Her discussions with William had led William to believe he had her endorsement if he should try and reform the church on a platform that was opposed to polygamy, something Emma was decidedly opposed to. However, before he even fled Nauvoo, she had withdrawn her support of his efforts, most likely because William had preached a public sermon advocating plural marriage at Nauvoo in August 1845.[5] William's ongoing conflict with leaders in Nauvoo probably distracted him from noticing that he had lost her favor, as she astutely detected his deceit and ambition. Emma also knew William's erratic history and conflicts with his brother Joseph and with other members of the Twelve, which impacted her trust of William and his motives.

Jenkins was absent from his family for the next five months. Katharine possibly worried whether Jenkins would ever return. There were other examples of sisters in Nauvoo whose husbands abandoned them, albeit rare, after leaving to work in St. Louis during this chaotic time. Like Jenkins, James Harris left his wife Emmeline (later known as Emmeline B. Wells) in Nauvoo to work in St. Louis because he was "restless, jobless, and overburdened with responsibility." Though James had promised to return in two weeks, those weeks stretched into months, until Emmeline eventually realized he was never coming home. She sank into an "emotional abyss," wrote her biographer, and "those months of empty waiting had left her morbidly reflective." Emmeline wrote that while she had been "brought to this great city by one to whom I ever expected to look for protection," instead she had been "left dependent on the mercy and friendship of strangers."[6] Unlike Emmeline, Katharine at least had the support and comfort of her sisters and mother, but she could assuredly relate to Emmeline's feelings of loneliness and worry about an uncertain future. Jenkins had been frequently absent for undetermined lengths of time and had been inconsistent as a provider.

William Smith and Jenkins Salisbury Vie for Nauvoo Property

In March 1846 William Smith hastily returned to Nauvoo from Cincinnati, stopping only briefly in St. Louis to pick up Jenkins. The timing of their return was not coincidental because most Saints had left the city just weeks earlier. Jenkins, in a letter intended for publication in Thomas Sharp's *Warsaw Signal*, wrote, "Wm. Smith, brother of the late Mormon Prophet, informs me, that he has returned here for the purpose of gathering his family together, with all such of the Mormons as are willing to be guided by his counsel and remove *immediately* out of the state." Jenkins further outlined his view that Smith's "patriarchal office" entitled him to "secure to the real church all *real estate* and other property which rightly belongs to the church."[7] To their dismay however, that plan did not materialize as smoothly as the two men hoped, as there were many Saints still loyal to the Twelve living at Nauvoo and trustees who remained in town to oversee the buying and selling of property. In the end, the only property William helped secure was a home that was deeded to his mother in the city—a residence he hoped to inherit after her death—after he intervened in negotiating between Nauvoo trustees and his mother.[8]

While at Cincinnati, William became distracted from launching his own church once he learned of James J. Strang's emerging branch of the church. Strang had established his headquarters in Voree, Wisconsin, and some of his early adherents in both Cincinnati and Nauvoo began to turn William to their cause. Even before his arrival in Nauvoo, William had shelved the idea of lineal succession in favor of Strang, who claimed Joseph Smith had sent him a letter appointing him as his successor just weeks before his death. As the two men struck up a correspondence, William received assurances from Strang of being appointed to prominent leadership positions within his church should the two link their aspirations.[9]

James J. Strang, 1813–56. Photograph ca. 1850, photograph of original by Sainsbury and Johnson, Salt Lake City. Courtesy of Church History Library.

While the Salisburys supported William's vacillating claims during the previous year and even for a time after he returned to Nauvoo in the summer of 1846, that support began to wane as he switched his loyalty to Strang. However, that did not prevent William from including the names of his mother, sisters, and their spouses in several letters he wrote to Strang in 1846, implying that the entire Smith family were unitedly supporting his church.[10] It was William's attempt to bolster his status in the new movement, and he assumed his remaining family members would follow his lead, but including their names without their consent caused confusion for the family. Katharine later issued an affidavit denying that she had the boy was only eight years old—Joseph his father was in jail at the time—the boy remembers the vision &c. Joseph before he was martyred, when on his way from the temple hill home, saw a vision, and his mother recollects that when he came home, he put his hands upon his eyes and prayed that the vision might pass, and that he stated he heard as it were music in the Heavens, but the notes were low and sad as though they sounded the requium of martyred prophets.

I remember myself that Joseph said; "My work is almost done, I feel that I shall rule a mighty host, but not in this world, the wolves are on the scent &c." Joseph bid his wife and mother farewell saying, I am going as a lamb to the slaughter; this was his impression. And I further state that Joseph did not appoint the twelve as his successor, and I was in the last council with him, and had an opportunity of knowing and hearing his sentiments in regard to these things.

I also heard Joseph say, that should the time ever come that Brigham Young and Heber C. Kimball would lead this church, that they would lead it to hell. This was said in the hearing of sister Emma Smith.— The whole Smith family of the Joseph stock join in sustaining J. J. Strang.

It is to be remembered that soon after Joseph and Hyrum's death, brother Green died, and he was heard by numerous individuals to say, that Joseph had appointed Strang.

WILLIAM SMITH.

This is to certify that the Smith family do believe in the appointment of J. J. Strang.

WILLIAM SMITH, Patriarch.
LUCY SMITH, Mother in Israel.
ARTHUR MILLIKEN.
NANCY MILLIKEN.
W. J. SALISBURY.
CATHERINE SALISBURY.
SOPHRONIA McLERIE.

Nauvoo, March 1st. 1846.

Letter from William Smith to James J. Strang, published in the *Voree Herald* 1, no. 7 (July 1846): 3, with his mother and his three sisters' names attached. Katharine later denied ever signing a statement in support of James J. Strang.

ever supported Strang: "I now in truth declare that I never signed my name to such [a] certificate or document; neither did I give my consent for anyone to sign it." She further recounted, "I never knew anything about Strang or his work," adding, "I do not believe that my mother, Lucy Smith, or my sisters, Lucy Millikin and Sophronia MCClerrie signed any such certificate."[11]

After affiliating with Strang for approximately one year and having been appointed an apostle and patriarch in Strang's church, William was excommunicated by Strang for practicing polygamy in 1847.[12] Following his break with Strang, William attempted to revive his earlier church organization with some marked success in the years 1847–53 near Amboy, Lee County, Illinois. That also came crashing down once his followers discovered he was secretly practicing polygamy in his church.[13] His brothers-in-law, Jenkins Salisbury and Arthur Millikin, acted as agents for his newspaper, but that was the extent of their involvement, and the Salisburys never removed to northern Illinois, providing evidence of only tacit support to his movement during those years.[14] However, during that decade after Joseph and Hyrum's deaths, William successfully laid the groundwork for a church organization based on lineal rights and opposed to polygamy among his family and followers. His supporters at Amboy and in southern Wisconsin almost immediately picked up where William had left off in the mid-1850s and provided a nucleus of leaders that ultimately formed the Reorganized Church of Jesus Christ of Latter Day Saints. Imbued with William's teaching on lineal succession, William's former disciples eventually persuaded Joseph III to assume leadership of their Church.[15] William's teachings on lineal succession and his narrative of injustice and maltreatment of the Smith family during the years 1845–53 profoundly impacted Katharine and her children in the ensuing decades.

Relocating in Missouri and Illinois

When William departed from Nauvoo in the spring of 1846 to follow James J. Strang, the Salisburys also left Nauvoo. Jenkins had been absent from Nauvoo the previous year and missed out on a prime opportunity to use his skill as a blacksmith in helping the Saints build and repair wagons for their journey west. With little work available in the city after the Saints' departure in February, Jenkins and Katharine loaded up all their belongings and decided to take their family south on the Mississippi River to try and obtain work in St. Louis.

In company with the family of Latter-day Saint Charles Kelley, whose friendship dated back to their time spent in Ohio,[16] the Salisburys purchased a weathered flatboat and the two families began their journey downriver. After a brief stop at Keokuk, Iowa, they continued their journey south until they were several miles below Alexandria, Missouri. As they rounded Fox Island, their flatboat collided with a large steamboat as it was launching from shore, destroying their smaller rig and spilling all their belongings and both families into the river. With the assistance from a group of men on shore, they managed to rescue the children along with the damaged flatboat, but only a portion of their belongings. The experience was traumatizing for the family, including the Salisburys' five children, who remembered details of the experience for the remainder of their lives.[17]

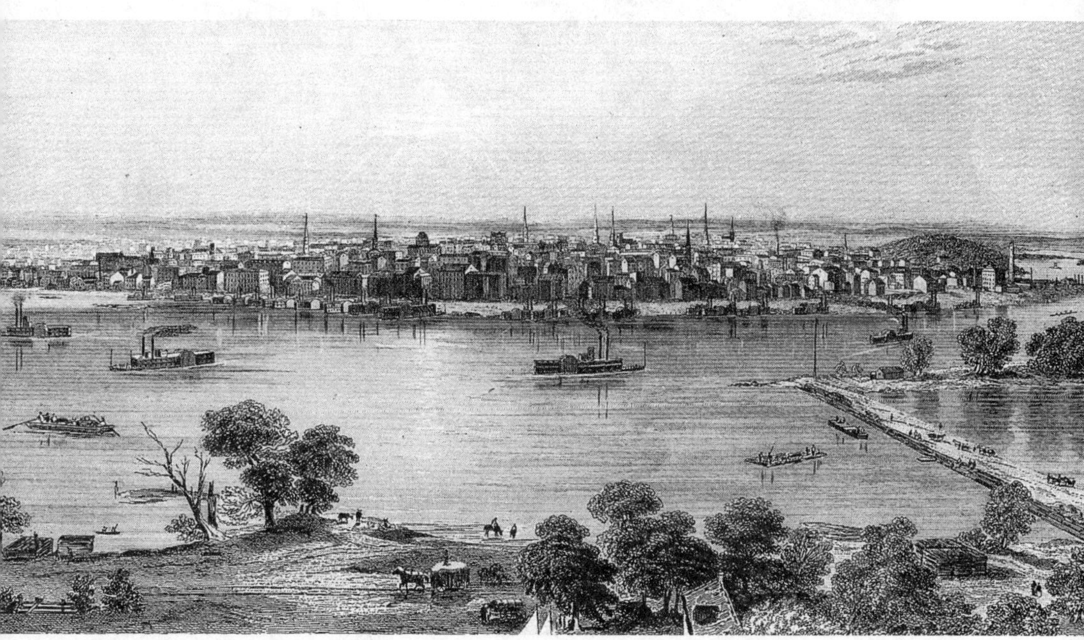

View of St. Louis in 1852, drawn by J. W. Hill, engraved by Wellstood and Peters, in the *Ladies Repository* 15, no. 1 (January 1855), x. Note the size of the smaller flatboats on the right side of the sketch in comparison to the much larger steamboats.

Lucy Salisbury Duke with her youngest daughter, Emma, ca. 1870s, photographer unknown. Courtesy of Carla Duke.

When Jenkins and Charles contemplated repairing the flatboat and continuing their journey, Katharine resolutely declared that she and the children had "had their last ride on that scow."[18] Katharine could be firm when she needed to be, as she recognized the precariousness of continuing the journey in the rickety vessel and was protective of her young children. Those who knew her well described her as being "very hale and strong" and possessing a "commanding presence," depictions which described both her stature and her temperament. Descendants recount how she could be resolute when necessary: "The kind of woman who would hen-peck a man that didn't have equal determination."[19] This was one of those instances, as Katharine was adamant the family remain in the area. Solomon recalled that once his mother refused to travel on the flatboat, "that ended the discussion," and "right there the Saint Louis trip ended."[20]

The Salisburys spent the remainder of the summer near Fox Island, where Jenkins and Charles cut cordwood for the steamships who docked in the vicinity. They managed to eke out a living until August, when the entire crew came down with the "shaking ague" (likely malaria). Kelley's wife died of the disease a short time later, and Charles departed for the East to be with family. The Salisburys moved their family into the town of Alexandria, but it did little to improve their health. Once Katharine also became ill, city authorities intervened to assist their family and "hired a colored lady to take care of us," and a local doctor was assigned to attend to the family.[21] Their two-year-old daughter, Emma, did not survive the winter, dying of malaria on October 10, 1846, and was buried "in the river bottom."[22]

The Salisburys' eldest daughter Lucy, who was only twelve years old at the time, had to grow up quickly during the chaos of the mid-1840s. She met Samuel Duke while the family was still living in Alexandria that same winter. Samuel worked alongside Jenkins at his trade as a blacksmith, perhaps laboring as an apprentice as Jenkins had done during his youth.[23] Samuel, who was born in North Carolina, was seventeen years older than Lucy. Perhaps she was taken in by the Duke family when the Salisburys became a ward of the town. The affection between them seemingly blossomed into romance, and the two wed a short time later, on January 21, 1847, in Alexandria.[24] Though not illegal to marry at age twelve in the state of Missouri, the union pushed the limits of societal propriety. Both Samuel and Lucy misstated their age each time the census was taken for several decades while they lived in Illinois, probably to avoid any legal complications and make the marriage appear more acceptable to neighbors.[25] At a much later date, Lucy's cousin Joseph Smith III summarized their marriage as an "unfortunate" union when she married Samuel Duke, "a man perhaps twice as old as she." While Samuel had initially made a favorable impression upon the family, according to Joseph III, he ultimately "proved to be a reckless and roistering fellow, unfitted to make her happy."[26] The newlyweds followed Lucy's parents each time they relocated over the next decade.

In the early months of 1847 and on advice from their attending physician, the Salisburys moved their family across the Mississippi River to Warsaw, Illinois. The family likely concealed their identity while in the area, as Warsaw was the hub of anti-Mormon sentiment in Hancock County, Illinois, in the 1840s and home to many of those who participated in killing Katharine's brothers and driving the Saints from the state just a few months earlier. Solomon recalled that his family "rented an old house on the bluff below the city" while they lived in Warsaw, slept on straw with no covers at night, and did not possess a change of clothing. A neighbor generously loaned them a stove to heat their home, but their only possession was Katharine's milk cow, which had somehow survived the family's migrations, even the flatboat accident on the Mississippi. Jenkins worked some at his blacksmith trade in town but evidently had not fully recovered his health. Nearing his twelfth birthday, Solomon contributed by obtaining work assisting with a local ferry boat operation, for which he was paid twenty-five cents a day.[27]

Adding to their difficulties, Katharine was in the late stages of pregnancy. The family recognized Warsaw would not be a permanent place of settlement, and by fall Jenkins wrote to a childhood friend named Donk Alexander, then living in McDonough County, Illinois, to see what assistance he could provide. Alexander immediately came to the family's rescue, bringing two wagons to pick up the family and transport them some forty-five miles east to his home. When he drove up to the house, Jenkins remarked, "Donk, what did you bring two teams for? All I've got are the wife and children." When Alexander saw what few belongings they possessed and observed their destitute circumstances, he wept in pity.[28]

The Salisburys lived with the Alexanders until their health improved, and probably remained there until after Katharine delivered a son they named Loren Ephraim on May 2, 1847.[29] Within months of Loren's birth, the Salisburys moved just across the county line into Hancock County, to the town of Webster, Illinois. The rural village had previously been the location of a flourishing branch of the church, known initially as Ramus and then renamed Macedonia during the first half of the decade, and where Sophronia and her family had resided during that time period. However, by the time the Salisburys moved to town, the name had been changed to Webster in an effort to erase any reminders of the church in their community.[30] It had only been a year since the Battle of Nauvoo had successfully driven most of the remaining Saints from the county.[31] By the summer of 1847 there were less than two hundred inhabitants in town,[32] and the community appeared desolate, with twenty-five or more abandoned homes that the Saints had left behind. The Salisburys moved quietly into one of one of these empty residences, and Jenkins began advertising his work as a blacksmith. With only a smattering of residents in the area, he would again have to travel to obtain money for the family. His efforts included several moves back and forth across the McDonough and Hancock County line, as well as spending time in Quincy and Warsaw, Illinois.[33]

It continued to remain a chaotic time for the family, as they sometimes remained in Webster, and other times the family relocated with Jenkins for months at a time. During this time their youngest child, six-month-old Loren, died at Webster on November 18, 1847, adding to the family's sorrow.[34] Katharine gave birth to their final child in Webster on January 27, 1850, a son whom they named Frederick Vilian.[35] Only five of the eight children born to the Salisburys survived to adulthood.

Wilkins Jenkins Salisbury
m. Katharine Smith in 1831

Elizabeth (1832–32)
Lucy (1834–92)
Solomon Jenkins (1835–1927)
Alvin (1838–80)
Don Carlos (1841–1919)
Emma (1844–46)
Loren Ephraim (1847–47)
Frederick Vilian (1850–1934)

During the period of 1844–51, the family had moved at least nine times, creating an environment of uncertainty for their growing family. Solomon moved in with his older sister Lucy and her husband, Samuel Duke, in McDonough County in the late 1840s, which provided him with more stability and work during the harvest season. By the early 1850s, the family settled more permanently in Webster. However, illness struck the family again in the year 1853, and this time it hit Jenkins the hardest. He contracted typhoid fever, and his condition quickly grew worse until his death on October 28, 1853, at the age of forty-four. Katharine was left a widow with four boys to raise between the ages of three and seventeen, residing in an area where her neighbors were hostile toward their faith.[36] The precariousness of her situation would bring tremendous challenges during the ensuing three decades.

Notes

1. William Small (St. Louis) to Benjamin Winchester, November 24, 1845, *Messenger and Advocate of the Church of Christ* (Pittsburgh) 2, no. 2 (December 1845): 407–8.
2. William Smith, *A Revelation Given to William Smith, in 1847, On the Apostacy of the Church and the Pruning of the Vineyard of the Lord* (n.p., 1848), 1–2, M293.1, CHL; Kyle R. Walker, *William B. Smith: In the Shadow of a Prophet* (Salt Lake City: Greg Kofford Books, 2015), 311–15, 352–54
3. Small to Winchester, November 24, 1845.
4. Valeen Tippetts Avery and Linda King Newell, "The Lion and the Lady: Brigham Young and Emma Smith," *Utah Historical Quarterly* 48, no. 1 (1980): 81–97.
5. "Brother Salsbury had just [come?] to St. Louis without obtaining your name [of support]," wrote William to Emma from St. Louis on October 21, 1845. "Judge my Serprise Emma when you now refuse to help me to reform the Church after the many times I have talked with you on this Subject and asked what I Should do to save my fathers family, . . . and the answer was for me to Come out and proclame against the Spiritual wife doctrine [and] the usurpation of the 12." William Smith (St. Louis) to Emma Smith, October 21, 1845, CHL. For information on William Smith's Nauvoo sermon advocating polygamy, see Dean C. Jessee, ed., *John Taylor Nauvoo Journal* (Provo, UT: Grandin Book, 1996), 97–99.

6. Emmeline eventually married Newel K. Whitney as a plural wife, on February 14, 1845. Carol Cornwall Madsen, *Emmeline B. Wells: An Intimate History* (Salt Lake City: University of Utah Press, 2017), 53–57.

7. W. J. Salisbury (Nauvoo, IL) to Mr. [Thomas] Sharp for the *Warsaw Signal, Warsaw Signal* 3, no. 2 (April 8, 1846): 2.

8. Orson Hyde (Nauvoo, IL) to Dear Brethren, March 27, 1846, Brigham Young Office Files, 1832–78, General Correspondence, Incoming, 1840–77, Letters from Church Leaders and Others, 1840–77, Orson Hyde, 1846, CHL; Kyle R. Walker, "Looking After the First Family of Mormonism: LDS Church Leaders' Support of the Smiths after the Murders of Joseph and Hyrum," *John Whitmer Historical Association Journal* 32, no. 1 (Spring/Summer 2012): 23–26.

9. William Smith (Nauvoo, IL) to Brother [James] Strang, March 17, 1846, James Jesse Strang Collection, 1832–1947, Beinecke Rare Book and Manuscript Library, Yale University, New Haven, CT; William Smith to Dear Brother Strang, April 12, 1846, *Voree Herald* 1, no. 6 (June 1846): 3–4. Strang published William's letters in his *Voree Herald* newspaper, and William was ordained as the presiding patriarch and as a member of Strang's First Presidency, per William's request. "The First Presidency," *Zion's Reveille* 1, no. 12 (December 1846): 3; "Patriarchs," *Zion's Reveille* 2, no. 1 (January 14, 1847): 3.

10. William Smith (Nauvoo, IL) to James J. Strang, March 1, 1846, *Voree Herald* 1, no. 7 (July 1846): 3; "Opinions of the Smith Family," *Voree Herald* 1, no. 6 (June 1846): 1.

11. Katharine Salisbury (Fountain Green, IL) to Editors Herald, March 26, 1899, *Saints' Herald* 46, no. 17 (April 26, 1899): 261.

12. In August, James J. Strang's *Zion's Reveille* reported, "It becomes our painful duty to give public notice that William Smith, the Patriarch, has been sometime since suspended, pending trial on charges of gross immorality." *Zion's Reveille* 2, no. 23 (August 26, 1847): 3. By October it was official, as the paper related that "William Smith, Patriarch, [has been] excommunicated for adultery. . . . And the whole congregation lifted their hands against him." "Conference of the Church of Jesus Christ of Latter Day Saints, at Voree," *Gospel Herald* 2, no. 30 (October 14, 1847): 2. For more information on Strang and Smith's alliance and subsequent fall out, see Walker, *William B. Smith*, 328–37.

13. Walker, *William B. Smith*, 339–403.

14. "List of Agents for This Paper," *Melchisedek and Aaronic Herald* 1, no. 5 (August 1849): 2.

15. Kyle R. Walker, "William B. Smith and the 'The Josephites,'" *Journal of Mormon History* 40, no. 4 (Fall 2014): 82–103.

16. Both Jenkins Salisbury and Charles Kelley (or Kelly) participated in the Zion's Camp expedition in 1834, were ordained to the office of Seventy and were excommunicated in May 1836 for neglecting their families.

After relocating to Illinois, the Kelleys also lived near the Salisburys in Plymouth. Brent M. Rogers et al., eds., *Documents, Volume 5: October 1835–January 1838*, vol. 5 of the Documents series of *The Joseph Smith Papers*, ed. Ronald K. Esplin, Matthew J. Grow, and Matthew C. Godfrey, (Salt Lake City: Church Historian's Press, 2017), 243–44; Solomon J. Salisbury, *Reminiscences of an Octogenarian* (self-pub., ca. 1926), 5; E. H. Young, *A History of Round Prairie and Plymouth, 1831–1875* (Chicago: Geo. J. Titus, Book and Job Printer, 1876), 87–88.

17. Salisbury, *Reminiscences of an Octogenarian*, 5.
18. Salisbury, *Reminiscences of an Octogenarian*, 5.
19. Herbert S. Salisbury, "Things the Prophet's Sister Told Me," 2–3, typescript, San Rafael, CA, June 30, 1945, CHL; "Sister of a Prophet," *Saints' Herald* 40, no. 36 (September 9, 1893): 1.
20. Salisbury, *Reminiscences of an Octogenarian*, 5.
21. Salisbury, *Reminiscences of an Octogenarian*, 5.
22. Dorothy D. Dean, Salisbury Family Group Sheet, n.d., copy of original in author's possession. Solomon said Emma died at Alexandria, Missouri, in 1847. The family continued to live in Alexandria in the early months of 1847, and it appears that Solomon's memory was a general recollection of the winter of 1846–47. Salisbury, *Reminiscences of an Octogenarian*, 5. Katharine said Emma died in 1856, but it appears to either have been a mistake by Katharine, or George A. Smith transcribed it incorrectly from Katharine's genealogy sheet. George A. Smith (Salt Lake City) to Cousin Catherine [Salisbury], August 17, 1865, Historian's Office letterpress copybooks, 1854–1879, Vol. 2, 1859–1869, CHL; John Smith Papers, 1833–1854, Journal, 1846 February–1854 May, CHL.
23. Richard P. Howard, *Memoirs of President Joseph Smith III (1832–1914)*, (Independence, MO: Herald Publishing House, 1979), 189.
24. The couple was married by M. J. Brown, justice of the peace, and the marriage record was not recorded until August 18, 1848. Marriage Records, Book A, 1837–54, p. 85, Clark County Courthouse, Kohoka, MO.
25. In the 1850 census, Samuel's age is correct, but Lucy's age is recorded as eighteen, when she was only fifteen at the time the census was enumerated. In the 1860 census, Lucy's age is correct, while Samuel's age is listed as thirty-two, ten years younger than his actual age. 1850 United States Federal Census, McDonough County, Illinois; 1860 United States Federal Census, Hire Township, McDonough County, Illinois. While I have been unable to locate Samuel Duke's birth record, Joseph Smith III confirmed that Duke was "a man perhaps twice as old as she [Lucy]." Richard P. Howard, ed., *The Memoirs of President Joseph Smith III (1832–1914)* (Independence, MO: Herald Publishing House, 1979), 189.
26. Howard, *Memoirs of President Joseph Smith III*, 189.
27. Salisbury, *Reminiscences of an Octogenarian*, 6.

28. Salisbury, *Reminiscences of an Octogenarian*, 6.

29. George A. Smith (Salt Lake City) to Cousin Catherine [Salisbury], August 17, 1865, Historian's Office letterpress copybooks, 1854–1879, vol. 2, 1859–1869, CHL; John Smith Papers, 1833–1854, journal, 1846 February–1854 May, CHL; Dorothy D. Dean, Salisbury Family Group Sheet, n.d., copy of original in author's possession; Lucy Mack Smith, *Biographical Sketches*, 43.

30. Charles J. Scofield, ed., *History of Hancock County Illinois* (Chicago: Munsell Publishing, 1921), 671; Susan Sessions Rugh, *Our Common Country: Family Farming, Culture, and Community in the Nineteenth-Century Midwest* (Bloomington: Indiana University Press, 2001), 52.

31. Kenneth W. Godfrey, "The Battle of Nauvoo Revisited," *John Whitmer Historical Association Journal*, Nauvoo Conference Special Edition (2002): 133–46.

32. Rugh, *Our Common Country*, 82.

33. Salisbury, *Reminiscences of an Octogenarian*, 6–7.

34. George A. Smith (Salt Lake City) to Cousin Catherine [Salisbury], August 17, 1865, Historian's Office letterpress copybooks, 1854-1879, vol. 2, 1859–1869, CHL; John Smith Papers, 1833–1854, journal, 1846 February–1854 May, CHL; Dorothy D. Dean, Salisbury Family Group Sheet. Solomon said his brother Loren died while the family was living in McDonough County. Orville F. Berry, "The Mormon Settlement in Illinois," *Transactions of the Illinois State Historical Society for the Year 1906*, no. 11 (1906), 94.

35. George A. Smith (Salt Lake City)to Cousin Catherine [Salisbury], August 17, 1865, Historian's Office letterpress copybooks, 1854–1879, vol. 2, 1859–1869, CHL; John Smith Papers, 1833–1854, journal, 1846 February–1854 May, CHL; Dean, Family Group Sheet.

36. Dean, Family Group Sheet. Jenkins's original headstone also has the date of October 28, 1853. Katharine said that Jenkins died on November 27, 1853. George A. Smith (Salt Lake City) to Cousin Catherine [Salisbury], August 17, 1865, Historian's Office letterpress copybooks, 1854–1879, vol. 2, 1859–1869, CHL; John Smith Papers, 18331854, journal, 1846 February–1854 May, CHL.

CHAPTER TWELVE

Destitution and Discrimination

I was called a Mormon, boycotted, abused, slandered. . . . All along the pathway of life I had to bear the reproach of Mormonism.
—Solomon J. Salisbury

KATHARINE HAD EXPERIENCED a very difficult marriage with Jenkins but always spoke respectfully of her husband in the years after his death. Others were less tolerant in their assessment of his character. Katharine's cousin George A. Smith summarized that Jenkins "never provided for her [Katharine's] wants during his lifetime[,] being drunken [and] licenscious," but observed that Katharine always remained "thoroughly attached to him."[1] There had been only minimal contact between the Salisburys and Jenkins's family in New York during their twenty-two-year marriage, but after his death Katharine wrote to the family informing them of his passing. She felt most comfortable reaching out to Jenkins's sister Samantha Salisbury Arnold, as she was only fourteen months older than Jenkins and seemingly the sibling he had been closest to in his youth.[2] "We feel Deeply to sympathize with you in your afflictions which are very great," Samantha responded in a letter written on New Year's Day 1854, encouraging Katharine to "look to him [God] who is able to sustain you and yours through this life."[3]

Samantha also sympathized with what she described as the family's "destitute" circumstances, which Katharine must have written about. It is also clear from Samantha's letter that she knew her brother well enough to know he had left her in that position. She referred to her brother's unsteadiness as a provider and supposed it "had made it very hard for you and the children." Samantha was unable to help financially, but her sympathy-filled letter must have brought some measure of comfort from the Salisbury side of the family. The two updated one another on their respective families, and Samantha expressed her hope that Katharine's boys would come visit them in New York after they reached adulthood. Katharine wrote again to her sister-in-law several months later, asking Samantha to gather funds from her Salisbury relatives so she could erect a proper gravestone for Jenkins. Samantha appears to have followed through with her plea, and that year Katharine was able to erect a notable marker in the Webster Cemetery that is still standing today. She included a lock of Jenkins's hair in her letter to Samantha per her request, a common practice in memorializing lost loved ones.[4]

Katharine leaned heavily on her two sisters in the immediate years after her husband's death. Arthur and Lucy Millikin lived in Fountain Green, Illinois, just two miles

Wilkins Jenkins Salisbury's gravestone, Webster Cemetery, Webster, Illinois. Photograph by Kyle R. Walker, 2019.

from Katharine's residence in Webster. Sophronia and her only surviving daughter, Mariah, lived with the Millikins in the early 1850s, before moving in 1856 some fifteen miles east to the town of Colchester, across the border in McDonough County.[5] Mariah married a successful merchant named Barnett Woolley in 1852, which likely prompted Sophronia to eventually follow the newlyweds to the budding town of Colchester.[6] Sophronia lived with her daughter's family in Colchester after she relocated, and Mariah's family then moved in with Sophronia once she purchased her own home for forty dollars from the Woolley family in 1858.[7]

The Millikins had led out in caring for Lucy Mack Smith in the years 1846–52, and she remained in their household until she moved back to the Mansion House at Nauvoo in 1852 to be cared for by her daughter-in-law Emma Hale Smith Bidamon, and Emma's second husband Lewis. Mother Lucy remained in Nauvoo until her death four years later. The Bidamons were attentive to her needs in her declining years, as she struggled with rheumatoid arthritis. During her final years, Lewis even constructed a wheelchair so she could be transported

Arthur Millikin, 1809–82. Photograph by Charles R. Savage, ca. 1875–82. Courtesy L. Tom Perry Special Collections, Harold B. Lee Library, Brigham Young University.

around the house and outside in the yard, an activity she always enjoyed.[8] In her final weeks, Lucy was cared for by Emma's son Joseph III and his wife Emmeline on the Smith farm, several miles outside of Nauvoo. "Grandmother died the morning of the 14th of May last easily with her senses to the last moment," Joseph III described of her final moments. "She appeared somewhat fearful of

Lucy Mack Smith gravestone, Smith Family Cemetery, Nauvoo, Illinois. Photograph by Kyle R. Walker, 2010.

death at a little while before he came [death] yet appeared resigned afterwards. I sat by her and held her hand in mine till death relieved her."[9] Katharine would sorely miss her mother's influence, as she remained her exemplar for the remainder of her life.

The Millikins lived within two miles of Katharine in those years after Jenkins's death, but they ultimately decided to follow Sophronia in relocating to Colchester in 1857.[10] Thus, while Katharine lived in Webster at her own residence, she was still within a twelve-mile radius of her two sisters in the decades that followed, and they lent their support after Jenkins's death. It is surprising that Katharine did not follow her sisters in removing her family further east. By relocating to the flourishing coal-mining town of Colchester and removing themselves from the turmoil the family had experienced in Hancock County, Katharine's two sisters raised their children in peace and away from the animosity that still existed in Webster and neighboring Fountain Green. Most residents at Colchester were immigrants and knew nothing about the conflicts between the Saints and their neighbors during the previous decade. Sophronia and Lucy's families also found much-needed work with the arrival of the railroad in 1855, and the corresponding businesses that grew up in the area, because they were some of the earliest residents in town.[11]

The Webster-Fountain Green community, on the other hand, had sent a contingent to Carthage at the time Katharine's brothers Joseph and Hyrum were killed and had participated in driving the Saints from the area. The Salisburys' nearby neighbors read like a who's who of anti-Mormons during the 1840s. Thomas Geddes, who lived just east of the Salisburys, had earlier served as colonel of the eighty-third regiment of the Illinois militia and had ordered the thirty-seven men of the Fountain Green Rifle Company to Carthage, Illinois, on June 17, 1844.[12] The following year, after the Smith brothers were killed at Carthage Jail, he and prominent local storeowner Stephen H. Tyler publicly declared their opposition to the Saints remaining in their community. Another was Jabez Beebe, the foreman of the jury that in 1845 had acquitted the accused murderers of Joseph and Hyrum.[13] These individuals were instrumental in successfully driving the Saints from their community in 1845–46, and Geddes and Beebe were among those who snatched up the Saints' properties at bargain prices.[14] Perhaps Katharine remained in the area because it allowed her to live in one of the abandoned homes of the Saints without paying rent, but the decision to raise her children in the area was fraught with challenges and would have a marked influence on their development.

Besides a year or so of schooling for the older children while the family lived in Plymouth, educational opportunities had been limited

Eagle schoolhouse, where Katharine's children attended school, Fountain Green, Illinois. Photograph by Kyle R. Walker, 2010.

for the Salisbury children due to their frequent moves. Once the children began attending school and securing employment during the harvest season, it became challenging to integrate with their peers. While they initially tried to keep their church ties a secret, locals quickly ascertained Katharine's identity as a sister of the prophet, and the family became targets of religious discrimination. Eldest son Solomon, fifteen in the year 1850, bore the brunt of the abuse during those early years. He recalled how the men he worked for "would often curse old Joe Smith" when he was within earshot and how their wives refused to let him eat with the others at their dinner table, even though he was often miles from his own home. In one instance, he

Solomon J. Salisbury, date and photographer unknown.
Courtesy of Estel Neff.

began taking Sunday walks and attending Sunday School with a girl who was about his same age, whom he described as "handsome as an artist's dream." Solomon felt the affection was mutual until she abruptly quit their excursions. When he finally encountered her and asked if he had done something wrong, the girl's little sister disclosed that their father "forbade [her] going with me [because he] . . . says you are a Mormon and he does not want anything to do with you." It was a deeply painful experience for Solomon, and he confided in his history, that even after seventy years "it was one of the wounds that has never healed."[15]

The Salisburys continued to experience alienation as a family as the children felt isolated from their peers. Solomon recalled that unlike the other children in the area, "there were no young folks that would invite me to parties or have anything to do with me." He recalled being shunned socially, and being "called a Mormon, boycotted, abused, [and] slandered."[16] As his younger brothers matured, they related similar experiences that, in at least some instances, were life-threatening. Don Carlos, who was age nine in 1850, recalled swimming in a creek below Webster when an older boy named Jack Broady sneaked up behind him, put him in a headlock, and began dunking him in the creek. Broady boasted that he had been in the mob that killed his uncles and crowed that it would be service to the community if he killed a Mormon—a statement meant to intimidate. Don Carlos felt that Broady would have killed him that day if it hadn't been for an older neighbor who happened upon the scene as Broady repeatedly held his head under water for an extended period.[17]

The bullying and ostracism the family faced increased to such an extent that Katharine felt it necessary to remove her children from school. Her youngest son Frederick, born in 1850, remembered that these challenges continued into the 1860s when he attended school. In a letter recounting his limited educational opportunities to a relative, Frederick wrote, "I am sorry to say that in my boyhood days I had not obtained an Education on the acount of persecution." He described how the other kids "would take My Dinner bucket and throw It away So I had no dinner to Eat" and then would "hiss at Me and Say your Mother was a Sister to Old Joe Smith the Mormon Prophet." Instead of attending public school, Katharine, who in her younger days was briefly hired to teach school, began instructing Frederick at home. Frederick said that his formal education was limited to three months at a district school at the age of twenty and often expressed embarrassment about his spelling in his holograph letters.[18]

Katharine also ensured her children received spiritual instruction, much like her mother Lucy had done during her own childhood. Not only did she read to her children from the Bible, but she also emphasized scriptural passages from the Book of Mormon, including her personal involvement in the publication of the book. Frederick recalled that his mother "read the Book of Mormon a great deal," "was well versed in the doctrine," and spoke often of

Katharine Smith Salisbury with her youngest son, Frederick, ca. 1870. Courtesy of Church History Library.

her brother Joseph as a prophet. "As she spoke as one who knew of what she was talking [about]," recalled Frederick, "I was impressed that he was a prophet [and] that impression from my boyhood days I never forgot."[19] Despite their complicated relationship with the church, the family continued to identify with at least some elements of the Restoration.

The boys were also occasionally privy to discussions between Katharine and her sisters about those early days. When Katharine's mother Lucy died on May 14, 1856, Sophronia stopped by the Salisbury home on her way to the funeral. Much like Katharine and Joseph had done during his visit to the Salisbury home in 1843, the two sisters reminisced about their girlhood days in Palmyra and how they had successfully protected the Book of Mormon plates during one tense experience when Joseph was being chased by a mob.[20] The children who were present listened attentively to the stories the Smith sisters recounted.

Widowhood and Poverty

Katharine struggled to keep things afloat financially for her family. Besides her family being socially isolated, being a widow in rural nineteenth-century America meant additional hardships. At some point, Katharine had acquired a large loom and began making and selling rugs that provided some income, but not enough to subsist on.[21] Solomon said that after his father's death, he and his next-eldest brother, Alvin, lent their best efforts in contributing to the family's support.[22] As early as 1850, at the age of twelve, Alvin was already living with various farmers during the summer to help provide income for the family.[23] Despite those efforts, Solomon remembered that "work was scarce and wages were low" in those immediate years after his father's death as the two boys worked at "haying, harvesting, and threshing."[24] Don Carlos joined his older brothers once he reached his teens, and the same would hold true for their youngest brother Frederick, but any income they provided was meager at best.

Women living in the mid-1800s knew to whom they would go for support if their husband should die long before that event occurred, explained social-historian Nancy Grey Osterud, and parents and their oldest children were clear about those "mutual obligations." "Inheritance practices that favored sons over daughters presumed that widows would live with sons, for men inherited the obligation to support their mothers at the same time that they inherited the family farm."[25] Though Jenkins had owned no property or a farm that he could bequeath to his boys, the Salisburys still followed that pattern. While Katharine's daughter Lucy and her husband lived nearby and were better established than her boys, Katharine still chose to live with her sons: first Solomon, then Alvin, and finally Frederick in her final years.

Marriage to Joseph Younger

In her attempt to mitigate financial hardship and assist her and the children during this difficult time, Katharine married a longtime member named Joseph W. Younger on May 3, 1857, in Carthage, Illinois, after only a brief courtship.[26] Younger's first wife, Susan McCurley, had died less than a year earlier, and Joseph was ten years older than Katharine.[27] She had waited four years after Jenkins's death to remarry, about the same period her sister-in-law Emma Hale Smith had waited to marry her second husband, Lewis Bidamon, after Joseph Smith's death. Younger had been affiliated with the Saints for more than thirteen years, having been converted by John Murdock in March 1832 in Greeneville, Illinois, and had weathered the Saints' difficulties in Missouri and Illinois.[28] After his excommunication from the main body of Saints for "apostacy" in December 1845, Younger had bounced around various factions of the church, much like Katharine's brother William had, including joining with James J. Strang, then James C. Brewster (Brewsterites), and afterward Charles B. Thompson

Mariah Stoddard Woolley, only surviving daughter of Katharine's sister Sophronia. Mariah assisted in raising Katharine's son, Don Carlos Salisbury. Date and photographer unknown. Courtesy of Mary Dennis.

(Baneeymites).[29] He was also likely drawn to William Smith's organization at some point because of his affinity for the Smith family. In 1850 he had unsuccessfully attempted to coerce a young Joseph Smith III to join him in following Charles B. Thompson's church, and nine years later Younger united with the RLDS Church.[30]

Salisbury descendants say this union was very brief, perhaps only lasting a few weeks, some denying that it had ever taken place.[31] When Katharine's nephew Samuel H. B. Smith visited Katharine's residence in Webster the same month as her marriage, he made no mention of Joseph Younger being present at her home. In a letter Samuel H. B. Smith wrote to his uncle George A. Smith about his visit with the Salisburys, he expressed his belief that Katharine (in the singular) would come west.[32] Perhaps Younger had married Katharine to strengthen his religious ambition, and when she refused to follow him, he moved on. One descendant recounted hearing that once Younger moved in with Katharine, he experienced immediate conflict with Katharine's sons and that caused him to leave Katharine and return to his family.[33] Her boys may have discerned Younger's ulterior motives and tried to protect her. Whatever the reason for this brief union, it evidently did not survive the summer, and Katharine quickly returned to using the surname of Salisbury.[34] Neither Katharine nor her children ever mentioned the marriage in any document or history, further evidence that the union was brief.

In need of support for her growing boys, Katharine's older sister, Sophronia, and her married daughter, Mariah (age twenty-five in 1857), offered to take Don Carlos into their home in Colchester, Illinois, and provide him with a quality education.[35] Don Carlos turned sixteen in 1857, the same year the first school was completed in Colchester, and he initially attended the common school and later a cadet school in nearby Middletown (later renamed Fandon).[36] The educational opportunity afforded Don Carlos had a significant influence on him and his posterity, something denied Katharine's other children. Don Carlos's children were highly educated, including a university president, a daughter who became a surgeon in Chicago, another an Illinois legislator, and a grandson who was a professor at

Harvard.[37] His aunt Sophronia, cousin Mariah, and Mariah's husband, Barnett Woolley, became a second family to Don Carlos, and he remained close to them throughout his life.

At the age of twenty-one, eldest son Solomon married Eliza Swisher on February 19, 1856.[38] Solomon said that he purchased a town lot in Webster on credit around the time of his marriage, and with the assistance of neighbors, he moved one of the abandoned log homes of the Saints on to his lot. Solomon eventually paid for his property and indicated it was the first home he or his parents had ever owned during his lifetime.[39] After Katharine and Joseph Younger separated, she went to live with Solomon and his new bride, bringing Alvin and Frederick with her.[40] Alvin married Mahala Aldrich several years later, on October 16, 1861.[41] By the early 1860s, Katharine's two eldest boys had obtained more secure work, enabling them to support themselves and their growing families. The three eldest boys all got together and decided they would collectively ensure their mother would never want for anything.[42] Despite those efforts, finances remained a hardship for both Katharine and her boys in the intervening years.

Notes

1. George A. Smith diary, 1872 May–November, files 1–20, entry for September 18, 1872, unpaginated, CHL.
2. The Salisbury Family Bible records Samantha's birthdate as August 6, 1807. Gideon Salisbury Family Bible, in Gideon Salisbury Revolutionary War Pension File, US, Revolutionary War Pension and Bounty-Land Warrant Application Files, 1800–1900, Ancestry.com. Samantha's grandson gives the date of her birth one year earlier, August 6, 1806. Paul W. Arnold, Application for Membership in the Empire State Society of the Sons of the American Revolution, National #40295, New York State #4150, US, Sons of the American Revolution Membership Applications, 1889–1970, vol. 202.
3. Samantha Arnold (n.p.), to Dear Sister [Katharine], January 1, 1853 [1854].
4. Samantha Arnold to Dear Sister [Katharine], January 1, 1853 [1854]; and Samantha Arnold to Katharine Salisbury, May 15, 1854, photocopies of originals, Katharine Smith Salisbury Correspondence, 1853–1879,

L. Tom Perry Special Collections, Harold B. Lee Library, Brigham Young University, Provo, UT.

5. Sophronia and Mariah were living in Colchester, Illinois, by the summer of 1856. Samuel H. B. Smith reported on the living situation of his relatives when he stopped in Illinois on his way to his mission in May of 1856. Samuel H. B. Smith, reminiscences and diary, 1856 April–1863 July, 14, entry for May 20, 1856, CHL.

6. Mariah Stoddard married Nathaniel Barnett Woolley on June 6, 1852, in Fountain Green, IL. Marriage License Book, vol. 2, p. 12, #1904, Hancock County Courthouse, Carthage, IL.

7. Mortgages, Book K, p. 29, McDonough County Courthouse, Macomb, IL.

8. 1850 US Census, Hancock County, Illinois, Lucy Smith, Arthur Milican, and Catherine Salisbury. Lucy Mack Smith was living in the Mansion House in Nauvoo by late November 1852. Perrigrine Sessions Reminiscences and Diaries, 1839–1886, vol. 4, entry for November 29–30, 1852, CHL; Lavina Fielding Anderson, ed. *Lucy's Book: A Critical Edition of Lucy Mack Smith's Family Memoir* (Salt Lake City: Signature Books, 2001), 211, 793–96.

9. Joseph Smith III (Nauvoo, IL) to John M. Bernhisel, August 6, 1856, John M. Bernhisel papers, 1818-1872, CHL.

10. Mortgages, Book J, 260, McDonough County Courthouse, Macomb, IL; John Smith (Colchester, IL) to Joseph F. Smith, December 21, 1859, L. Tom Perry Special Collections, Harold B. Lee Library, Brigham Young University, Provo, UT.

11. During the 1850s Colchester's population was rapidly expanding due to the coal-mining industry. The Quincy Burlington Railroad (QBR) passed through the middle of town, and the Quincy Canal Company would eventually employ 130 men and 60 boys. The greatest year of growth in town was 1856–57, the same time the Millkins relocated to the community. Arthur Millikin and his boys would work in the mines and with the railroad. June Moon, *"Multum in Parvo," A History of Colchester, Illinois* (Colchester, IL: Colchester Chronicle, 1956), 14–15; Nathan H. Williams, "Lucy Smith Millikin," in *United by Faith: The Joseph Sr. and Lucy Mack Smith Family*, ed. Kyle R. Walker (American Fork, UT: Covenant Communication and BYU Studies, 2006), 417–19.

12. Fountain Green Rifle Company Roll, January 25, 1849, Hancock County Historical Society, Carthage, IL; Thomas Geddes, Certificate, January 25, 1849, Fountain Green Vertical File, Hancock County Historical Society, Carthage, IL.

13. Susan Sessions Rugh, *Our Common Country: Family Farming, Culture, and Community in Nineteenth-Century Midwest* (Bloomington: Indiana University Press, 2001), 51.

14. Deed Record, Town of Webster, Hancock County Clerk's Office, Carthage, IL, as cited in Rugh, *Our Common Country*, 220n135.

15. Solomon J. Salisbury, *Reminiscences of an Octogenarian* (self-pub., ca. 1926), 7, 9.

16. Salisbury, *Reminiscences of an Octogenarian*, 7.

17. H.[erbert] S. Salisbury, "The Western Adventures of Don Carlos Salisbury," San Rafael, CA, unpublished typescript, ca. 1945, 5.

18. Frederick Salisbury to Audentia Anderson, June 2, 1930, Audentia Anderson Genealogy Research Letters, Miscellaneous, P78-4, folder 37, Community of Christ Library-Archives, Independence, MO.

19. Frederick V. Salisbury, "The Teachings and Testimonies of My Mother," unpublished typescript, ca. 1926–1928, 1–2, 14, Warren L. Van Dine Papers, Hancock County Historical Society, Carthage, IL.

20. Emma M. Phillips, *Dedicated to Serve: Biographies of 31 Women of the Restoration* (Independence, MO: Herald House, 1970), 17.

21. Warren L. Van Dine, "Catharine Smith Salisbury," unpublished typescript, 1972, 14, Community of Christ Library-Archives.

22. Salisbury, *Reminiscences of an Octogenarian*, 7.

23. At the age of thirteen, Alvin was living with a local farmer named John Thompson in the summer of 1850. 1850 United States Federal Census, Alvin Salisbury, Hancock County, Illinois.

24. Salisbury, *Reminiscences of an Octogenarian*, 7, 9.

25. Nancy Grey Osterud, *Bonds of Community: The Lives of Farm Women in Nineteenth Century New York* (Ithaca, NY: Cornell University Press, 1991), 134.

26. The two were married by justice of the peace Kendrick N. Leach at Carthage, IL. Marriage Book A-2, 1849-1857, #2937, Joseph Younger and Catharine Salisbury, Hancock County Courthouse, Carthage, IL.

27. Joseph Younger was born December 10, 1803, at Chatham County, NC. H. Michael Marquardt, ed., *Early Patriarchal Blessings of the Church of Jesus Christ of Latter-Day Saints* (Salt Lake City: Signature Books, 2007), 341–42.

28. John Murdock Diary, 1832 February–September, entry for March 15, 1832, in John Murdock Journal and Autobiography, 1830–1867, CHL.

29. "Notice," *Times and Seasons* 6, no. 19 (December 15, 1845): 1065; "Withdrawal.—Joseph Younger," *Olive Branch* (Springfield, IL) 2, no. 11 (May 1850): 12 [172].

30. Joseph Smith III (n.p.) to Caroline Case, March 27, 1894, Joseph Smith III Letterbook #5, Vault Collection, P6, folder 102–218, 172–75, Community of Christ Library-Archives, as cited in Mark Scherer, *Journal of a People: The Era of Reorganization, 1844 to 1946* (Independence, MO: Community of Christ Seminary Press, 2013), 59. For Younger's conversion to the RLDS Church, see W. W. Blair Journal, March 4, 1859–January 14, 1860, entry for July 20, 1859, P2, J1, Community

of Christ Library-Archives, Independence, MO. Katharine's brother William had given Joseph Younger a patriarchal blessing at Nauvoo, on July 23, 1845. Younger's wife, Susan McCurley, and the couple's twenty-year-old daughter, Polly Jane, also received their blessings on the same day. Marquardt, *Early Patriarchal Blessings*, 341–42. Younger appears to have followed Smith's lead when he affiliated with James J. Strang's church because they both traveled to Voree, Wisconsin, in the summer of 1846 and were ordained to offices in Strang's hierarchy on the same day. "Chronicles of Voree, 1844–1849," typescript, June 11, 1846, CHL. Joseph and Susan had married at Maury, Tennessee, on September 28, 1824, and had five children by the year 1850. Tennessee Marriage Records, 1780–2002, Tennessee State Library and Archives, Nashville, TN; 1850 United States Federal Census, Sangamon County, IL, Joseph Younger; 1850 United States Federal Census, Sangamon County, IL, under "Joseph Younger."

31. Van Dine, "Catharine Smith Salisbury," 15; Estel G. Neff, interview by the author, May 17, 2002, Nauvoo, IL.

32. Samuel H. B. Smith to George A. Smith, June 2, 1857. George A. Smith Papers, 1834–1877, General Correspondence, Incoming Letters, 1857, CHL

33. Warren Van Dine, "Statement by Warren L. Van Dine about certain points sometimes brought up in connection with Mrs. Salisbury after his [her] death," unpublished typescript, 1, n.d., n.p., Hancock County Historical Society, Carthage, IL.

34. Van Dine, "Catharine Smith Salisbury," 15. The last-documented reference to Katharine being referred to by the surname of Younger was made by Katharine's niece Mary Bailey Smith Kelteaux in August 1857, just three months after the couple married. However, it is also possible that Mary, who lived some distance away in Iowa at the time, had not yet have been informed that the two had separated. Mary Bailey Smith Kelteaux to Dear Aunt Catharine Younger, Katharine Smith Salisbury Correspondence, 1853–1879, L. Tom Perry Special Collections, Harold B. Lee Library, Brigham Young University, Provo, UT. Younger was living in Decatur, Iowa, in the summer of 1859. W. W. Blair Journal, March 4, 1859–January 14, 1860, entry for July 20, 1859, Community of Christ Library-Archives.

35. Mary Salisbury Hancock, "The Three Sisters of the Prophet Joseph Smith, Part III," *Saints' Herald* 104, no. 4 (January 25, 1954), 11; Salisbury, "Western Adventure of Don Carlos Salisbury," 5.

36. "Don Carlos Salisbury. Died," *Carthage Republican* 46, no. 16 (April 16, 1919): 1. The first school in Colchester was completed by 1857, and the first schoolteacher was Cyrus Holt. *History of McDonough County, Illinois* (Springfield, IL: Continental Historical Co., 1885), 614.

37. Salisbury, "Western Adventure of Don Carlos Salisbury," 18.

38. Salisbury, *Reminiscences of an Octogenarian*, 9.
39. Salisbury, *Reminiscences of an Octogenarian*, 8. George A. Smith, who delivered five hundred dollars from Brigham Young to Katharine in September 1872, also indicated this was the first home she could ever call her own. George A. Smith diary, 1872 May–November, files 1–20, entry for September 18, 1872, CHL.
40. 1860 United States Federal Census, McDonough County, Hire Township, Illinois, under "Solomon Salisbury."
41. Alvin married Mahala Aldrich on October 31, 1861, in McDonough County, Illinois. Marriage License 1704, McDonough County Courthouse, Macomb, IL.
42. Warren L. Van Dine, "Information on the Smith and Salisbury Families, 1966–1975," typescript from a taped interview conducted by Norma Hiles, Burnside, IL, 1975, 33, CHL.

CHAPTER THIRTEEN

Mountain Saints

*The memory of our beloved Prophet is deeply cherished in the hearts of
the Saints, and for his sake, his relations and members of his family,
notwithstanding differences of opinion, are kindly regarded.*
—Brigham Young, 1871

IN THE DECADE AFTER THE SAINTS fled Nauvoo in the
spring of 1846, there had been no documentable interaction between
the Salisburys and their Smith relatives who had settled in the Salt
Lake Valley under Brigham Young's leadership. That began to
change by the mid- to late-1850s as members of the Smith family in the West began serving missions to the eastern United States
and Europe. While en route to their missions, Katharine's cousins
George A. and John Lyman Smith, as well as sons of her brothers
Hyrum and Samuel Smith, stopped in Nauvoo and sought out their
Smith relatives who had remained in the Midwest. These interactions reveal much about Smith family relations, attitudes toward

succession in the church, and the family's sense of privilege in being part of the founding family of the Latter-day Saint movement.

One of the first to return to the Midwest and seek out his relatives in the area was seventeen-year-old Samuel H. B. Smith, the only son of Katharine's elder brother Samuel and his first wife, Mary Bailey Smith.[1] Katharine had developed an attachment to Samuel H. B. when he was a child because both families lived in Plymouth, Illinois, in the early 1840s. His mother had died in 1841, and he was orphaned after his father died of bilious fever in the summer of 1844.[2] Though he had a stepmother (Levira Clark) at the time of his father's death, he and his two older sisters must not have been close to her. They did not live with her for any substantial amount of time after their father died, and Samuel H. B. rarely, if ever, mentioned her in his journal. Instead, Samuel H. B. lived with various relatives in the ensuing decade, including with his stepmother's parents at Winter Quarters. He was the only one of his siblings to move to the Salt Lake Valley in the decade after the deaths of Hyrum and Joseph, immigrating in the year 1848.[3] His sister Mary remained in the Midwest, helping care for her grandmother Lucy Mack Smith, and after Lucy died in 1856, she lived with Katharine and her sisters until she married.[4]

Samuel H. B. was appointed to a mission in 1856 at the youthful age of seventeen, traveling with a large contingent of missionaries who crossed the plains that spring and arriving in St. Louis, Missouri, in June. On the journey east, he was tutored by more experienced missionaries, including his father's cousin George A. Smith, who turned thirty-nine that summer and was a member of the Quorum of the Twelve Apostles. "I had considerable talk with George A., in

Samuel H. B. Smith, photograph by Charles R. Savage, Salt Lake City, ca. 1860s. Courtesy of Church History Library.

reference to the Smith family," recorded Samuel H. B. during the overland journey. In returning to the Midwest, both were concerned about the well-being of their Smith relatives who stayed in Illinois and were determined to reconnect. After arriving in St. Louis, Samuel H. B. remained in the city just a few days before he caught a steamer upriver to Nauvoo, where he headed immediately to the home of his aunt Emma Hale Smith Bidamon.[5] He had missed seeing his grandmother Lucy Mack Smith by only a month, because she had passed away on May 14, 1856.[6]

Emma had remarried Lewis Bidamon a decade earlier. When Samuel visited, all four of Emma's sons and her adopted daughter Julia were residing together at the Mansion House in Nauvoo.[7] He found Emma and her family "comfortably situated" but expected a friendlier reception than he received. "They manifested some interest in so unexpected a visit," wrote Samuel H. B. of their initial greeting, "but at the same time appeared a little shy."[8] His use of the word *shy* as recorded in his journal meant that Emma and her family were restrained in their warmth and affection toward him. Wounds created in the aftermath of her husband's death had been slow to heal for Emma, and her typical welcoming attitude was absent when interacting with those from the West. Katharine's cousins John Lyman Smith and George A. Smith, as well as nephew Joseph F. Smith, all visited Emma in the years 1855–60, and each separately recorded her reception as "cool" and "distant."[9] Emma's reserve toward her orphaned nephews Samuel H. B. and Joseph F. must have been psychologically painful to the youths.

After staying in Nauvoo for just a few days, Samuel H. B. then headed east to locate the three Smith sisters and found Katharine and her sister Lucy Millikin living on farms near Fountain Green, Illinois. Here he also found his older sister Mary Bailey Smith, who was "busily engaged" in working in the Millikins' home. It was a joyous reunion with his sister Mary, whom he had not seen in nearly a decade, and he found a much warmer reception among his relatives here than he had in Nauvoo. After laboring as a missionary in Illinois for several months, Samuel H. B. was drawn back to

Fountain Green, where he spent the winter living with his relatives before leaving for a mission to England in June 1857.[10]

George F. A. Spiller, Samuel H. B.'s missionary companion, recorded the hospitable reception they experienced when visiting the three Smith sisters in Illinois. "I accompanied Elder Samuel H. B. Smith in his visits to his relations and formed a very agreeable acquaintance with Mrs. Sophronia McClarie, Mrs. Catherine Salisbury, and Mrs. Lucy Millkin," he recounted. "I remained with them over two nights and they made me heartily welcome." Spiller was anxious to record that although the three Smith sisters had not gone west, they still "testified that they knew that their brother Joseph was a prophet of God." When they prepared to leave the area, Spiller recounted how the sisters "earnestly requested" them to return to stay with them as soon as they could.[11]

In a letter he penned to George A. Smith, Samuel H. B. summarized his memorable stay with his relatives in the area that winter. He enthusiastically expressed his view that he had "partly persuaded" his sister Mary "to go to the [Salt Lake] Valley with me." Among the three Smith sisters, he felt that Katharine was most open to the possibility of gathering with the Saints in the West. "Aunt Katharine I believe will go next year if her way opens," he opined, "for She has a desire to be amongst the Saints ever more, but has to keep rather still about it, for it beats all how the Peoples minds are tethered against the Saints in that place [Fountain Green]. The very name Mormons is almost poison to them and there is nothing to[o] bad to say about the Saints."[12] Though his youthful missionary enthusiasm probably overstated the likelihood of Katharine relocating to Salt Lake City, Samuel H. B.'s efforts that winter assuaged some of the animosity between branches of the Smith family and paved the way for additional relatives and traveling missionaries who visited the Smith sisters in subsequent years.

By the late 1850s, Katharine felt comfortable enough with her nephews that she struck up an ongoing correspondence with three of them—Samuel H. B., John Smith[13] (who visited in the year 1859), and Joseph F. Smith[14] (who visited in the year 1860). The traveling missionaries also occasionally preached in the area. One such occasion happened in the summer of 1860, when Samuel H. B. and Joseph F. stayed with their Smith relatives for a week on their way to their missions in England. Joseph F. reported that there was a small LDS branch in McDonough County, where two of the Smith sisters resided. Joseph F. invited his Smith relatives in the area to attend several of his sermons directed to that branch. Katharine, Sophronia, and Lucy's families all joined the small congregation of Saints that week, and Joseph F. recorded that he "did some tall preaching to them." Joseph F. thought that the three Smith sisters "all though[t] I was prejudiced against them for certain causes which they themselves have imagined," but by the time he left, felt that he and Samuel H. B. "got them to think very differently of a great many things."[15]

Just a few months earlier, Joseph Smith III had been installed as president of the Reorganized Church of Jesus Christ of Latter Day Saints (RLDS) at Amboy, Illinois, and the three Smith sisters had been distantly apprised of those proceedings. Joseph F. reported the reservations among the three Smith sisters regarding Joseph III's efforts to organize. "They all seemed to feel very shy about Joseph [III]'s step," Joseph F. summarized in a letter he wrote to George A. Smith, but "at the same time they seemed to want it to be right." He sensed there was a mix of apprehension and hopefulness among the Smith sisters for Joseph III's success. Perhaps their fear stemmed from the possibility that animosity might increase toward Latter-day Saints in the communities where they lived and what that might mean for them personally and for their expanding posterity. But they had also observed their brother William's failed attempts at organizing within the state and possibly remained skeptical that Joseph III's organization would succeed.[16] The three Smith sisters would wait more than twelve years after Joseph III was ordained president before they affiliated with the RLDS Church.

Katharine's third eldest son Don Carlos went overland in the year 1864 initially to participate in the California Gold Rush. His elder cousin, Mariah, who had helped raise Don Carlos, along with her husband, Barnett Woolley, had given him a deed to a gold mine in Idaho. Instead of mining, Don Carlos spent the next year and a half driving a stage line route through northern Nevada for the Wells Fargo Express Company. He was paid the lucrative sum of fifty dollars a month in gold for his services and returned to Fountain Green, Illinois, in the fall of 1866 with five hundred dollars in gold. On his journey home, he decided to visit relatives in Salt Lake City, because his Smith cousins had often encouraged him to visit when they had stayed at the Salisbury home in Illinois. Once word spread that Don Carlos was in the city, he was welcomed by his first cousins Joseph F. Smith and John Henry Smith and his mother's first cousin George A. Smith, whom he said "treated him like a brother." Brigham Young also welcomed him to the city, fed and entertained him at his home, and then gave him a tour of the city. He described how they collectively gave him "a friendly and hearty welcome and treated [me] like a member of the royal family." Young then arranged for Don Carlos to be transported to Council Bluffs with one of his own mule teams.[17]

Financial Support from Latter-day Saint Leaders

After learning of Don Carlos's positive interactions in Salt Lake City and establishing warm relationships with her nephews for more than a decade, Katharine felt comfortable enough with the Saints in the West to reach out to Brigham Young for financial assistance. On April 29, 1871, she wrote directly to Young, petitioning him for two hundred dollars to help her build a home just a few miles northeast of Fountain Green. Young promptly responded to her request, writing that "the memory of our beloved Prophet is deeply cherished in the hearts of the Saints, and for his sake, his relations and members of his family, notwithstanding differences of opinion[,] are kindly regarded."[18] Young sent the two hundred dollars with a traveling missionary named Warren Dusenbery, who arrived with the money less than a month after her initial request. Katharine immediately wrote to Young, indicating that the money was "thankfully received" and that she was certain the money would prove to be "the Blessing

Salt Lake City. U.T.
May 17. 1871.

Mrs Katharine Salisbury,
Fountain Green, Hancock Co. Ill.
Dear Sister:

Your letter of the 29th April was duly received. I send you Two hundred (200) dollars at your request. and I sincerely trust it will prove the blessing you anticipate.

Elder Warren N. Dusenbury, who has been instructed to bear it to you, will give you all the news, much of which will doubtless prove interesting; you will find him a gentleman worthy of your consideration, and as he is well acquainted with the leaders of the Church, and many others, possibly with whom you are acquainted. I think you will appreciate his society. He will convey to you our best regards. The memory of our beloved Prophet is deeply cherished in the hearts of the Saints, and for his sake, his relations and members of his family, notwithstanding differences of opinion are kindly regarded and would be welcomed among us and received with open arms, were they willing to adhere to the principles taught by the Prophet and become one with those who are striving night and day with all their hearts to carry out those principles he held so sacred and taught his brethren.

May peace be with you and the blessings of Heaven attend you all the remnant of your days upon the earth, and a happy

hereafter be your lot in eternity.
Your Bro. in the Gospel

Brigham Young

Letter from Brigham Young to Katharine Smith Salisbury, dated April 29, 1871. Original now housed in the L. Tom Perry Special Collections, Harold B. Lee Library, Brigham Young University.

I desired of it, and I feel shure the Lord will bless the doner for the gift."[19]

Her home was under construction by January 1872, and Katharine described how workers were "putting it up as fast as they can." However, Katharine underestimated the costs associated with constructing her home, and she continued to write to Latter-day Saint leaders in Salt Lake City in the ensuing months requesting additional funds. The excitement over the prospect of owning a home and property spilled out in her letters. "I send my respects to you," she wrote to Brigham Young and George A. Smith, "and my thanks to[o] for the help you have rendered me in sending me the amount to build my house [where] I can spend my remaining days in." Though she described the home as modest, she indicated "that lumber is very dear and carpenters work is verry high" and feared she would not have enough funds to complete construction.[20] In several different

Sketch of Katharine's home in Fountain Green, Illinois, with (left to right) Katharine; her son, Frederick; and Frederick's wife, Mary Brewer. *Salt Lake Tribune* 44, no. 57 (June 24, 1894): 16.

payments, Young eventually sent several additional payments totaling thirteen hundred dollars so that Katharine could finish her home and purchase twenty acres of land.[21]

Katharine continued to correspond with Brigham Young and George A. Smith throughout the decade of the 1870s. For a time, at least, President Young's generosity seemed to heal former misunderstandings. Katharine wrote to Young, "My gratitude to you is unbounded and i shall ever pray for blessing[s] to rest uppon your venerable head. . . . I will send you my likeness [photograph] . . . and wish you would send me yours in return that i may look uppon [it] with thankfullness for the great help you have rendered to me in the hour of my greates[t] need."[22] Her home was finished by June. George A. Smith visited Katharine in the latter part of 1872 and wrote to Brigham Young, describing her home and her gratitude for the financial gift. "[K] atherine is living on the place, that you furnished her means to purchase," he explained, "and is . . . the happiest Woman I have seen on the journey." He depicted her property as "a piece of Timber land, which your last bounty enables her to increase to twenty acres. And as in all her live [life] she has never been

Above: Brigham Young, ca. 1855, by Savage & Ottinger, Salt Lake City. Courtesy of L. Tom Perry Special Collections, Harold B. Lee Library, Brigham Young University. Below: George A. Smith, ca. 1872, by Charles R. Savage, Salt Lake City. This photograph was in Katharine Salisbury's photobook. Courtesy of Mary Dennis.

Katharine Salisbury (far right) next to her grandson, Herbert S. Salisbury. Alexander Hale Smith, son of Joseph and Emma Hale Smith, is on the far left. Don Carlos Salisbury is seated fourth from left. Photograph ca. 1893. Courtesy of Mary Dennis.

able to enjoy a home of her own for a single hour, her gratitude to you seems unbounded."[23] She moved into her home just a month before her fifty-ninth birthday and after all her children were grown.

Following Brigham Young's death in 1877, Katharine continued to petition Latter-day Saint leaders for financial assistance. During the 1870s Katharine still struggled financially and at one point borrowed money against her house to meet her financial obligations. When a new owner then assumed her mortgage, he threatened to evict her from the property if she could not make regular payments.[24] That series of events certainly reminded Katharine of what had happened to her parents when she was still a teenager, when her family had lost their Palmyra farm under similar circumstances. Katharine anxiously wrote to several Latter-day Saint leaders in the years 1877–79, including church president John Taylor and apostle Orson Pratt begging for assistance to retain her property.[25] Joseph F. Smith, now a member of the Quorum of the Twelve, who became aware of the request, was less inclined to use church funds to support Katharine than had been Young, for he knew that she and her sons were now members of the RLDS Church. He felt Katharine should first try and petition RLDS leaders for support. Notwithstanding these reservations, through Joseph F. Smith's intercession, he persuaded John Taylor to send another three hundred dollars to Katharine to ensure creditors would not foreclose on her property.[26] The monies enabled her to remain in her home and expand her property to forty acres, where she lived with her youngest son Frederick for the remainder of her life, nearly thirty years after Young's initial gift.

In time, the circumstances surrounding the monies sent from Latter-day Saint leaders to purchase her home and property were reinterpreted. The gift apparently did not fit RLDS rhetoric about Young's caricature as being hostile and neglectful toward the Smith family, and Katharine's descendants in turn surmised that the monies were instead sent to pay for her to gather with the Saints in the West. As Katharine's grandson Herbert Salisbury summarized, "Brigham Young sent my grandmother, [K]atherine Smith Salsibury, several hundred dollars . . . telling her that he was sending that money to her and that he would like to have her remove to Utah. My grandmother [instead] took that money and stayed right there among the mobocrats and bought 40 acres of land and built a house with her money." However, this version of events that was perpetuated in the Salisbury family does not align with contemporary statements, as Katharine specifically had requested the money to build a home in Fountain Green, Illinois, and Young sent the money for that express purpose. What makes the later reinterpretation further puzzling is that Young's initial holograph letter sent to Katharine with the two hundred dollars and signed by Young remained a treasured heirloom

BIOGRAPHICAL SKETCHES

OF

JOSEPH SMITH,

THE

PROPHET,

AND HIS

Progenitors for many Generations.

BY

LUCY SMITH,

MOTHER OF THE PROPHET.

Liverpool:
PUBLISHED FOR ORSON PRATT BY S. W. RICHARDS,
15, WILTON STREET.

London:
SOLD AT THE LATTER-DAY SAINTS' BOOK DEPOT,
35, JEWIN STREET;
AND BY ALL BOOKSELLERS.

1853.

Title page of Lucy Mack Smith's *Biographical Sketches of Joseph Smith the Prophet and His Progenitors for Many Generations* (Liverpool: S.W. Richards, 1853).

among her descendants.[27] During the decade of the 1870s, Katharine responded to each financial gift by expressing her appreciation to Latter-day Saint leaders, including her desire that she "would like very much to See you all once more before we depart this life. May the blessings of heaven rest upon you and all the church."[28] After uniting with the RLDS Church, Katharine's public comments about Latter-day Saint leaders probably contributed to her descendants' misunderstanding of the purpose of the funds. Towards the end of her life, Katharine indicated that she had been entitled to the monies, stating on several occasions that "Brigham restored to me $500 of the Smith estate."[29] It was a similar view as her brother William held and promoted in the aftermath of his brothers' deaths—namely, that due to sacrifices the family had made in laying the foundations of the church, they were entitled to financial remuneration.[30] One specific example Katharine recounted was that she believed that Orson Pratt or other leaders were receiving profits from the sale of her mother's history, published in 1853.[31]

Perhaps Emma and her sons ongoing disagreements with Brigham Young influenced Katharine's views as Emma's sons' negative missionary experiences with leaders in the Salt Lake Valley reignited differences between branches of the Smith family.[32] Katharine's perspective on those Saints in the Salt Lake Valley appear to have been closely aligned with Emma's. The two remained close in those decades after Joseph's death, evidenced by Katharine's sons serving as pallbearers at Emma's funeral in the year 1879.[33]

These differences notwithstanding, Katharine's personal letters and in-person interactions with Latter-day Saint members and traveling missionaries remained remarkably positive. Victor E. Bean and Herbert H. Bell's visit to Katharine in the summer of 1885 provides another example. Bean recounted how he and his companion were received with kindness and were invited to stay several nights at her home. "She is living with her son on a 20 acre farm that she says Pres Young bought for her," recounted Bean in his journal, and Katharine described to them in detail how Young "sent her $13000.00 [$1,300] which bought her the place she now lives on." Bean said that during their religious discussion that day that he "found them pretty strong in the Josephite faith," but afterward asked Katharine "what I should tell the folks in Utah." "She began to sob in tears," described Bean, as seeing the missionaries "carried her mind back to early days when her Brothers used to go in the same way to preach the gospel. She said she would be very glad to see her folks in Utah but that she was poor and about worn out and thought that she wouldn't live to ever visit Utah. She invited us and any of our brethren to always call and see her when passing through."[34]

Her recounting of Young's gift to the traveling missionaries seems at odds with some of her public statements during the final twenty years of her life. Perhaps her public rhetoric, as expressed in letters intended for publication in the RLDS official newspaper, the *Saints' Herald*, were more divisive than her true feelings. In her personal letters to those in the West, she frequently included them as being one with her in the faith, often closing her letters with phrases such as "your sister in the gospel," or "your sister in the church of God."[35] She obviously considered those in the West her fellow Saints. Before Bean and his companion left their home that summer, the Salisburys requested them to pray over Katharine's two granddaughters—perhaps a reference to a priesthood blessing—who were sick with the measles in her home. As the missionaries then prepared to depart, Bean said "we bid them good bye [and] we left Mrs. Salisbury in tears."[36] It was her last documentable interaction with the Saints headquartered in Salt Lake City.

Notes

1. Samuel said he was born at Marrowbone, Caldwell County, MO, on August 2, 1838. Lucy Mack Smith, in her history, recorded the date as August 1. Samuel H. B. Smith Reminiscences and Diary, 1856 April–1863 July, CHL; Lucy Mack Smith, *Biographical Sketches of Joseph Smith the Prophet and His Progenitors for Many Generations* (Liverpool: S. W. Richards, 1853), 43.
2. "Died," *Times and Seasons* 5, no. 14 (August 1, 1844): 606–7. For more information on the circumstances leading to Samuel's death, see Mary Bailey Smith Norman, "Samuel Harrison Smith," reminiscence, typescript, June 24, 1914, CHL; J. Winter Smith, taped interview by Dean

Jacobs, transcription by Tom Duke, Smith Family Reunion, August 18–19, 1972, Nauvoo, IL; Dean L. Jarman and Kyle R. Walker, "Samuel Harrison Smith," in *United by Faith: The Joseph Sr. and Lucy Mack Smith Family*, ed. Kyle R. Walker (American Fork, UT: Covenant Communications; Provo, UT: BYU Studies, 2006), 230–31.

3. Samuel H. B. traveled with Truman O. Angell's contingent of Brigham Young's 1848 company, arriving in the Salt Lake Valley on September 22, 1848. Samuel H. B. Smith Reminiscences and Diary, 2–4.

4. Mary Bailey Smith was born March 27, 1837, and died October 13, 1916. "Records of Early Church Families," *Utah Genealogical Magazine* 26, no. 19 (July 1835): 103–4. After two unsuccessful marriages, Mary eventually married John Norman and the two migrated to Salt Lake City, where Mary was rebaptized into the Church of Jesus Christ of Latter-day Saints. Ruby K. Smith, *Mary Bailey* (Salt Lake City: Deseret Book, 1954), 97.

5. Samuel H. B. Smith Reminiscences and Diary, 12–14.

6. Buddy Youngreen, "The Death Date of Lucy Mack Smith: 8 July 1775–14 May 1856," *BYU Studies* 12, no. 3 (Spring 1972), 318.

7. Linda King Newell and Valeen Tippetts Avery, *Mormon Enigma: Emma Hale Smith*, 2nd ed. (Chicago: University of Illinois Press, 1994), 261–66.

8. Samuel H. B. Smith Reminiscences and Diary, 14.

9. Joseph F. Smith (Colchester, IL) to Levira Smith, June 28, 1860, Joseph F. Smith Papers, 1854–1918, Family Correspondence, CHL; George A. Smith Papers, 1834–1877, Autobiographical Writings, journal, 1856 April–1857 May, entry for October 30–31, 1856; John Lyman Smith, a first cousin to Joseph Smith, had also visited Emma's family the previous year, on July 2, 1855, and similarly described her as "very cool and distant." David Francis Haight, ed., "Biography of John Lyman Smith," entry for July 2, 1855, CHL.

10. Samuel H. B. Smith Reminiscences and Diary, 14–16.

11. George F. A. Spiller (St. Louis, MO) to T. B. H. Stenhouse, December 8, 1856, *Mormon* 2, no. 44 (December 20, 1856): 2–3.

12. Samuel H. B. Smith (New York City) to George A. Smith, June 2, 1857, in George A. Smith Papers, 1834–1877, General Correspondence, Incoming Letters, 1857, CHL. Samuel H. B. also spent three weeks with his sister Susannah in Wisconsin during his missionary travels in the fall of 1856 and felt that both his sisters would follow him to Salt Lake City when he visited them again after his mission was complete. Samuel H. B. Smith Reminiscences and Diary, 14–15.

13. John Smith (1832–1911) was the son of Hyrum and Jerusha Barden Smith, and served as the presiding patriarch for the Church of Jesus Christ of Latter-day Saints headquartered in Salt Lake City from 1855 to 1911.

14. Joseph F. Smith (1838–1918) was the son of Hyrum and Mary Fielding Smith, and later became president of the Church of Jesus Christ of Latter-day Saints headquartered in Salt Lake City from 1901 to 1918.

15. Joseph F. Smith (Hull, England) to George A. Smith, August 22, 1860, George A. Smith Papers, 1834–1877, General Correspondence, Incoming Letters, R–Y, 1860, CHL.

16. Joseph F. felt that Lucy Millikin and her family appeared most receptive to his preaching and purpose. Lucy took her nephew warmly by the hand, and Joseph F. recorded that she "was the first one to receive me in the true spirit of friendship." Joseph F. Smith to George A. Smith, August 22, 1860.

17. Herbert S. Salisbury, "The Western Adventures of Don Carlos Salisbury," unpublished typescript, San Rafael, CA, 1945, 1–2, 12–13, 17, CHL.

18. Brigham Young (Salt Lake City) to Katharine Salisbury, May 17, 1871, Brigham Young Office Files, box 8, Letterpress Copybook vol. 12, 684–85, CHL.

19. Katharine Salisbury (Fountain Green, IL) to Brigham Young, May 28, 1871, Brigham Young Office Files, 1832–1878, General Correspondence, Incoming, 1840–1877, Re–Sn, CHL.

20. Katharine Salisbury (Fountain Green, IL) to Dear Cousin [George A. Smith] and Brigham Young, January 14, 1872, Brigham Young Office Files, 1832–1877, box 34, folder 15, CHL.

21. Brigham Young and George A. Smith (Salt Lake City) to Daniel H. Wells, October 26, 1871, Brigham Young Office Files, box 73, folder 34; D. McKenzie (Salt Lake City) to Mrs. Katharine Salisbury, November 13, 1871, Brigham Young Office Files, box 8, vol. 12, CHL. Katharine wrote to Brigham Young and George A. Smith on January 14, 1872, indicating she had received an additional $200 "from the hands of brother [Cyrus] Sanford." Salisbury to Smith and Young, January 14, 1872. For evidence of an additional $400 sent by Young to Salisbury, see E. Cecil McGavin, *The Family of Joseph Smith* (Salt Lake City: Bookcraft, 1963), 105.

22. Katharine Salisbury (Fountain Green, IL) to Brigham Young, October 20, 1872, Brigham Young Office Files, 1832–1878, General Correspondence, Incoming, 1840–1877, General Letters, N–Sn, 1872, CHL.

23. George A. Smith (New York City) to Brigham Young, November 1, 1872, Brigham Young Office Files, 1832–1878, General Correspondence, Incoming, 1840–1877, Letters from Church Leaders and Others, George A. Smith, 1872–1873, CHL.

24. Katharine Salisbury (Fountain Green, IL) to George A. Smith and Brigham Young, July 25, 1873, George A. Smith Papers 1834–1875, Incoming Letters, folder 13, CHL; Katharine Salisbury (Fountain

Green, IL), to John Taylor, August 15, 1879, First Presidency (John Taylor) correspondence, 1877–1887, CHL.

25. Salisbury to Taylor, August 15, 1879; Katharine Salisbury (Fountain Green, IL) to Orson Pratt, December 20, 1877, Historian's Office correspondence files, 1856–1926, CHL; Katharine Salisbury (Fountain Green, IL) to Orson Pratt, January 23, 1878, Historian's Office correspondence files, 1856–1926, CHL.

26. Joseph F. Smith (Salt Lake City) to Catherine Salisbury, August 29, 1879; Joseph F. Smith (Salt Lake City) to Catherine Salisbury, September 7, 1879; Joseph F. Smith (Salt Lake City) to Arthur Millkin, September 7, 1879, all in Joseph F. Smith Letterpress Copybooks, 1875–1917, CHL.

27. Brigham Young to Katharine Salisbury, May 17, 1871. Katharine's grandson Herbert S. Salisbury owned this letter from Young for a time, which he described as being written by his secretary in a "nice spencerian hand." Despite the contents of the letter in his possession, Herbert still insisted that the money was intended to have her relocate to Utah and that his grandmother wrote back to Young in "positive and insulting language, as she was angry at him for claiming that her brother authorized polygamy," something that never occurred. Isaac Birkenhead Ball, "The Prophet's Sister Testifies She Lifted the B. of M. Plates," typescript interview with Herbert S. Salisbury, ca. 1954, 2, CHL; Herbert S. Salisbury, "Reminiscences of Joseph Smith as Told by His Sister, Catherine Smith Salisbury, to Her Grandson, Herbert S. Salisbury," *Saints Herald* 60, no. 41 (October 8, 1913): 983–84. In the year 2003, the author discovered this letter, along with many of Katharine's surviving letters and personal photobook, at the home of one of her descendants living in Burlington, Iowa. The author helped facilitate the acquisition of this collection, which is now housed in the L. Tom Perry Special Collections at Brigham Young University.

28. Katharine Salisbury to Brigham Young, May 28, 1871.

29. Salisbury, "Reminiscences of Joseph Smith as Told by His Sister," 983–84.

30. Kyle R. Walker, "Looking After the First Family of Mormonism: LDS Church Leaders' Support of the Smiths after the Murders of Joseph and Hyrum," *John Whitmer Historical Association Journal* 32, no. 1 (Spring/Summer 2012): 20–26.

31. Katharine Salisbury to Orson Pratt, December 20, 1877.

32. Valeen Tippetts Avery, *From Mission to Madness: Last Son of the Mormon Prophet* (Urbana: University of Illinois Press, 1998), 88–113.

33. Joseph Smith III said that all four of Katharine's boys served as Emma's pallbearers. Richard P. Howard, ed., *The Memoirs of President Joseph Smith III (1832–1914)* (Independence, MO: Herald House, 1979), 186.

34. Victor E. Bean Journals, 1884–1889, vol. 2, 1885 January–October, entries for July 4–5, 1885, 117–19, CHL.

35. Katharine Salisbury to Brigham Young, October 20, 1872; Katharine Salisbury (Fountain Green, IL) to George A. Smith and Brigham Young, July 25, 1873, George A. Smith Papers 1834–1875, Incoming Letters, folder 13, CHL. Katharine continued to refer to LDS leaders as being one with her years after she had joined the RLDS Church. See, for example, Katharine Salisbury to Orson Pratt, January 23, 1878.
36. Victor E. Bean Journals, entry for July 5, 1885, 119.

CHAPTER FOURTEEN

Smith Family Rights and the Reorganized Church

*I think you & all of the Smith family should look into this matter &
see if you are not the successors of Joseph the Prophet & Hyrum the
Patriarch & should lead & govern the Church in the last days.*
　　—Arthur and Lucy Smith Millikin to John Smith, 1863

IN THE TWENTY-FIVE YEARS since the Saints had left Nauvoo,
the three Smith sisters and their families remained unaffiliated with
any church. Both Katharine's and her descendants' retrospective recollections make it appear that the entire family was eagerly awaiting Joseph III's appointment as his father's successor and that they
were linked with the Reorganized Church from the first.[1] In fact,
it would be more than twelve years after Joseph III was ordained
president of the Reorganization until the sisters allied themselves
with the RLDS Church. Contemporary letters written by Katharine
and her sisters help to sort out their religious leanings and attitudes
related to succession in those decades after their brother Joseph's
death. While none of them had lost faith in the Restoration, their

brother's prophetic calling, or the divinity of the Book of Mormon, there was no Restoration branch in the areas they resided where their faith could find expression during the years 1846–72. However, with the traveling Latter-day Saint missionaries now proselyting the family, and Joseph III assuming leadership of the Reorganization, the Smith sisters were now confronted with several competing options.

Writing to her nephews living in the Salt Lake Valley in the fall of 1865, Katharine vented her frustration that Joseph III and his brothers had not shown more interest in involving her family with the Reorganization. It had been more than five years since Joseph III had been appointed president, and thus far "they have entirely forsaken us," wrote Katharine pointedly. "They manife[s]t no interest in our eternal welfare [and] they have never invited us to come and take a helping hand with them." At that juncture, she appeared open to uniting with the Saints in the West if the circumstances were right. "For my part I would be escedind [exceedingly] glad if all of us the

connexcion one and all could live in a Society together and believe in one Lord one Saveioure one faith one baptisem." The challenge was how to bring that desire to fruition as she seemed unwilling to relocate but emphasized that it was the "sincere desire of my heart" that all the family could "see eye to eye and rejoice in the holy one of isreal."[2]

Arthur and Lucy Millikin also wrote a letter to their nephews in the West in the year 1863 and were even more explicit in disclosing their views on succession. Writing at Lucy's instigation, and certainly with her input, Arthur directed their letter to John

John Smith, 1832–1911, eldest son of Hyrum and Jerusha Barden Smith. Photograph ca. 1850s and located in Katharine's photobook. Courtesy of Mary Dennis.

Smith, just after Samuel H. B. and Joseph F. Smith had visited their home upon the completion of their missions to Europe. The Millikins mentioned Joseph Smith III's modest success since assuming the presidency of the Reorganization and their belief that he would eventually "gather a large church around him." Then, rather revealingly, the Millikins wrote: "I think you & all of the Smith family should look into this matter & see if you are not the successors of Joseph the Prophet & Hyrum the Patriarch & should lead & govern the Church in the last days. I do not see how you boys can preach Brigham the successor to Joseph or that he has eny more

Joseph F. Smith, 1838–1918, eldest son of Hyrum and Mary Fielding Smith. Photograph by Edward Martin, ca. 1860s. Courtesy of Church History Library.

authority than he had when Joseph died. I never believed it nor never shall believe it."[3] That view doubtless represented the position of all three of the Smith sisters and their families. While they longed for unity in the Smith family, they remained reluctant to accept Young as the head of the Church.

These letters written in the 1860s reveal the Smith sisters' attitudes toward succession and how their views on succession differed from the Saints who had gone West, before their affiliating with the RLDS Church. What was most important to the Smith sisters was that leadership remain in the Smith line, something their brother William Smith had promoted after he split with Brigham Young's leadership in the year 1845, and in his attempts to form his own church.[4] Yet the seedbed for the notion of lineal succession probably came much earlier. Joseph Smith frequently installed his family members in positions of leadership, teaching on at least one occasion during the mid-1830s, "my family have been chosen to preside over the quorums of the priesthood."[5] There was a sense of privilege in being part of the founding family of Mormonism due to the sacrifices they made in helping launch the Restoration, which, at least for some, included an expectation of leadership and church financial support.[6] Thus, it clearly did not matter to the sisters which of their nephews should assume that role, as long as it was a Smith. Joseph III and Joseph F. were the most likely candidates among the succeeding generation due to their leadership abilities and charisma, and the prominent roles their fathers had played in the early church. It wouldn't come as a surprise to the Smith family then when both men would ultimately be president of their respective churches as the two organizations transitioned to the twentieth century, but the Smith sisters had all died by the time Joseph F. was eventually installed as the president of the Church of Jesus Christ of Latter-day Saints.[7]

As Katharine's sons grew to maturity during the 1850s, they also did not attend any church. Religious discrimination against the Restoration and the family's known connection to its founder were likely factors as to why her family avoided attending other denominations who held their meetings near Fountain Green. Their primary religious instruction came from their mother in the home. Youngest son Frederick recalled how his mother frequently read and taught the children from the Book of Mormon, recounting to them the role she personally played in protecting the plates in her youth and of her firm belief in her brother Joseph's role as a prophet.[8] Katharine would similarly perpetuate her faith to her grandchildren, several of whom recorded details of what she shared with them about her faith and participation in the early Restoration.[9]

Yet Katharine's strict religious upbringing, and the accompanying spiritual values she sought to perpetuate, did not always transfer easily to her boys. Growing up without a father no doubt influenced their developing personalities as Solomon, Alvin, and Don Carlos were eager to chart their own course in life. But Katharine also inadvertently contributed to their religious indifference. She was, at times, too prescriptive in her religious instruction to her children, perhaps a result of trying to overcompensate in the absence of their father. In letters she wrote to the *Saints' Herald*, for example, she would repeatedly chide sisters for adopting modern fashions in dress and grooming, urging them to adopt to more traditional style of fashion.[10] Though most of her surviving writings underscoring these values were often directed to female Saints, those strict traditional values from her childhood were undoubtedly directed to her sons as well. This was compounded by the fact that she seemingly had not adjusted to the societal softening of religious norms typical of religious families in the second half of the nineteenth century, as she held rigidly to a more traditional view of religious practice.[11] Like others in the Smith line, her boys were independent, and they would not be coerced into accepting their mother's faith and values. When Alvin and Don Carlos left for the gold fields of California in November 1864, it only increased Katharine's anxiety about how that environment might impact their moral rectitude.[12]

The apathy she observed in her boys was part of the reason she was frustrated with Joseph III and his brothers. She thought that if they had shown more interest in proselytizing her boys, "my Sons would be on a mission now instead of hunting for gold." "For my part," she confided to her nephews in the West, "I should feel Safer about them if they were in the employ of their hevenly father."[13] Perhaps Joseph III was consumed with building up the newfound church in other areas of the Midwest during those early years of the Reorganization, preventing him from reaching out to his immediate cousins. Whatever his reasoning for not including the Salisburys, Katharine felt neglected and excluded by Joseph III during the decade of the 1860s. Observing the dedication of her Utah nephews who visited her home as they came and went from their various missionary assignments brought uncomfortable spiritual comparisons to her own boys. Though they respected their mother, her boys viewed their mother's conservative views outdated. Katharine agonized over their lack of spirituality, especially with her eldest son Solomon, who had been blessed by Joseph Smith Jr. when an infant that he would grow to be a missionary and preach the restored gospel.[14] By the late 1860s, when Solomon was in his thirties, that must have seemed like an impossibility to his family. Attempting to increase his religiosity, Katharine would chide her son by rehearsing the details of the blessing he received from his Uncle Joseph, an approach that was not well received. Solomon's response to his mother's lectures on these occasions was that he would "prove to her that her brother was a false prophet."[15] Solomon was old enough to observe his father's religious skepticism during his youth, and adopted a similar mindset regarding organized religion. He described himself as a "wild, reckless boy" whose lack of interest in religion continued well into adulthood.[16] Yet even after her sons had married and had families of their own, Katharine was unrelenting in reproving her sons to accept her faith and the values she espoused.

The Salisburys' RLDS Conversion

She and her boys might have remained at an impasse but for an unexpected event that occurred in the fall of 1872. During an episode of severe illness where he was confined to his bed for the better part of a year, Solomon related how he was visited by a heavenly messenger during one particularly difficult night. The angelic visitor questioned him as to whether he wanted to get better, and that if he were to be healed, what he wanted to live for. Solomon answered, "I would like to live to raise my family." The Spirit pressed him further, "is that all you want to live for?" "No," responded Solomon, "I would like to do some good in the world," adding, "I think I never have." The messenger then directed him to send immediately for Joseph Smith III, who would provide him further direction. Learning of his cousin's sickness, Joseph III came directly to

Joseph Smith III, 1832–1914, ca. 1870s. Photograph by Charles W. Carter, Salt Lake City. Courtesy of Community of Christ Archives.

Solomon's home, gave him a healing blessing, and instructed him to get baptized in the RLDS faith. The following day, on October 23, 1872, before his health had even recovered, Solomon was baptized in nearby Crooked Creek by his ministering cousin. His health soon improved.[17] The experience was life-altering for Solomon and set him on a different course for the rest of his life.

Katharine was elated at this turn of events as she also embraced her nephew's leadership during the year 1872 and lent her full support for her son Solomon, who began to preach in the area and accepted leadership responsibilities in the RLDS Church in the ensuing months. She came to accept the Reorganization as the answer to her pleadings to unite her family around her long-held religious values. Some twelve years after accepting the presidency of the RLDS Church, Joseph III finally reached out to the three Smith sisters and their families, which was formalized during a preaching tour through Hancock and McDonough Counties during the week of December 9–17, 1872. Don Carlos Salisbury carried Joseph III in his wagon on a preaching tour through the countryside to visit all his Smith relatives, and Arthur Millikin arranged for him to use the Christian Church when they arrived in his hometown of Colchester, Illinois. All three Smith sisters, with several of their children, attended the services that were held throughout that week.[18] The influence of Joseph III's preaching during that week, along with Solomon's conversion and Katharine's abiding faith in the Restoration, influenced Don Carlos and Frederick to accept the Reorganization. They were both baptized the following spring, in May 1873. Though already an adherent, Katharine formally demonstrated her belief in the Reorganization by requesting baptism and confirmation under Joseph Smith III's hands the following month, which occurred on June 17, 1873.[19] She was just a month shy of her sixtieth birthday.

RLDS Pilot Grove Branch

Joseph R. Lambert, a newly installed apostle in the RLDS Church, supervised the organization of the Pilot Grove Branch of the RLDS

Church near Fountain Green that same summer, on July 13, 1873. The expanding Salisbury family made up the core of the branch's membership, with Solomon being appointed the branch's first president at the meeting, and Don Carlos being ordained a deacon. Solomon had some success in those early years, eventually building up the branch to eighty-seven members by the end of the decade.[20] Considering the animosity that persisted toward the Saints in Hancock County, Solomon's success in building up a thriving branch in the area was a remarkable accomplishment. His success brought Solomon some notoriety in the county and within the RLDS Church, and his church role was later expanded to district president, which included Nauvoo. Though he was always modest about his achievements, Solomon was celebrated as a respected church and community leader and a capable preacher.[21]

Over the next decade, Katharine continued to be influential in ensuring the rest of her children and their families united with the RLDS Church.[22] She was also the only one of the Smith sisters who was formally rebaptized, an expression of her devotion to the Reorganization for regenerating her faith. Sophronia and Lucy expressed their support of their nephew's leadership by being received on their original baptisms in April 1873, a common practice among those who were members of the earlier church organization before Joseph Smith's death in 1844.[23] The extent of their involvement was limited to hearing an occasional RLDS sermon in their community and securing a location where traveling RLDS ministers could preach on those infrequent visits to their hometown of Colchester. The closest RLDS congregation was the Salisburys' Pilot Grove Branch that had been organized in the year 1873. That was still likely too far for Sophronia and Lucy's families to make the thirty-mile round trip with any regularity, and neither of their names appear on the Pilot Grove Branch membership roster. Sophronia died in 1876, only three years after being received into the church, and both Arthur and Lucy in the year 1882.[24]

The Pilot Grove Branch went through its own ebbs and flows of activity, peaking at eighty-seven members, then dissolving at one point in the 1880s due to lack of interest, only to be revived a few years later in 1890 through Solomon's labors.[25] Seeing her growing posterity unite around a common belief system brought Katharine great satisfaction.

Adopting RLDS Beliefs:
Antipolygamy and Lineal Succession

Katharine and her sisters were unaware that their brother Joseph had introduced plural marriage at Nauvoo prior to his death. None of their spouses ever served in any significant leadership capacities, and both Sophronia and Katharine lived in remote branches of the church during the Nauvoo period, far removed from the day to day happenings at Nauvoo. Additionally, for the Salisburys, Jenkins was outside the faith during those years and would not have been aware of teachings which were reserved only for Joseph's most trusted followers. While Katharine may have heard or read about the rumors of plural marriage during the early 1840s, to her they were simply hearsay. Katharine confirmed her lack of knowledge about plural marriage in later years, attesting that it wasn't until after she moved her family to Nauvoo in the summer of 1845 when she first learned that church leaders were engaging in the practice in the city. "I heard nothing of such a doctrine existing until a year after his [Joseph's] death," she recounted, and that on "coming to Nauvoo, I was informed that Brigham Young and others were practicing that system."[26]

The source of her information was likely her brother William, because his excommunication from the Church coincided with Katharine's return to Nauvoo and his subsequent expose of polygamy in his writings and sermons that fall during the time he and Jenkins attempted to gather adherents in St. Louis, Missouri. William attempted to place responsibility on Brigham Young for inventing polygamy to bolster a lineal claim to leadership in the mid- to late-1840s. William knew better because he had taught and practiced plural marriage during the Nauvoo period before his brother's death,[27] but neither Jenkins or Katharine knew that, and they accepted William's statements as further evidence that Joseph

THE TRUE

LATTER DAY SAINTS'

HERALD.

"WHEN THE RIGHTEOUS ARE IN AUTHORITY, THE PEOPLE REJOICE: BUT WHEN THE WICKED BEARETH RULE, THE PEOPLE MOURN."—*Prov.* 29 : 2.
"HEARKEN TO THE WORD OF THE LORD, FOR THERE SHALL NOT ANY MAN AMONG YOU HAVE SAVE IT BE ONE WIFE: AND CONCUBINES HE SHALL HAVE NONE."—*Book of Mormon.*

No. 8.—VOL. 11.] PLANO, ILL., APRIL 15, 1867. [WHOLE No. 123.

"HEARKEN TO THE WORD OF THE LORD, FOR THERE SHALL NOT ANY MAN AMONG HAVE SAVE IT BE ONE WIFE: AND CONCUBINES HE SHALL HAVE NONE."—*Book of Morm*

never adhered to that practice. Once Joseph III revived the idea that Young had invented plural marriage, a claim that became a founding tenet of the Reorganization, that idea aligned with Katharine's and her sisters' understanding because of what they had already been taught by their brother William. If Katharine was familiar with Emma Hale Smith's later denials of plural marriage, it served only to reinforce that belief.[28] Joseph III was determined to establish a church free of polygamy and clear his father's name from any connection to the practice, something which clearly differentiated the RLDS faith from the Saints headquartered in Salt Lake City.[29]

As the Salisburys began to affiliate more extensively with the RLDS Church in the 1870s, animosity toward Brigham Young and the Saints in the West was at its height. Katharine could not personally reconcile the perception that Young had denigrated her brother's name and teachings surrounding polygamy in an apparent attempt to strengthen his claim to leadership. "Brigham Young

Masthead of the *Saints' Herald*. Note the scripture on marriage quoted on each issue of the newspaper, a defining tenet of the RLDS Church.

invented polygamy after my brother's death," Katharine succinctly summarized of her understanding of the history of the practice, "and then tried to saddle its authorship upon my brother."[30] Descendants recounted hearing that sentiment expressed by Katharine on various occasions. That perceived slander repeated in RLDS circles rekindled her animosity towards Young, despite her positive interactions with Young, LDS missionaries, and family members from the West. Among succeeding generations of Salisburys, resentment toward Young over polygamy and the perception that he had betrayed Joseph overshadowed the Salisburys' gratitude for his generous financial gifts during the 1870s. Antipathy toward Young grew to such an extent that veiled statements Joseph had made about enemies existing within the church, just before his death, were reattributed to Brigham Young by the Salisburys.[31] Katharine and her descendants sometimes took that a step further, insinuating that Brigham Young played a role in both Joseph and Samuel H. Smith's demise.[32]

In the final decades of her life, Joseph III used Katharine's recollections in the early church to strengthen RLDS ideology. On several occasions he solicited sworn affidavits on topics that included her denying the Smith family knew Sidney Rigdon until after the Book of Mormon was published, that her brother Joseph ever practiced polygamy, and repudiating that the Smith family ever supported James J. Strang's leadership. Katharine's denial that the family had known Rigdon prior to the latter part of the year 1830 helped the RLDS Church undercut theories that Rigdon helped to compose the Book of Mormon text.[33] In her sworn statement on plural marriage, Katharine recounted, "I was at his [Joseph Smith's] house in Nauvoo a great many times, . . . but I never heard him at any time mention such a thing as the plural-wife system or order."[34] It was a conversation to which Katharine would not have been privy, because plural marriage was not spoken of openly during the Nauvoo period and the Salisburys were not among Joseph's trusted inner circle. Regarding Strang's leadership, Katharine denied that she and her mother and sisters ever signed a certificate supporting his movement, something her brother William Smith claimed in several letters he

Print of RLDS Church leadership, including images of Lucy Mack Smith, Emma Hale Smith, and Katharine Smith Salisbury, by William Crick, ca. 1897. Courtesy of Community of Christ Archives.

sent to Strang in 1846.[35] Such statements strengthened Joseph III's claim to leadership, underscoring that he was the rightful successor of his father. Joseph III ensured that her sworn statements were distributed to church members via the church's newspaper—the *Saints' Herald*.[36] Her affidavits regarding polygamy and about Strang were again used in the twentieth century by RLDS tour guides, who used her statements to strengthen the church's position on these issues.[37]

During the final twenty years of her life, Katharine was quickly becoming an influential voice in RLDS circles, most especially in her counsel directed to women and with her recollections of the early Restoration. Her greatest contributions to the Reorganization would come during the final decades of her life, after she had reached her seventieth birthday.

Notes

1. In a letter written just a year before her death, Katharine stated that she knew her husband "looked forward to Joseph Smith [III] taking his father's place," and that she and her family all "waited patiently for him to take his place." Katharine Salisbury (Fountain Green, IL) to Editors Herald, March 26, 1899, reproduced as "Testimony of Katharine Salisbury," *Saints' Herald* 46, no. 17 (April 26, 1899): 261. Katharine's youngest son Frederick similarly recorded that "when young Joseph took his father's place at the head of the church . . . at Amboy, Illinois, in 1860, my mother and her two sisters . . . joined the movement of reorganization. They had waited from June 27th 1844 until the year 1860 for young Joseph to take his father's place." Frederick was also mistaken in assuming that the three Smith sisters had been present when Joseph III was ordained president. Frederick V. Salisbury, "The Teachings and Testimonies of My Mother," 1926/1928, unpublished typescript, 14–16, Hancock County Historical Society, Carthage, IL.

2. Katharine Salisbury (n.p.) to Dear Nephews [Joseph F. Smith, John Smith], September 11, 1865, L. Tom Perry Special Collections, Harold B. Lee Library, Brigham Young University, Provo, UT.

3. Arthur Millikin (Colchester, IL) to Dear Nephew [John Smith], July 25, 1863, L. Tom Perry Special Collections, Harold B. Lee Library, Brigham Young University, Provo, UT.

4. In the year after his brother Joseph's death, William's view on succession had shifted from fully supporting Brigham Young's leadership, to advocating that Joseph Smith III was the rightful successor, to then promoting his own right to leadership. Kyle R. Walker, "William B. Smith

and the 'Josephites,'" *Journal of Mormon History* 40, no. 4 (Fall 2014): 73–83. As early as August 1845, William was began explicating the idea of lineal succession, when he wrote to a friend, "Emma is well and also little Joseph his fathers successor although some people would fain make us believe that the Twelve are to be the perpetual heads of this church to the exclusion of the Smith family, but everyone who has read the book of Doctrine and Covenants must be aware that Priesthood authority is hereditary and descends from father to son and therefore Josephs oldest son will take his place when he arrives at the age of maturity." William Smith (Nauvoo, IL) to Jesse C. Little, August 20, 1845, Jesse C. Little correspondence, 1845–1846, CHL.

5. Joseph Smith made this statement during a debate about whether Joseph's brother Don Carlos should be appointed as president of the high priests in Kirtland when he was only age nineteen. After making the statement, Don Carlos was unanimously sustained. Erastus Snow quoted in John Henry Smith, *Church, State, and Politics: The Diaries of John Henry Smith*, ed. Jean Bickmore White (Salt Lake City: Signature Books, 1990), 84.

6. Kyle R. Walker, "Looking After the First Family of Mormonism: LDS Church Leaders' Support of the Smiths after the Martyrdom," *John Whitmer Historical Association Journal* 32, no. 1 (Spring/Summer 2012): 20–26; Herbert S. Salisbury, "Reminiscences of Joseph Smith as Told by his Sister, Catherine Smith Salisbury, to her Grandson, Herbert S. Salisbury," *Saints' Herald* 60, no. 41 (October 8, 1913): 983–84; Katharine Salisbury (Fountain Green, IL) to Orson Pratt, December 20, 1877, Historian's Office correspondence files, 1856–1926, CHL.

7. Joseph F. Smith served as president of the church from 1901 to 1918. Katharine, the last surviving member of the Smith family, died on February 2, 1900.

8. Salisbury, "The Teachings and Testimonies of My Mother," 14.

9. Herbert S. Salisbury, "Reminiscences," 982–84; Mary Salisbury Hancock, "The Three Sisters of the Prophet Joseph Smith, Part 1," *Saints' Herald* 101, no. 2 (January 11, 1954): 10–12.

10. Katherine Salisbury (n.p.) to Sister Frances, December 24, 1886, *Saints' Herald* 34, no. 6 (February 5, 1887): 84; Katharine Salisbury (n.p.) to Dear Sisters, July 2, 1895, *Saints' Herald* 42, no. 30 (July 24, 1895): 473.

11. Kyle R. Walker, "Katharine Smith Salisbury: Purveyor of Women's Values in the Early Restoration," *John Whitmer Historical Association Journal* 40, no. 2 (Fall/Winter 2020): 91–92.

12. Alvin and Don Carlos spent the winter of 1864–65 in Council Bluffs. Don Carlos made the overland journey that next year, while Alvin returned home to Fountain Green, Illinois. Herbert S. Salisbury, "The Western Adventure of Don Carlos Salisbury," unpublished typescript, 1945, 2, CHL; Katharine Salisbury to Dear Nephews.

13. Katharine Salisbury to Dear Nephews.

14. Salisbury, "Teachings and Testimonies of My Mother," 20.

15. Salisbury, "Teachings and Testimonies of My Mother," 20–21.

16. Solomon J. Salisbury, *Reminiscences of an Octogenarian* (self-pub., ca. 1922), 8.

17. Salisbury, *Reminiscences of an Octogenarian*, 10–11; Salisbury, "Teachings and Testimonies of My Mother," 20. The episode is reminiscent of his namesake great grandfather, Solomon Mack, who was similarly converted to the Christian faith in later life after experiencing a painful illness. Solomon Mack, *Narraitve* [sic] *of the Life of Solomon Mack* (Windsor, VT: self-pub., 1811), 18–24.

18. "Hail the New Year!," *True Latter Day Saints' Herald* 20, no. 1 (January 1, 1873): 17–18; *History of the Reorganized Church of Jesus Christ of Latter Day Saints*, 8 vols. (Independence, MO: Herald House, 1973), 3:719–20.

19. Pilot Grove Reorganized Branch Minutes, holograph, 5–25, Community of Christ Library-Archives, Independence, MO.

20. Pilot Grove Reorganized Branch Minutes, 122; *History of the Reorganized Church of Jesus Christ of Latter Day Saints*, 8 vols. (Independence, MO: Herald House Publishing, 1952), 4:698.

21. Salisbury, *Reminiscences of an Octogenarian*, 11–12; "Tells of Solomon Salisbury's Life," *Saints' Herald* 74, no. 5 (February 2, 1927): 136–37.

22. Alvin was baptized on January 19, 1878, but was cut off for apostasy a year later. He was outside of the RLDS faith at the time he was murdered in 1880. Though no record exists documenting the baptisms of Samuel and Lucy Duke, Katharine's daughter and son-in-law, there are records documenting the baptism of their children into the Pilot Grove Branch and evidence that Lucy attended RLDS conferences with her mother. Pilot Grove Reorganized Branch Minutes, 49, 120; Fred Salisbury (Fountain Green, IL) to Editors Herald, November 7, 1891, *Saints' Herald* 38, no. 48 (November 28, 1891): 763.

23. At the RLDS general conference held in April 1873, "Sophronia McClary, Arthur Millikin, and Lucy Millikin, were received on their original baptisms." *History of the Reorganized Church*, 4:4.

24. Jessie Salisbury, "Died," *True Latter Day Saints' Herald* 23, no. 19 (October 1, 1876): 607; "Died—Millikin," *Saints' Herald* 29, no. 11 (June 1, 1882): 180; S. J. Salisbury, "Died—Millikin," *Saints' Herald* 30, no. 2 (January 13, 1883): 23.

25. Alex[ander] Hale Smith (Kewanee, IL) to Editors Herald, June 9, 1890, in *Saints' Herald* 37, no. 25 (June 21, 1890): 407; Pilot Grove Reorganized Branch Minutes, 122.

26. "Aunt Katharine Salisbury's Testimony," *Saints' Herald* 40, no. 18 (May 6, 1893): 275.

27. William Smith, "A Proclamation," *Warsaw Signal* 2, no. 32 (October 29, 1845): 1, 4; Mary Ann [Covington Sheffield] West, Testimony, in United

States Testimony 1892, Court of Appeals Eighth Circuit, 495–96, MS 1160, CHL. William was sealed to Mary Elizabeth Jones by Brigham Young during the summer of 1845. Ibid., 497, 509. Under the date of August 8, 1845, Brigham Young recorded in his journal, "In the evening went to Wm. Smiths and sealed [him] to Miss [Henriette] Rice." Brigham Young Office Files 1832–1878, Brigham Young Journals, 1832–1846, CHL. For more information on William's sanctioning plural marriages as president of the eastern branches of the Church, see Kyle R. Walker, *William B. Smith: In the Shadow of a Prophet* (Salt Lake City: Greg Kofford Books, 2015), 180–207.

28. "Last Testimony of Sister Emma," *Saints' Herald* 26, no. 19 (October 1, 1879): 1.

29. Contemporary Community of Christ [formerly RLDS] histories acknowledge Joseph Smith's teachings and involvement in plural marriage. Mark A. Scherer, *The Journey of a People*, 2 vols. (Independence, MO: Community of Christ Seminary Press, 2013), 1:398–409. See also Richard P. Howard, "The Changing RLDS Response to Mormon Polygamy: A Preliminary Analysis," in Maurice L. Draper and Debra Combs, eds., *Restoration Studies III: A Collection of Essays About the History, Beliefs, and Practices of the Reorganized Church of Jesus Christ of Latter Day Saints* (Independence, MO: Herald Publishing House, 1986), 145–62.

30. Salisbury, "Reminiscences of Joseph Smith as Told by His Sister," 983.

31. In his history, Frederick Salisbury recorded a story that had been perpetuated in the Salisbury line about his Uncle Joseph Smith, which stated that if Brigham Young "ever became the leader of the church that he would lead it to hell." Salisbury, "Teachings and Testimonies of My Mother," 12. See also Katharine Salisbury (Fountain Green, IL) to Dear Friend [unknown], February 26, 1889, Community of Christ Library-Archives. Katharine's grandson Herbert Salisbury, whose own resentment toward Brigham Young appears to have been greater than his grandmother's, recounted that Katharine remained very angry at Young "for claiming that her brother authorized polygamy," implying the two had a strained relationship throughout her later years. Salisbury, "Reminiscences of Joseph Smith as Told by His Sister," 983–84.

32. Gay Davidson, "Anniversary of Carthage," *Salt Lake Daily Tribune* 44, no. 57 (June 24, 1894): 16; Salisbury, "Teachings and Testimonies of My Mother," 12–13. See chapter 10 for a discussion on the cause and circumstances of Samuel's death.

33. "Testimony of Katherine Salisbury," *Saints' Herald* 28, no. 11 (June 1, 1881): 169. For sources on Sidney Rigdon helping to manufacture the Book of Mormon, see, for example, Pomeroy Tucker, *Origin, Rise, and Progress of Mormonism* (New York: D. Appleton, 1867), 121–25; Benjamin G. Ferris, *Utah and the Mormons: The History, Government,*

Doctrines, Customs and Prospects of the Latter-day Saints (New York: Harper & Brothers, 1854), 50–55.

34. "Aunt Katharine Salisbury's Testimony," 275.

35. "Testimony of Katharine Salisbury," 261; Josephine Salisbury (Fountain Green, IL) to George Lambert, February 10, 1899, Community of Christ Library Archives; William Smith (Nauvoo, IL) to James J. Strang, March 1 [*date incorrect*], 1846, *Voree Herald* 1, no. 7 (July 1846): 3; "Opinions of the Smith Family," *Voree Herald* 1, no. 6 (June 1846): 1.

36. "Aunt Katharine Salisbury's Testimony," 275; "Testimony of Katharine Salisbury," 261.

37. Both the following sources were used by RLDS tour guides in the twentieth century and are contained in a folder at the Community of Christ Library Archives titled "For the Guides[,] Library at the Auditorium, Independence, Missouri": Salisbury to Lambert, February 10, 1899 (denying that the Smith sisters or Lucy Mack Smith ever signed a letter that supported James J. Strang leadership); and a copy of "Aunt Katharine Salisbury's Testimony" (quoted exactly the same as "Aunt Katharine Salisbury's Testimony," 275, cited above).

CHAPTER FIFTEEN

Political Strife and Alvin's Murder

Most of us [the Saints] were persons of education and refinement, from the best New York and New England families, and were people of progressive ideas and strong antislavery sentiments.
—Katharine Smith Salisbury

DURING HER YOUTH IN PALMYRA, New York, Katharine had witnessed the social tensions engendered by slavery. Cultural anthropologist Mark L. Staker documented the influence of racial tensions on the Smith family during their fourteen-year stay in Palmyra. Although in 1817 the state had more slaves than Missouri, by the time Saints immigrated to Ohio in 1831, the practice was virtually nonexistent in New York. Staker noted that New York had the highest concentration of Blacks in the country during the 1820s, a situation that would have made the Smiths keenly aware of their plight, and that in their first neighborhood in Palmyra, "free blacks and runaways congregated in noticeable numbers. . . . Because the region had an open, sparsely populated border with Canada, it was attractive to slaves seeking freedom; but the sympathetic attitude of the local population also helped to make the area a magnet for runaways."[1]

In addition, abolitionist thought infiltrated religious ideology throughout western New York, including sermons in church and camp meetings in which the Smiths participated. Methodists in New York were so outspoken against slavery that they refused to license "preachers, exhorters, or traveling preachers who were slave-owners."[2] While Presbyterians were typically less sympathetic to the antislavery movement than Methodists, Staker noted that Presbyterians in Palmyra were an exception: "The Reverend George R. H. Shumway of Palmyra's Western Presbyterian Church was a 'conductor' on the Underground Railroad and regularly hid runaways in his church buildings."[3] This was the same church which Katharine's mother and her siblings affiliated in the mid-1820s and where Katharine regularly attended Sunday School during her youth. Slavery and abolitionist thought were hotly contested issues everywhere during Katharine's formative years. Such sentiments continued once the family moved to northeastern Ohio, where many escaping slaves also passed through the area on their way to Canada by crossing Lake Erie.[4]

Those experiences appear to have had a profound impact on the Smith family. In subsequent decades, two of Katharine's brothers, Joseph and William, bestowed the priesthood on several Saints of Black African descent. William's liberality towards Blacks was particularly noteworthy. During his tenure as the presiding authority over the eastern branches in the years 1843–45, he ordained Black Saints Q. Walker Lewis an Elder and Joseph T. Ball a high priest in the church's priesthood, later installing Ball as the presiding elder over a church branch in Boston, Massachusetts. Both men were radical abolitionists in Massachusetts.[5] William later resided with the Restoration's most renowned Black couple, Elijah and Mary Ann Ables, while he was preaching in Cincinnati in the year 1850.[6]

The Smith brothers' progressiveness in extending full privileges of priesthood and leadership positions to nineteenth-century Black

A Slave Auction, in Edmund Ollier,
Cassell's History of the United States,
3 vols. (London: Cassell Petter & Galpin,
1874–77), 3:199.

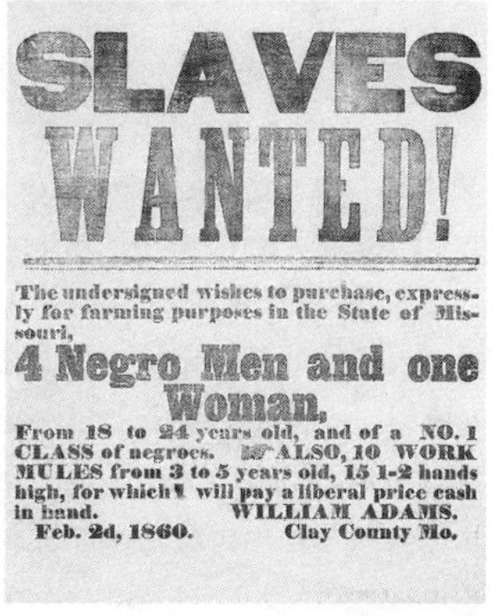

Broadside printed in Clay
County, Missouri, 1860.

Saints was notable, and Katharine shared those views. When the Salisburys were driven from Missouri in the winter of 1838–39, Katharine felt that the principal reason was due to the differing political ideologies of the Saints and the Missourians, most especially regarding the issue of slavery. Her recollection was that "most of us [the Saints] were persons of education and refinement, from the best New York and New England families, and were people of progressive ideas and strong antislavery sentiments." Katharine went so far as to describe the Saints as "New England abolitionists," which stance, if true, obviously conflicted with her Missouri neighbors, whom Katharine described as being "mortal enemies to all persons endowed with New England ideas in regard to the iniquity of negro slavery."[7]

For Katharine's children, the realities of slavery became decidedly more poignant during the family's brief stay in Alexandria, Missouri, in 1846. Solomon described how his family was living in town that fall when they happened upon a town square auction for people who were enslaved. The ten-year-old youth vividly recalled witnessing more than eighty enslaved people being sold at auction that day, describing the "heart-breaking sobs and pleadings of the mothers as their children were torn from their arms and sold to distant parts of the country." The trauma of that scene left an indelible impression on Solomon and presumably other members of the family, something he never forgot.[8]

Political Clash

The area of Webster and Fountain Green, where the Salisburys had long resided, was first settled by Southerners. The first permanent White settlers in town were the family of Ute and Sally Perkins in the year 1826, who were born in North Carolina and joined the Saints in 1839.[9] They were soon followed by other Southern families, who ended up dominating local government in those early decades, until the time of the Saints' influx in the 1840s. By the 1850s the number of those from the South made up only 25 percent of households, and that number had shrunk to 17 percent by the 1860s, but the convergence of those from North and South created tension within Hancock County during the time of the Civil War and continued for decades thereafter.[10]

Don Carlos Salisbury's Civil War Service

The Salisburys' political ideology meant they were decidedly on the Union side. Two of Katharine's children, Alvin and Don Carlos, enlisted for Civil War service early in 1861. Don Carlos was mustered in as part of the 16th Illinois Volunteer Infantry on May 24, 1861, at Quincy, Illinois, enlisting for a three-year commitment.

Alvin had enlisted at the same time but was sent home before being sworn in, probably because he could not make the three-year commitment required of recruits at that time.[11] In a twist of fate, the commander of Don Carlos's regiment was none other than Robert F. Smith of Carthage, Illinois. Smith was the justice of the peace during the time Joseph and Hyrum Smith were arrested in June 1844 and served as Captain of the Carthage Greys, the troop left in charge of protecting the Smith brothers on the day they were murdered in Carthage Jail.[12] Don Carlos never recorded if he was treated any differently by Captain Smith during his time as a soldier due to his being a nephew of Joseph Smith. Perhaps he kept his identity hidden from his commanding officer. The 16th Illinois Infantry apparently stood out from other regiments, the local newspaper reporting that "the men drill six hours and the officers twice each day. All are improving very fast, and with the determination to have this regiment among the best in the state."[13]

Photograph ca. 1861 of Don Carlos Salisbury, 1841–1919. Don Carlos served in the Civil War from 1861 to 1864. Courtesy of Mary Dennis.

Don Carlos enlisted in the war out of a sense of duty. During his three years of service in the states of Missouri, Tennessee, and Georgia, he participated in battles at Utica, Missouri, the Battle of Island Number Ten, and battles at Shiloh, Farmington, Resaca, and Rome.[14] During his training at Quincy, Salisbury indicated that

Confederate flag captured by Don Carlos Salisbury when he led the charge at Utica, Missouri, driving the Confederates from the region. Courtesy of the Illinois State Military Museum in Springfield, Illinois. Department of Military Affairs, Springfield, Illinois.

his company was in "good spirits for we think we may have a little fun with Missouri."[15] His supposition was correct, and the high-point of his military service was securing the railroad line that ran from Hannibal to St. Joseph, Missouri, and participating in a battle with Confederates at Utica, Missouri. During the latter battle, Don Carlos led the charge that drove out the Confederates, where he personally captured the enemies' flag. He was promoted for his bravery to the office of corporal, and for many years thereafter the flag he captured would hang in a museum in Springfield, Illinois, with a label crediting Don Carlos with its capture. Much like the Saints in Utah, the Salisburys felt the fierce fighting in northwest Missouri was a kind of divine retribution on the state for having driven out the Saints in the 1830s.[16]

Writing in 1862 to his brother Alvin, Don Carlos expressed how much he longed to see his family. However, his sense of duty outweighed his desire to return home and gave him grit to endure the hardships of the war. "When I think of you I think of my country," wrote the young soldier, "and the thought strikes me that I would not enjoy myself at home until peace is restored to this once happy country." He linked his military service with his commitment to God: "I have set my heart on something higher than worldly affairs," he wrote ardently, praising the faith that allowed him to find happiness "under all misfortunes." Like thousands of others enmeshed in this ambiguous and bloody war, he found in his faith strength to face even death: "There is one happy thought that bear them [Christians] up and that is if they don't meet again in this world they will meet in heaven."[17] Don Carlos also wrote to his older cousin Mariah, instructing her to assure her mother, Sophronia, that he was "a second Lamoni [Moroni] to her."[18] Sophronia and Mariah and been instrumental in raising Don Carlos during his late teens, which included enrolling him in a cadet school near their home, which had prepared him for success as a soldier.[19] He had not forgotten the upbringing and education they had provided for him.

Like most mothers, Katharine worried about her son during his three years of service, sending Frederick or Alvin to the post office each week to retrieve his letters and to purchase a Chicago newspaper, which the family anxiously scanned to see if Don Carlos's name appeared on the list of soldiers killed in battle.[20] That fear was warranted, because Don Carlos fought in some of the bloodiest battles of the war, especially during the Battle of Shiloh. Katharine prayed intently during those years that God would spare her son's life.[21] He fulfilled his three-year enlistment, being discharged in the month of May 1864 at Rome, Georgia, while suffering simultaneously from pneumonia, scurvy, and a case of the measles at the time of his release.[22]

Alvin's Murder

By the decade of the 1870s, the animosity towards the Salisburys had softened some, mainly due to the improved reputation of the family, whose respect from their neighbors had been hard earned. An apparent exception was their closest neighbors, the Joshua and

Martha Louisa Duff family, who had migrated from the southern states of Kentucky and Tennessee and built their home just east of Katharine's in Fountain Green. Political differences that divided Hancock County during the Civil War became more personal as the two family's differing ideologies collided living in such proximity. Hostility toward the Salisburys might have also had a religious undercurrent, as Joshua Duff's mother Mary and his sister Frances had both joined the branch at Macedonia decades earlier, received their endowments in the Nauvoo Temple in 1846, and migrated with the branch to Iowa in 1847. Both Frances and Mary eventually returned from Iowa to Fountain Green, but their earlier affiliation with the Saints had created a religious split in the family and likely contributed to the animosity the Duffs held for the Salisburys.[23]

Frederick Salisbury (left), with his nephew, Newton Duke, ca. 1860s. Photographer unknown. Courtesy of Carla Duke.

In the early 1870s, political and religious differences between the two families spilled into violence. The Salisburys described the Duffs as "roughs from Tennessee," and had heard them boast on occasion that they were "half alligator and half horse."[24] Not long after Katharine's home was finished in Fountain Green in 1872, she and her son Frederick celebrated its completion by hosting a dance party at their residence. One of the Duff sons, probably twenty-two-year-old Thomas Duff, was so crude during the evening's festivities that Frederick felt it necessary to have him removed from the premises. Frederick didn't feel as though hard feelings would persist beyond that evening, but when he visited the Duff home a few weeks later, the family returned the slight. According to a later account, several of the Duff boys "attacked him [Frederick] violently, at first with their tongues, and afterwards with hammer and tongs."[25] Frederick managed to escape the scene without significant injury but grew increasingly more vigilant about his safety when dealing with his near neighbors thereafter. Katharine and her children began referring to the stretch of road between her home and the Duff place as "Devil's Lane."[26] The situation was developing into something akin to the Hatfields versus the McCoys, characteristic of the animosity that persisted between Northerners and Southerners in post–Civil War America.[27]

Late one evening in the ensuing summer, Frederick, his older sister Lucy, and one of Lucy's small children were walking down "Devil's Lane." As they passed by the Duff home, members of the Duff family unexpectedly began firing pistol shots from inside their home at the three. Their target was Frederick, but one bullet came so near killing Lucy that it passed through her hair, singing her scalp, while another passed through Frederick's coat collar, grazing his neck. Lucy grabbed her child and fled for her mother's home a few hundred yards away. After Frederick's earlier violent exchange with the Duffs, he was prepared for just such an encounter and had armed himself for his protection. After recovering his senses, Frederick returned fire toward the Duff home. He overheard Joshua Duff, the family's father, call for his rifle, swearing that he "could bring the d——d scoundrel down with that [gun]," causing Frederick to make a sprint for his mother's home.[28]

While no one was materially harmed on either side in the skirmish, the incident obviously increased Katharine's worry for her family's safety. Though her boys were now adults, being a widow in a rural location adjacent to hostile neighbors brought additional fear for her own safety. Katharine and Frederick attempted to prosecute the Duffs over the incident, and Thomas Duff and his father Joshua were each required to pay eight hundred dollars bail. The Duffs, in turn, attempted to defend themselves by prosecuting Frederick.[29] Katharine frantically wrote to her first cousin George A. Smith and Brigham Young in the Salt Lake Valley for money to hire a lawyer to prosecute the case against the Duffs, whom she described as "men that will Swear to anything to clear themselves."[30] Although Brigham Young and George A. Smith had paid for Katharine's home the previous year, they declined getting involved in her legal difficulty.[31] Neither lawsuit was successful, and the case was eventually dropped, but animosity between the two families persisted.[32]

Sometime later, Frederick spotted Thomas Duff hiding behind a tree in the woods near the property line, possibly intending to ambush him. However, Frederick discovered his hiding spot before Duff saw him, sneaked up behind him, pulled out his revolver, and pointed it in his direction. This time it was Frederick's turn to intimidate Duff. He marched him out of the woods some distance ahead of him, assuredly threatening Duff to keep his distance from Frederick's family before eventually letting him go.[33] Frederick's nephew Herbert Salisbury, who was only a boy during the developing feud, recounted his belief that "we could have tamed them [Duff boys]" during the 1870s, "but the damned old rebel county would not have been easy on us."[34]

By the time he reached maturity, Katharine's second-eldest son, Alvin (Frederick's older brother), was tall and muscular like all his Smith uncles. Standing over six feet in height, he held in common with his Smith predecessors a love of wrestling and was described as one of the strongest men in Hancock County.[35] When Alvin's cousin Samuel H. B. Smith visited the Salisburys during his missionary travels, Alvin's first inclination was to test his strength against his stout cousin, who was his same age. Samuel H. B. recalled that almost immediately after he arrived at his aunt Katharine's home in the summer of 1860, he found that Alvin was "very anxious to try his strength with me, being taller and every way stronger than myself." The two tussled back and forth for some time, with neither man claiming victory. Samuel H. B. expressed his relief in his journal at how Alvin had somehow failed in his several attempts to throw him despite Alvin's superior strength.[36]

Alvin was quick-tempered and because of his physical prowess, did not shy away from conflict. The religious and political discrimination he had experienced during his formative years had an influence on his developing temperament. Descendants speculated that growing up without a father also had an effect.[37] When all his family linked themselves with the RLDS Church in the 1870s, he remained distant for another seven years. When he eventually joined in 1879, his commitment was short-lived because he was excommunicated a few months later for "apostasy."[38]

Because the Salisburys had been instrumental in the resurgence of the Restoration in the Fountain Green area in the early 1870s, that development increased fears for a time among some of the old settlers. "Now, don't think the people had forgotten who we were, for they had not," recalled Solomon of that post–Civil War era. Once he and his brothers began laboring to build up the Pilot Grove RLDS Branch in the region, Solomon recalled how "the fun commenced in earnest now. I was the first convert baptized in Pilot Grove Township since they had driven the Mormons out. Oh, horror! They could not stand for that!" Solomon was also serving as the township's tax collector at the time and recounted how rumors swirled that he would somehow steal all their tax money. Some of his neighbors used that as an excuse not to pay their taxes.[39] Though Alvin wasn't affiliated with the RLDS Church

Alvin Salisbury, 1838–80. Photograph ca. 1870, photographer unknown. Courtesy of Carla Duke.

during the first half of the 1870s, he resented the way his brother Solomon had been treated.

Frederick married Mary J. Brewer on December 3, 1874. Alvin incredulously watched as Mary's parents, Thomas and Sarah Brewer, disowned her for "marrying into the Smith family of Mormonism." The antipathy directed towards the Salisburys was likely intensified due to political differences because the Brewer family hailed from South Carolina and Kentucky.[40] These resurgent experiences of religious and political prejudice, along with the repeated exchanges between his brother Frederick and the Duffs, rekindled Alvin's animosity toward these families.

During the summer of 1880, forty-two-year-old Alvin experienced his own clash with Thomas Duff. Although the circumstances of that encounter are unknown, Thomas Duff, who was ten years younger than Alvin, had threatened Alvin with bodily harm on that occasion, something Alvin would not have received well.[41] Alvin appears to have demonstrated uncharacteristic restraint at the time, as Duff was described as being short and portly, and both men knew Duff would not stand a chance in a scuffle with Alvin.[42] Judging from previous encounters between the families, if Alvin brushed off his threat during this exchange, it probably served only to increase Duff's wrath. Tensions were brewing between the two men.

On the late summer evening of August 20, 1880, Republicans held a political rally at Fountain Green's Presbyterian Church in support of James A. Garfield's run for the presidency. Alvin had only recently switched his loyalty to the Republican Party and had been involved in the festivities that evening, donning a uniform and carrying a lamp as part of the procession of the local "Garfield and Arthur Club." The festivities brought out most of the town folk from Fountain Green and nearby Webster, Republicans and Democrats alike, and the church was filled to overflowing, with many standing in the churchyard listening to the proceedings. During one of the speeches that evening, Alvin stood just outside the front doors visiting with Jack Mull, a Democratic leader in the area, who questioned Alvin about why he turned Republican. After sharing a few thoughts

Presbyterian Church, Fountain Green, Illinois, ca. 1906.

with Mull, Alvin quipped, "Show me a democrat and I will show you a drunkard." Unbeknown to Alvin, Thomas Duff was within earshot of his conversation and interjected loudly, "My old father is a democrat, and he is not a drunkard, and I don't like to hear his party abused." Alvin responded, "Keep your mouth shut, I am not talking to you, [and] if you don't I'll make you shut it." Duff retorted, "My mouth is my own, and I will use it when I please."[43] Duff then insulted Alvin's deceased father, referring to Jenkins as the one who was a drunk.[44]

That comment was the tipping point for Alvin, and from there all mayhem broke loose. While Alvin simply expected a fist fight with his belligerent neighbor, Duff had come that night prepared for something more sinister. Still smarting from the quarrel he had with Alvin weeks earlier, Duff chose that night to follow through on his earlier threat, and Alvin's political comment was just the opening he needed.[45] Duff had previously tried to shoot Frederick over a minor disagreement, and he now similarly sought revenge against Alvin.

Alvin asked for someone to hold his lamp, but bystanders had retreated by this point. He instead threw his lamp to the ground and came at Duff. Little did Alvin know that Duff was carrying a large, double-sided bowie knife and, in the dusk of evening, apparently did not see him extract it from its sheath. Bowie knives were a common weapon in nineteenth-century America, and some were more than ten inches in length.[46] As Alvin swung, Duff slashed Alvin's left forearm with his knife, severing all the muscles in that arm and causing it to fall limply by his side. Duff then swung his knife again, cutting Alvin's chest, making a four-inch gash that nearly penetrated his sternum. As Alvin reeled back in pain, hunched over, Duff struck a fatal blow, sinking his knife deep into Alvin's forehead, spinning Alvin nearly around. Alvin then "put his hand to the wound and reeled away saying 'I am cut,' and mistaking the edges of [his] the fractured skull for the knife blade, which he evidently thought had been broken off in the wound, asked those who were present to take it [the knife] out." During the fray, Duff had attempted to make it look as though Alvin had been the aggressor, and even after the final stabbing kept repeating, "take that man away [from me]." After the final blow, Duff quickly mounted his horse and hurriedly rode to his home in the countryside several miles away.[47]

As evidence of Alvin's strength, he never fell to the ground. Holding his hand over his head wound, he walked the thirty yards back to the church unassisted, where the political rally was still underway. What a sensation it created as Alvin entered the standing-room-only church, bleeding profusely from multiple wounds and calling out, "Is there a doctor in the house?" Alvin remained conscious just long enough to identify his assailant as Thomas Duff, whom bystanders had also recognized. Alvin held on for several more hours, passing away under the care of local physician Leonard T. Ferris, between ten and eleven that same night.[48] If Katharine was not present at the rally, she likely arrived in time to see her son before he passed. The gruesome scene was forever etched in her memory.

In the interim, Thomas Duff rode home and picked up his father, Joshua, and the two galloped immediately to Carthage that same evening to obtain a constable. Duff recounted to the Carthage authority a version of the fight that made him look like the victim. Duff's rendering of the incident didn't hold much credibility once the constable arrived in Fountain Green the next morning, however, as there were dozens of witnesses to the incident, and Duff had gone into hiding. Duff was immediately located and arrested in the nearby town of La Harpe and, in another twist of irony, was held in Carthage Jail, the same location where Katharine's brothers had been murdered decades earlier. Here Duff remained for the next six months, awaiting trial for the murder of Alvin Salisbury.[49]

1880 Sketch of Carthage Jail. Thomas Duff was held in Carthage Jail while awaiting trial for the murder of Alvin Salisbury. It is the same jail where Salisbury's uncles Hyrum and Joseph Smith were murdered thirty-six years earlier. Thomas Gregg, *History of Hancock County, Illinois* (Chicago: Chas. C. Chapman, 1880), 279.

During the trial in March 1881, the prosecution argued that Thomas Duff provoked the assault to commit the deed, which meant the killing was premeditated. Duff's lawyers argued it was self-defense, contending that Alvin, a much larger man, had initiated the fight and that Duff was simply defending himself. Had Duff been convicted of the earlier shooting incident with Frederick seven years earlier, it would have strengthened the prosecution's case. After persuasive arguments on both sides, Duff was ultimately convicted of the lesser crime of manslaughter and was sentenced to only five years in the penitentiary.[50]

The verdict was obviously upsetting to the Salisburys, who felt Duff's light sentence was due to the jury being composed of "southern sympathizers and children of the men that mobbed Joseph and Hyrum Smith."[51] That sentiment regarding religious prejudice was possible, as anti-Mormon sentiment in Hancock County persisted among long-time residents well into the twentieth century.[52] Ten of the twelve jurors either had ties to the South or were from Carthage, Illinois, possibly contributing either to political or religious bias.[53] Not long after Thomas's conviction and to the great relief of the Salisbury family, the Duff family moved from the area, probably due to their tarnished reputation.[54]

According to family members, Katharine was prostrate with grief from Alvin's death.[55] Like most parents who have lost a child, it was something she never fully recovered from, especially as she tried to comprehend the unexplainable death of her son that fateful August night. His murder in the county and Duff's incarceration in Carthage Jail while awaiting trial, brought painful reminders of the murder of her brothers Joseph and Hyrum thirty-six years earlier. Not long after his murder, Alvin's widow, Mahala, and their four children left Illinois for Kansas, never to return, and their involvement with Katharine and the rest of the family was minimal after they relocated.[56] That must have been additionally painful for Katharine, because she felt bereft of Alvin's entire family after his murder.

Alvin Salisbury gravestone, Webster Cemetery, Webster, Illinois. Photograph by Kyle R. Walker, 2021.

Fountain Green's residents were sympathetic to the Salisburys' loss. That compassion seemingly overrode former animosities regarding her connection to Joseph Smith. On Sunday, August 22, an immense crowd gathered to pay their respects to the Salisbury family, the crowd being so large that Alvin's funeral had to be moved from the Majorville Methodist Church, where Alvin occasionally attended, to the much larger Presbyterian Church in Fountain Green. It was the same location where his murder had taken place, and after the funeral the large entourage followed the family to Webster Cemetery, some two miles away, where Alvin was interred.[57] The outpouring of support the Salisburys received from the community was especially comforting to Katharine and her surviving children. The funeral procession and packed church revealed an acceptance and support that the family had not experienced since moving to Fountain Green some thirty years earlier.

Notes

1. Staker added, "Palmyra operated at least four stations on the Underground Railroad where slaves moved north to the border." Mark Lyman Staker, *Hearken, O Ye People: The Historical Setting for Joseph Smith's Ohio Revelations* (Salt Lake City: Greg Kofford Books, 2009), 120.
2. Quoted in Staker, *Hearken, O Ye People*, 121.
3. Staker, *Hearken, O Ye People*, 122.
4. According to Staker, *Hearken, O Ye People*, "Geauga County was the last stop on the Underground Railroad just before runaways crossed over Lake Erie into Canada" (29–30).
5. W. Paul Reeve, *Religion of a Different Color: Race and the Mormon Struggle for Whiteness* (New York: Oxford University Press, 2015), 106–9; Connell O'Donovan, "The Mormon Priesthood Ban and Elder Q. Walker Lewis: 'An Example for His More Whiter Brethren to Follow,'" *John Whitmer Historical Association Journal* 26 (2006): 66–71; Connell O'Donovan, "Joseph T. Ball, 1804–1861: Mormonism's First African American High Priest," unpublished manuscript, 2011, 6, copy in author's possession courtesy of O'Donovan; "Religious Notices," *Prophet* 1, no. 12 (October 12, 1844): 3; Kyle R. Walker, *William B. Smith: In the Shadow of a Prophet* (Salt Lake City: Greg Kofford Books, 2015), 436–38. Joseph and Emma Smith also befriended Jane Manning James, an early Black convert who was invited to live and work with them at the Mansion House in Nauvoo. Joseph offered to have Jane adoptively

sealed as a child into his family, an offer she refused due to misunderstanding about what the ordinance entailed. Quincy D. Newell, *Your Sister in the Gospel: The Life of Jane Manning James, A Nineteenth-Century Black Mormon* (New York: Oxford University Press, 2019), 48–50.

6. Toward the end of his life, William shared his views on race during a time when there was ongoing debate among RLDS leaders regarding ordaining Blacks to the priesthood in the latter part of the nineteenth century. William explicated his perspective in a letter he wrote to the *Saints' Herald* in 1892: "The constitution of these United States makes no distinction in the human family; all men are born free and equal." Smith quoted the apostle Paul that "God has made of one blood all nations." "If such are the facts founded upon a just law," Smith argued, "by what authority have we the right to say that a colored man has no right to be ordained to all the powers of the priesthood, necessary for the building up of the Church of Christ in any part of the world, among any race of people, whether black or white." "Extracts from Letters," *Saints' Herald* 39, no. 40 (October 1, 1892): 631. William D. Russell documented how Joseph III retreated from his initial (1860s) liberality toward Blacks and that by the 1890s he warned "against haste in ordaining Negro men," instead advocating for "separating the races in church and establishing separate branches where practicable so that black priesthood could minister to their own race." William D. Russell, "A Priestly Role for a Prophetic Church: The RLDS Church and Black Americans," *Dialogue: A Journal of Mormon Thought* 12, no. 2 (Summer 1979): 39–41, 45–46. William Smith thus took a decided stance against his nephew's position during this period. W. Paul Reeve, *Religion of a Different Color*, 21–23, 195–97, 205–6; Walker, *William B. Smith*, 435–42.

7. "Reminiscences of Joseph Smith: As Told by His Sister, Catherine Smith Salisbury, to Her Grandson, Herbert S. Salsibury," *Saints' Herald* 60, no. 41 (October 8, 1913): 982–84. Herbert quotes his grandmother at length in this article.

8. "Celebrated S. J. Salisbury's 89th Birthday, Sunday," *Carthage Republican* 71, no. 38 (September 17, 1924): 2.

9. Ute was a Revolutionary War veteran, and he and his extended family formed the nucleus of Saints in the community that eventually expanded to approximately five hundred by the year 1842. Susan Sessions Rugh, *Our Common Country: Family Farming, Culture, and Community in the Nineteenth-Century Midwest* (Bloomington & Indianapolis: Indian University Press, 2001), 3; Thomas Gregg, *History of Hancock County, Illinois* (Chicago: Chas. C. Chapman, 1880), 232.

10. Rugh, *Our Common Country*, 25, 40–41.

11. H.[erbert] S. Salisbury, "The Western Adventures of Don Carlos Salisbury," San Rafael, CA, unpublished typescript, ca. 1945, 5, Hancock County Historical Society, Carthage, IL; Charles J. Scofield, ed., *History*

of Hancock County Illinois (Chicago: Munsell Publishing, 1921), 1347. On Alvin's enlistment and early discharge, see "Camp Wood," *Quincy Whig and Republican* 24, no. 9 (June 1, 1861): 3; Solomon J. Salisbury, *Reminiscences of an Octogenarian* (self-pub., ca. 1922), 9; Frederick V. Salisbury, "Teaching and Testimonies of My Mother," Unpublished typescript, ca. 1928, 18, Hancock County Historical Society, Carthage, IL.

12. Dallin H. Oaks and Marvin S. Hill, *Carthage Conspiracy: The Trial of the Accused Assassins of Joseph Smith* (Chicago: University of Illinois Press, 1975), 18–21, 218. For an alternative view of Robert F. Smith's role at Carthage, see Alex D. Smith, "The Day Joseph Smith was Killed: A Carthage Woman's Perspective," *BYU Studies* 58, no. 2 (2019): 105–12.

13. "Camp Matters," 24, no. 11 *Quincy Whig and Republican* (June 15, 1861): 3. Katharine's older brother William also enlisted for Civil War service just seventy miles upriver at Rock Island, IL, in the year 1863. While he was too old to enlist, he misstated his age making it appear that he was ten years younger than his actual age. He served primarily in the state of Arkansas during his year and a half of service. Kyle R. Walker, *William B. Smith: In the Shadow of a Prophet* (Salt Lake City: Greg Kofford Books, 2015), 442–57.

14. Newton Bateman, Paul Selby, and Charles J. Scofield, eds., *Historical Encyclopedia of Illinois and History of Hancock County* (Chicago: Munsell Publishing, 1921), 1347.

15. Don Carlos Salisbury (Quincy, IL) to Mother, Brothers, and Sister, May 8, 1861. L. Tom Perry Special Collections, Harold B. Lee Library, Brigham Young University, Provo, UT.

16. Herbert S. Salisbury, "The Western Adventures of Don Carlos Salisbury," 1, unpublished typescript, San Rafael, CA, Hancock County Historical Society, Carthage, IL. Don Carlos was "promoted to the rank of a non-commissioned officer for gallantry at Utica." Bateman, et al., *Historical Encyclopedia of Illinois and History of Hancock County*, 1347. Brett D. Dowdle, "'What Means This Carnage?': The Civil War in Mormon Thought," in *Civil War Saints*, ed. Kenneth L. Alford (Provo, UT: Religious Studies Center, Brigham Young University, 2012), 107–25.

17. Don Carlos Salisbury (Tuscumbia, AL) to Dear Brother Alvin [Salisbury], August 28, 1862, L. Tom Perry Special Collections, Harold B. Lee Library, Brigham Young University, Provo, UT.

18. D.[on] C.[arlos] Salisbury (Tuscumbia, AL) to Mariah Woolley, August 28, 1862, L. Tom Perry Special Collections, Harold B. Lee Library, Brigham Young University, Provo, UT. Since Lamoni was a convert-king in the Book of Mormon, it seems most likely that, in a mental slip, he confused Lamoni with "Moroni," the latter a noted military hero in the Book of Mormon.

19. "Don Carlos Salisbury. Died," *Carthage Republican* 46, no. 16 (April 16, 1919): 1.
20. Salisbury, "Western Adventures of Don Carlos Salisbury," 2.
21. Warren L. Van Dine, "Catharine Smith Salisbury," unpublished typescript, 16, paper presented at the Smith Family Reunion, 1973, CHL.
22. Bateman et al., *Historical Encyclopedia of Illinois and History of Hancock County*, 1347; Salisbury, "Western Adventures of Don Carlos Salisbury," 1 and n5 added by Winfield W. Salisbury.
23. Mary Duff, a widow, along with her daughter Frances joined the Church of Jesus Christ of Latter-day Saints while living near Fountain Green, IL, and received their endowments in the Nauvoo Temple on February 7, 1846. They migrated with the Macedonia Branch when the Mormons were driven out of the area and appear in the Macedonia Branch minutes in Council Bluffs, IA, in 1847. However, they returned to Hancock County, IL, by the late 1840s and did not migrate with other members of the branch to the Salt Lake valley. Macedonia Branch Record, 1839–1850, 67, CHL; Devery S. Anderson and Gary James Bergera, eds., *The Nauvoo Endowment Companies, 1845–1846: A Documentary History* (Salt Lake City: Signature Books, 2005), 615; 1850 United States Census, Hancock County, IL, James and Frances Westfall.
24. Herbert S. Salisbury (San Rafael, CA) to Catherine Groom, February 24, 1944, Community of Christ Library-Archives, Independence, MO.
25. "Shooting Affair Near Fountain Green," *Carthage Gazette* 8, no. 52 (June 11, 1873): 3.
26. Herbert S. Salisbury, "History of Salisburys, Part II, Life of Don Carlos [Salisbury] after His Return to Illinois [1866], Including Herbert's Description of His Own Life (1870 up to 1945)," unpublished typescript, ca. 1945, 4, copy in author's possession.
27. While the family and community structure was more expansive in the feud between the Hatfields and McCoys, there are a number of parallels to the ongoing conflict between the Salisburys and the Duffs. One of the earliest clashes between the Hatfields and McCoys also occurred at a large political gathering where an argument ensued, where a knife was used in the scrap, and where Ellison Hatfield was murdered after being stabbed twenty-four times. Altina L. Waller, *Feud: Hatfields, McCoys and Social Change in Appalachia, 1860–1900* (Chapel Hill: University of North Carolina Press, 1988), 3–4.
28. "Shooting Affair Near Fountain Green," 3.
29. "Shooting Affair Near Fountain Green," 3.
30. Katharine Salisbury (Fountain Green, IL) to George A. Smith and Brigham Young, July 25, 1873, George A. Smith Papers, 1834–1875, Incoming letters, R-Y, CHL.

31. George A. Smith (Salt Lake City) to Catherine Smith Salisbury, August 6, 1873, Historian's Office letterpress copybooks, 1854–1879, vol. 3, CHL.

32. "Shooting Affair Near Fountain Green," 3; "Further Particulars of the Affair," *Carthage Gazette* 16, no. 13 (September 4, 1880), 3.

33. Salisbury to Groom, February 24, 1944.

34. Salisbury to Groom, February 24, 1944.

35. Salisbury to Groom, February 24, 1944.

36. Samuel H. B. Smith, Reminiscences and Diary, 1856 April–1863 July, entries for late June and early July 1860, p. 19, CHL.

37. Van Dine, "Catharine Smith Salisbury," 23.

38. Pilot Grove Reorganized Branch Minutes, holograph, 60, Community of Christ Library-Archives, Independence, MO.

39. Salisbury, *Reminiscences of an Octogenerian*, 10–12.

40. Van Dine, "Catharine Smith Salisbury," 24–25.

41. "The Duff Trial Concluded, Verdict of the Jury," *Carthage Gazette* 16, no. 42 (March 26, 1881): 3.

42. "Terrible Tragedy," *Carthage Gazette* 16, no. 12 (August 28, 1880): 3.

43. "Terrible Tragedy," 3; "The Duff Trial Concluded," 3.

44. "The Tragedy at Fountain Green Last Friday Night—Duff Held to Answer, Without Bail," *Quincy Daily Whig* 29 (August 27, 1880), 2.

45. "The Duff Trial Concluded," 3.

46. Robert M. Ireland, "The Problem of Concealed Weapons in Nineteenth-Century Kentucky," *Register of the Kentucky Historical Society* 91, no. 4 (Autumn 1993): 370–85.

47. "Further Particulars of the Affair," 3.

48. "Terrible Tragedy," 3.

49. "Terrible Tragedy," 3.

50. "The Duff Trial Concluded," 3.

51. Salisbury to Groom, February 24, 1944.

52. See interviews with longtime Hancock County residents John LaCroix, Paul J. McKoon, James W. Moffitt, Estel Neff, and Louis Pilkington in *Modern Perspectives on Nauvoo and the Mormons: Interviews with Long-Term Residents*, comp. Larry E. Dahl and Don Norton (Provo, UT: Religious Studies Center, Brigham Young University, 2003), 121, 168, 182–87, 193, 200–201, 295–96.

53. The twelve jurors were S. B. Dodd (born in Tennessee), Joe Kirkendoll (from Ohio, spouse from Kentucky), Nathan Dowd (born in Connecticut), James Roseberry (from Carthage), Reuben Garnett (parents born in Kentucky), Lemuel Crow (born in Missouri), Isaac Willy (from Carthage), William G. Allison (born in Virginia), James Ewing (from Carthage), Wesley Lane (from Carthage), Emile Kunz (unknown), and William McClellan (from Warsaw, spouse born in Kentucky). For the

list of jurors, see, "Circuit Court," *Carthage Gazette* 16, no. 41, March 19, 1881, 3.

54. Joshua Duff, Iowa, U.S., Wills and Probate Records, 1871–1952, Probate Case Files, 1873–1926, boxes 28–30, Decatur County Courthouse, Decatur, IA; Marriage Record of Thomas B. Duff and Sophia Johnson, March 2, 1889, Custer County, NE, Marriage Records, State Library and Archives, Nebraska State Historical Society, Lincoln, NE.

55. Warren L. Van Dine, "Statement About His Salisbury Family," unpublished typescript, 1975, 30–34, copy in author's possession.

56. Salisbury to Groom, February 24, 1944; Van Dine, "Statement About His Salisbury Family," 34.

57. "Terrible Tragedy," 3; Susan Sessions Rugh, *Our Common Country: Family Farming, Culture, and Community in the Nineteenth-Century Midwest* (Bloomington: Indiana University Press, 2001), 154.

CHAPTER SIXTEEN

A Season of Peace, 1885–1900

There is something in the aged woman, in the knowledge of her long and strange experiences, that attracts the attention of all who hear her.
—Reporter from the *Kansas City Daily Journal*

THE TRAGEDY OF ALVIN'S DEATH paradoxically marked a turning point for Katharine and her descendants. That softening towards the Salisburys was evident in the way neighbors interacted with Katharine and her children in subsequent decades. The religious animosity so evident in earlier years began to subside, allowing the family to fully integrate into their community. Katharine gradually gained esteem with locals because of her connection to the earliest history of Hancock County, and her closing years were the most peaceful of her life. All her children lived within forty miles of her home, and her health was robust enough that she was able to visit regularly. Two of her adult children preceded her in death, Alvin in 1880, and her only surviving daughter Lucy, who died of malaria on October 18, 1892, at age fifty-eight.[1]

Of all her children, she remained closest to her youngest child Frederick and his family, who shared Katharine's home for the last thirty years of her life; the little home and property Brigham Young and other Latter-day Saint leaders in the West had funded for her. She set up two rooms for herself, a small bedroom just big enough for a rocking chair and her bed, and a larger room where she kept a large loom. A grandson recalled that when they went to Katharine's home, "we would find grandmother spinning yarn to knit stockings from, weaving linsey-woolsy at her loom, or braiding straw hats."[2] She also continued to make rugs which she sold for extra income, as she had done in earlier days, and the clothing items she made became treasured heirlooms for her grandchildren.[3] Like her mother, Katharine was said to have recovered her "second sight" in later years, allowing her to read fine print without the aid of glasses.[4] She would meticulously peruse the RLDS *Saints' Herald* newspapers, often responding to issues she felt passionate about.

Some of her surviving letters to her posterity during her final years frequently had to do with the ordinary day-to-day activities related to her skill with a needle. "I wish that you would get me some calico to finish my quilt," she wrote to a granddaughter, "two and half yards of green . . . a half of light calico and one yard of handsome dark to finish my other one [quilt] and one spool of thread." She hoped to have all these materials before she traveled to a church conference in Lamoni, Iowa, where she would work on finishing the quilts.[5]

Perpetuating Faith and Values

After her eightieth birthday, Katharine felt a keen responsibility to perpetuate feminine virtues to the Saints. When she received her patriarchal blessing in 1834, not long after her marriage in Kirtland, she listened to what she held as her father's heaven-inspired counsel: "Thou shalt teach the young of thy sex virtue and sobriety, and those things which are duties of wives and mothers."[6] She was apparently intent about fulfilling that charge, which became especially evident once she was afforded a platform to express her values. Far

Quilt made by Katharine Salisbury, ca. 1880. Photograph by Lachlan Mackay, 2024. Courtesy of Community of Christ.

removed from RLDS Church headquarters after her baptism, the primary outlet she had to spread the gospel message was through the medium of letter-writing to the editors of the *Saints' Herald* newspaper. While she expressed regret that she was unable to contribute financial support to traveling missionaries, as she picked up her pen and expressed these feminine ideals it fulfilled her desire to assist in building the kingdom.[7]

During her final years, Katharine emphasized the virtues that she had learned during her youth, including prayer and scripture reading, an emphasis on supporting missionary work, and even addressing such practical matters as parenting, dress, and hairstyle. Of all these values Katharine extolled in her letters, the theme most repeated in her writings was that of appearance and dress. It was one way of demonstrating her religious piety. Most of the religions that the Smiths affiliated in Katharine's childhood stressed plainness in apparel and hairstyle. While some were less descriptive than others, the underlying reasoning was similar—maintaining unpretentiousness in appearance reflected one's devotion to the faith. Some denominations also taught that simplifying material needs demonstrated a willingness to dedicate resources to religious service, such as missionary work, while others stressed that simple dress indicated preparedness to labor in building up the kingdom of God.[8] By the middle of the nineteenth century however, attitudes about dress and grooming were shifting, so that women could now choose more widely how they would implement scriptural teachings about clothing and hairstyle. Despite this shift, many of the older generation, including Katharine, still clung to the more traditional view.[9]

Katharine felt impelled to instruct the younger generation in this more conservative fashion. She believed in dressing simple and remonstrated with those whom she perceived to be caught up in the ever-changing fashions she had witnessed during her lifetime, which spanned the entirety of the nineteenth century. In the early days of the church, all the sisters "dressed plain," described Katharine in a letter she sent to the *Saints' Herald*, directing sisters in the church to adopt a conservative fashion. Citing the New Testament teachings of Paul and Peter (1 Timothy 2:9–10; 1 Peter 3:3–4), Katharine stated that a woman's hair was to "adorn the woman" and that it was a "shame to cut it off and make bangs to dangle over the forehead and in your eyes."[10]

She also stressed the importance of keeping bonnets and dresses simple. Katharine felt clothing should be designed to be comfortable and not ostentatious, emphasizing the utility of such clothing in a pious commitment to work and serve others. At times, Katharine could be uncompromisingly strict in her writings, recommending in one instance that bonnets should be miniature, and that it was excessive to load hats with flowers or other ornamentations. She additionally reproved those who wore ruffled sleeves for being wasteful, and whose dresses had "cloth enough in them to make a child a dress!"[11] She valued the process of producing her own clothing, referencing

Katharine Salisbury, ca. 1894, by Gillett, at Lamoni, Iowa. Katharine presumably had this photo taken when she attended the RLDS general conference held at Lamoni in April 1894. Courtesy of Buddy Youngreen.

a revelation proclaimed by her brother Joseph that instructed Saints to "let your garments be plain and the workmanship of your own hands."[12] She felt that the money saved from the waste of all these "needless trimmings," could instead be utilized in supporting missionary work.[13] Katharine repeatedly emphasized these strict guidelines regarding dress and grooming in the final decade of her life.

Dressing simply was a form of religious commitment that, for her, materially demonstrated a willingness to sacrifice worldly desires and avoid pride.

One can only guess what the response was from younger generations of women in the church when they read her letters containing these strict guidelines. Her own children had grappled with their mother's conservative values earlier in life, but Katharine's notoriety and influence within the church was increasing as she moved into her eighties. Her fellow Saints appeared willing to tolerate some of her antiquated standards, which, instead of ostracizing her from the younger generation, appears to have instead had the opposite effect of endearing her to her fellow Saints. That held true within her family as well, as her posterity began looking to her for counsel and direction during her final years. She frequently instructed her grandchildren on how to launch a successful marriage as they arranged to wed, and as they prepared for parenthood, she would often cite the Biblical injunction in Proverbs 22:6, to "train up your children in the way they should go and when they are old they will not depart from it."[14]

Recollections of Early Mormonism

The other theme she most frequently addressed in her letters to the *Saints' Herald* was her reminiscences of the early church. Joseph III's publication of her sworn affidavits on topics such as polygamy, and on other items of early church history that strengthened his claim to leadership, heightened interest in her memories. She was subsequently sought out by fellow Saints and newspaper reporters alike for her recollections of these events. With her brother William's death in 1893, her last surviving sibling, it prompted her to share more of her recollections as the only surviving member of the family, ensuring that the story of early Mormonism was preserved for her family and fellow Saints. Many of these instances came when she attended the annual RLDS Conference, such as in the year 1894 in Lamoni, Iowa, when she stayed with her nephew Joseph Smith III at his spacious home, Liberty Hall. While staying there that week, she

Community of Christ (RLDS) Stone Church, Independence, Missouri, ca. early 1900s, photographer unknown.

was approached by Hubert and Oscar Case, brothers who had only recently been baptized into the RLDS Church and who were preparing for missionary service.[15] The Case brothers eagerly approached the elderly matriarch, requesting her to share "her personal testimony of the story of the Smith family, and all about the coming forth of the Book of Mormon." According to Oscar, Katharine began by telling the brothers of Joseph's First Vision, and then shared details of the coming forth of the Book of Mormon, and the spiritual peace that permeated her childhood home when they had the sacred record in their possession. An interaction with a member of the founding family of their faith was an experience the Case brothers never forgot.[16]

By the 1890s Katharine began traveling to both district and general conferences of the RLDS Church. Despite her age, she especially looked forward to traveling by train to Lamoni, Iowa, or Independence, Missouri for the annual RLDS conference, and fellowshipping with the Saints on these occasions was among her most treasured memories.[17] Her most notable contribution came at the annual conference held at the Stone Church in Independence, Missouri, during the week of April 6–14, 1895. Katharine's presence was noted by local newspaper reporters who attended the conference, where she conspicuously sat on the front row near the rostrum. Either by previous invitation, or of her own volition, Katharine spoke several times during the week-long conference. The first occasion came on Monday, April 8, and she directed her remarks to the youth who were present, encouraging them to "be faithful and true" and to "lead true and pure lives" to secure their salvation. "I have always found that to be faithful was to be loved by the Lord Jesus Christ," she reflected. She kept her remarks brief that day, disclosing that "my heart is full to overflowing and I cannot speak further."[18]

Two days later during a testimony meeting, Katharine removed her shawl from her shoulders and slowly rose from her chair, receiving assistance as she climbed the stairs to the rostrum. She was the first and most notable speaker during the meeting that day, and this time spoke for a full half hour recounting details of Moroni's visits to her brother Joseph Smith and the coming forth of the Book of Mormon. According to a reporter from the *Kansas City Times*, she was again "several times overcome with emotion during her allusion to former scenes, incidents and characters so dear to her heart and mind," and the congregation listened with "rapt attention." While she followed the general outline of Restoration history as contained in her mother's history, Katharine added unique supplementary details. She shared that when Moroni appeared to Joseph, he wore a girdle about his waist; she recounted that, following the loss of the 116 pages, Joseph fasted for several days to have the plates and Urim and Thummim returned to him; and she stated that her father and two of her brothers were the first to hear Joseph's recital of Moroni's visitations. She also identified Alvin and then Emma Hale Smith as the individuals identified by Moroni who were to accompany Joseph to the Hill Cumorah to obtain the Book of Mormon plates,[19] a detail her mother had not included in her history. The congregation was

Left: *Lucy Mack Smith*, painting by Sutcliffe Maudsley, ca. 1840s. Courtesy of the Museum of Church History, Salt Lake City. Lucy has a copy of the Book of Mormon in her right hand. Center: Katharine, presumably holding a copy of the Book of Mormon in her left hand, photography by A. T. Holmes, Indpendence, Missouri, ca. 1895. Courtesy of Community of Christ Archives. Right: Lucy Salisbuy Duke, ca. 1870s. Lucy appears to have continued the tradition of being photographed with a copy of the Book of Mormon, held in her right hand. Courtesy of Mary Dennis.

captivated. Her reminiscences made front-page news the next day in the *Kansas City Times*, and "prayers of thankfulness were offered by many members . . . for allowing the conference the privilege and blessing of having Mrs. Salisbury present."[20] "There is something in the aged woman," recounted the reporter who had listened to Katharine's gripping narrative, "in the knowledge of her long and strange experiences, that attracts the attention of all who hear her."[21]

Katharine's experience at the RLDS annual conference was remarkably like her mother's some fifty years earlier, when Lucy spoke to the Saints in Nauvoo during a general conference of held in October 1845. In both instances, mother and daughter not only recounted the early history of the Restoration from a family perspective but also sought to perpetuate spiritual values to the younger generation of sisters.[22] It was an unusual occurrence for a woman to speak at a general conference meeting in any Restoration branch during the nineteenth century, and it revealed the esteem Saints held for both Katharine and her mother.

During the final decade of her life, RLDS leaders began requesting Katharine sit with them on the stand during conferences. Though she was frail and spoke with a trembling voice, she continued recounting as many details of the early Restoration to RLDS Saints in the ensuing years as her health would allow.[23] In 1896, at the age of eighty-three, Katharine spoke to a congregation of more than two hundred RLDS Saints who had gathered for a district conference in Montrose, Iowa, across the Mississippi River from Nauvoo. She once again related the story of the "early life of her brother [Joseph] in connection with the angel's visit to him and the coming forth of the Book of Mormon, the trials and persecutions that were endured by their family from the very first claims made by her brother."[24]

By the 1890s Katharine was regarded as a living link between the early church her brother had founded and the Reorganization led by his son. Her presence on the stand was visible evidence that the Reorganization was the true successor to the original church her brother had established. Her photograph, along with images of Lucy Mack Smith and Emma Hale Smith, was even included with photos of RLDS leadership on a large stand-alone print published by the church in 1897, designed to be displayed in meetinghouses and homes throughout the church.[25] (See image on page 210.)

Last Member of the Smith Family

Katharine had benefited markedly from the support of her sisters after she had settled in rural Fountain Green. Descendants remembered that before Sophronia and Lucy's deaths, the Smith sisters often traveled together to important events or jointly supported their married children in their activities in their later years. Katharine's granddaughter Mary Salisbury Hancock recalled one such occasion when Mary's parents attended a wedding and she and her brother

Katharine with RLDS Church leaders, ca. 1896, at Burlington, Iowa. Katharine is seated front row, third from left. To her right is Alexander Hale Smith. Courtesy of Mary Dennis.

were to be babysat by Katharine and Sophronia. "This arrangement was readily acceptable at the time it was made," recalled Mary, "but not so later. Seeing me happily occupied with my blocks on the floor, my parents had slipped away. Disturbed by the void and the quiet atmosphere of the room, I looked up. There they were! Those two tall women dressed in black alpaca, hoop skirts reaching to the floor, lace neckerchiefs over their shoulders and clasped at their throats with great cameo brooches above which were the severely chiseled Smith features looking down on us. There were two outside doors in the room, and against each stood one of these black figures as though daring us to run out on them."[26] Mary thought it best not to test the resolve of her grandmother and great-aunt on that occasion.

Katharine would greatly miss the companionship of her two sisters as they each preceded her in death. Sophronia passed in the year 1876 of unknown causes.[27] Tragically, Sophronia's only surviving

Gravestone of Sophronia Smith Stoddard McCleary, Mount Auburn Cemetery, Colchester, Illinois. Photograph by Kyle R. Walker, 2003.

daughter Mariah, her two daughters and one granddaughter, all died by the year 1884, leaving Sophronia with no posterity.[28] Arthur and Lucy Millikin both died in the year 1882. Arthur of rheumatic brain fever, and Lucy of a respiratory illness. Linking Lucy with the greater Smith family, Solomon Salisbury preached Lucy's funeral sermon, summarizing her life as a continual round of being "mobbed, hated and reviled, because [she] had feared God more than man. Few have loved them [the Smiths], many have hated them. The world to come will be for them a rest; for here there was none found."[29] Fortunately for Katharine, she was surrounded by her growing posterity during the last eighteen years of her life after her sisters passed.

Left: Gravestones of Lucy Smith Millikin and Arthur Millikin, Widow Moore Cemetery, Colchester, Illinois. Photograph by Kyle R. Walker, 2003.

Below right: William B. Smith, ca. 1893. Photographer unknown. Courtesy of Gracia Jones.

Below left: William B. Smith's gravestone, Bethel Cemetery, Osterdock, Iowa. Photograph by Kyle R. Walker, 2015.

Katharine's only surviving sibling after the deaths of her sisters was William, who had also linked himself with the RLDS Church in the year 1878. He spent the final fifteen years of his life supporting his nephew's leadership, even traveling as a missionary on several occasions in his old age.[30] He occasionally visited Katharine, though those stays were infrequent due to his living hundreds of miles away in northeastern Iowa. When he came to Fountain Green, William

Katharine's photobook, housed at the L. Tom Perry Special Collections, Harold B. Lee Library, Brigham Young University. Photograph by Kyle R. Walker.

stayed at Katharine's home, where "he and [K]atharine talked long hours day after day reliving the early years of Latter Day Saintism." The two were united in their support of the Reorganization until the end of their lives, and Katharine's posterity observed how "in their old age they clung to each other like a couple of children." When William was in town, Katharine's boys arranged for him to preach in the Eagle or Hickory schoolhouses, which were within a few miles of Katharine's home.[31] Katharine lived another seven years after William's death in 1893.

Katharine also remained close to Emma and her children. The first photograph in her personal photobook was an image of Emma, and Katharine's boys acted as pallbearers at Emma's funeral in 1879, evidence of the bond between the two families.[32] While Katharine had occasional interactions with Joseph Smith III, both she and her children were closest to Joseph and Emma's third son, Alexander. Alexander often preached in Fountain Green in response to Katharine's pleadings and kept connected through writing letters and attending Katharine's annual birthday celebrations.[33] When Alexander preached in eastern Hancock County, he often shared the pulpit with his cousin Solomon, and Alexander baptized members of the Salisbury family in the decade of the 1890s.[34]

Birthday Picnic Celebrations

During her final years, the Salisburys gathered each year on July 28 for a grand birthday celebration to honor Katharine at her rural home in northeast Fountain Green. As early as 1891, newspaper reporters had learned of the gathering and were eager to interview Katharine about her reminiscences of church history within the state of Illinois. Correspondents noted her tall stature, blue eyes, and her gray hair, "in which there are yet traces of gold." "The charming old lady is a bright conversationalist," described a reporter from the *Chicago Record*, "has an excellent memory and a rich store of historical facts." She was once again depicted "as a woman who would be noticed anywhere, and in her earlier years was of a commanding presence."[35]

Katharine Salisbury birthday reunion, ca. 1890s. Katharine is seated in the second row, sixth from the left. Alexander Hale Smith, son of Joseph and Emma Hale Smith, is in the third row, fifth from left.

More than fifty relatives would typically gather on these occasions, which expanded to include friends and dignitaries in the ensuing years. "In later years, all the clan gathered," recalled Katharine's grandson Herbert S. Salisbury of these memorable birthday celebrations, "with presents for her and baskets filled with cakes, pies, fried chickens etc., for a grand picnic and feast in the house and yard."[36] The festivities included music and singing, a "bounteous" dinner, concluding with light refreshments while listening to "Aunt Katharine" share her reminiscences.[37]

Katharine prepared weeks in advance for the celebration by making a dozen or more mincemeat pies, which she stored in a thick wooden barrel that doubled as a pie safe, kept in a cool location on her property. Katharine's granddaughter Mary Salisbury Hancock said that the large oak barrel "took the place of a cave cellar & contained grandmother's meat as she usually had a well fatted calf or pig butchered each fall or winter for winter's use." When Mary peeked into the barrel on one occasion, she saw that it contained not only meat but "a large stove jar of pumpkin butter, & another of apple butter & sometimes a dozen or more mince pies which grandmother made up from the beef scraps & apples in the fall at butchering time. These pies she would always bring in one or two to heat up for our dinner."[38] If she managed the temperature correctly, these pies and other storable food items could be stored for weeks and be protected from vermin. Mary and her brother Herbert often debated over who was Katharine's favorite grandchild, largely determined by who received the largest slice of her mincemeat pie.[39] Descendants remember her laboring for days over her large cookstove in preparation for her birthday celebration, which she managed with expert skill.[40] After Katharine passed in 1900, Solomon continued the

Katharine Salisbury birthday reunion, ca. 1893, at Katharine's home in Fountain Green, Illinois. Courtesy of Mary Dennis. Katharine is seated in the middle surrounded by her grandchildren.

tradition of a Salisbury gathering on his own birthday, held each year until his death in 1927.[41]

These large Salisbury gatherings also afforded Katharine an opportunity to perpetuate her faith. Toward the end of the day's activities, she would gather her grandchildren around her and rehearse the account of her brother's First Vision and of the coming forth of the Book of Mormon. She included stories about how she personally helped protect the plates during those tense months in the fall of 1827 and recalled the ostracism and animosity that came to the family because of Joseph's theophany. When Katharine recounted how the minister rejected Joseph's First Vision experience, it aroused the ire of her posterity. Granddaughter Mary Salisbury Hancock described that when "grandmother told the story we would sit at [in] rapt attention until mention of the unbelieving preacher and the great uproar that followed." At that juncture in the story, she described how she and the other grandchildren would collectively "straighten our backs and clench our fists" in protest. The rejection of Joseph's First Vision by a Methodist minister marked the beginning of the Salisbury family narrative of persecution and religious discrimination. Notwithstanding, Katharine remained temperate when recounting the story to her grandchildren. "Now remember, children," she cautioned, "it is not for us to judge these people. It was a strange thing your uncle [Joseph] was telling them."[42]

Toward the end of her life, Katharine enjoyed riding from one end of Hancock County to the other visiting her expanding posterity. One descendant remembered that when Katharine came to visit, she would stay most of the day, and then "about four o'clock in the afternoon she would get her wraps and say to my father, 'Carry me on home, Jimmy.'" Before bed, she would have "a cup of tea, fix the latch, and go to bed at sundown."[43] In her elderly years she kept herself busy by regularly baking bread, making apple and pumpkin butter, weaving, sewing, and fixing her own meals. Not long after settling on her property, she had sent Frederick into town to purchase a good milk cow and a few chickens. Not only did the chickens provide eggs for the family, but Katharine would sell the extras to purchase groceries and material for sewing. Her cow became a pet to her, following her around the yard, and she continued the chore of morning and evening milking up to twenty-four hours before her death, an indication of her remarkable physical strength.[44]

During the final year of her life, Katharine was suffering from breast cancer. While her family feared the cancer would take her life, Joseph III, learning of her condition, promised her that condition would not lead to her death. In the closing months of 1899, she contracted a cold, which developed into pneumonia and eventually was the cause of her death on February 2, 1900.[45] James McKiernan, a prominent member of the RLDS Quorum of the Seventy, preached Katharine's funeral sermon two days later at the Webster church. Rather fittingly, her funeral was on the same site as the Saints' meetinghouse built at Ramus (later renamed Macedonia and then Webster) in the early 1840s, though no longer extant.[46] She was buried just a few blocks away in the Webster Cemetery, next to her husband and her two deceased children, Alvin and Lucy.

Katharine's life had been riddled with hardships, filled with disappointment, financial poverty, religious discrimination, and the premature death of numerous family members. Despite these overwhelming challenges, she remained remarkably resilient. She managed to raise five children to adulthood as a widow living in rural Illinois, and at the time of her death, her posterity deeply revered her as the matriarch of the family. She had experienced insufferable difficulties due to her familial connection to Joseph Smith but firmly retained her belief in his mission and successfully perpetuated that faith to her descendants.

Unlike the remainder of her siblings, religious prejudice persisted for Katharine and her children long after her brothers were murdered in nearby Carthage Jail. She watched as her sons were gradually trusted to serve in prominent civic positions in the community where they had long resided. Katharine looked on her four sons with admiration and noted the irony as each of them was appointed a justice of the peace in their respective townships and in the same county where she had endured so much injustice.[47] They also served in leadership

Katharine Salisbury gravestone, Webster Cemetery, Webster, Illinois. Photograph by Alexander L. Baugh, 2005.

positions in the RLDS Church, making dozens of converts among their former hostile neighbors and expanding the Pilot Grove RLDS branch to eighty-seven members at its height.[48] Katharine must have been gratified that, despite all the hardships she had endured, she lived long enough to see former prejudice give way to acceptance and admiration of her growing posterity.

In one interview with a newspaper reporter during her birthday celebration in the year 1894, Katharine remarked that there had been both newspaper reporters and historians that "have not always treated us right in their stories of Mormon times." Her judicious statement grossly underestimated all she had endured as a sister of the Latter-day Saint founder. She might have elaborated on the mistreatment she and her family had experienced in Fountain Green since the 1840s but chose instead to avoid the antagonism that this might have created with her neighbors. Experience had taught her to speak temperately of the past. "All we ask is justice," Katharine implored of the reporter.[49]

Solomon shared in the experience of overcoming religious discrimination in common with his mother, eventually winning over his neighbors. Initially viewed with skepticism and fear, his exemplary life ultimately led to respect for his character among neighbors. Warren H. Orr, a Hancock County attorney who later served as a judge on the Illinois Supreme Court, encapsulated the Salisburys' experience in the county in a tribute he wrote to Solomon some twenty-five years after Katharine's death. "Your life exemplifies the truth of the sometimes doubted statement that right will prevail in the end," wrote Orr. "When one reads of your early hardships and the persecutions and impositions you suffered at the hands of ignorance and poison-minded intolerance, and yet sees that you had courage enough to stand up and tolerate the weaknesses of others and finally conquer their love and respect by your own good living, it gives one greater hope for the future."[50] Illinois state senator Orville F. Berry, who had been at the Salisbury home on numerous occasions, similarly wrote, that "the world would be wonderfully

Solomon J. Salisbury and Frederick Salisbury in front of the Kirtland Temple, ca. 1915. Courtesy of Carla Duke.

well off if everyone was as good as [K]atherine Smith Salisbury."[51] These tributes evidence the way Katharine and her children eventually won the respect of their neighbors through decades of steady living. For Katharine, it was her faith that had seen her through life's challenges. She had earlier counseled Saints, "Be faithful, for there is a crown laid up for them that come up through great tribulation and faint not by the way."[52] It was a paradigm that enabled her to endure the unrelenting adversity of her remarkable life.

Notes

1. "Died—Whalen," *Saints' Herald* 39, no. 47 (November 19, 1892): 756; "Mrs. Lucy Whalen," *Upper Des Moines* (Algona, IA) 27, no. 31 (October 26, 1892): 1.

2. Herbert S. Salisbury, "History of Salisburys, Part II, Life of Don Carlos [Salisbury] after His Return to Illinois [1866], Including Herbert's Description of His Own Life (1870 up to 1945)," unpublished typescript, ca. 1945, 4, copy in author's possession.

3. Warren L. Van Dine, "Catharine Smith Salisbury," unpublished typescript, 1972, 34, Hancock County Historical Society, Carthage, Illinois.

4. Herbert S. Salisbury, "The Prophet's Sister Testifies She Lifted the B. of M. Plates," *Messenger* (Berkeley, CA) (October 1954): 1, 4. Lucy Mack Smith, *Biographical Sketches of Joseph Smith the Prophet and His Progenitors for Many Generations* (Liverpool: S. W. Richards, 1853), 208–9.

5. Katharine Salisbury (Fountain Green, IL) to unnamed granddaughter, February 11 [no year], original in possession of Estel Neff, Nauvoo, IL, copy in author's possession.

6. H. Michael Marquardt, comp., *Early Patriarchal Blessings of The Church of Jesus Christ of Latter-Day Saints* (Salt Lake City: Smith-Pettit Foundation, 2007), 18.

7. Katherine Salisbury (n.p.) to Sister Frances, December 24, 1886, *Saints' Herald* 34, no. 6 (February 5, 1887): 84.

8. Mary Anne Caton, "The Aesthetics of Absence: Quaker Women's Plain Dress in the Delaware Valley, 1790–1900," in *Quaker Aesthetics: Reflections on a Quaker Ethic in American Design and Consumption*, ed. Emma Jones Lapsansky and Anne A. Verplanck (Philadelphia: University of Pennsylvania Press, 2003), 257–58; Matthew Simpson, *Cyclopedia of Methodism* (Philadelphia: Everts & Stewart, 1878), 311; William B. Sprague, *Annals of the American Pulpit* (New York: Robert Carter & Brothers, 1858), 139; Norman Fox, "George Fox and the Early Friends," *Baptist Quarterly* 11, no. 4 (October 1877): 437.

9.   Miss Hannah Frances Rumball, "The Relinquishment of Plain Dress: British Quaker Women's Abandonment of Plain Quaker Attire, 1860–1914" (PhD thesis, University of Brighton, 2016), 132–40, 163; Caton, "The Aesthetics of Absence," 262; Karen J. Kriebel, "From Bloomers to Flappers: The American Women's Dress Reform Movement" (PhD diss., Ohio State University, 1998), 2–4.

10. Salisbury to Sister Frances, December 24, 1886.

11. Katharine Salisbury (n.p.) to Dear Sisters, July 2, 1895, *Saints' Herald* 42, no. 30 (July 24, 1895): 473.

12. Katharine wrote "workmanship," while the revelation read "work." Salisbury to Dear Sisters, July 2, 1895; Michael Hubbard MacKay et al., eds., *Documents, Volume 1: July 1828–June 1831*, vol. 1 of the Documents series of *The Joseph Smith Papers*, ed. Dean C. Jessee et al. (Salt Lake City: Church Historian's Press, 2013), 252; Doctrine and Covenants 42:40.

13. Salisbury to Dear Sisters, July 2, 1895; Salisbury to Sister Frances, December 24, 1886.

14. Van Dine, "Catharine Smith Salisbury," 33; Katharine Salisbury (Fountain Green, IL) to Dear Sisters, March 10, 1886, *Saints' Herald* 33, no. 17 (May 1, 1886): 260.

15. Earlier that same year, at an RLDS meeting held in Logan, Iowa, an elderly man arose from the audience who was seated just behind Hubert and Oscar Case. Speaking in tongues, the unnamed man laid his hands upon the two brothers and prophesied the two brothers would "be sent to far places" to preach the gospel." Hubert served a lengthy mission to French Polynesia that next year, and both Hubert and Oscar were renowned missionaries in the RLDS faith. Alice Montague Case, "A Missionary of the Church: The Life of Hubert Case," *Saints' Herald* 100, no. 1 (January 5, 1953): 10; "Oscar Case Preaches at Campus—He's Only 96," *Saints' Herald* 115, no. 17 (September 1, 1968): 606.

16. Oscar Case Reminiscence, unpublished typescript, ca. 1894, Tom and Carla Duke Papers, Burlington, IA, copy in author's possession.

17. Mary Salisbury Hancock, "The Three Sisters of the Prophet Joseph Smith, Part III," *Saints' Herald* 101, no. 4 (January 25, 1954): 23.

18. "Says He Saw Christ," *Kansas City Times* 50, no. 99 (April 9, 1895): 1.

19. Only Katharine and early supporter and convert Joseph Knight Sr. recounted the details about both Alvin and Emma being designated by the Angel Moroni to accompany Joseph to the Hill Cumorah. Dean C. Jessee, "Joseph Knight's Recollection of Early Mormon History," *BYU Studies* 17, no. 1 (1976): 31.

20. "An Angel Told Him," *Kansas City Times* 1, no. 101 (April 11, 1895): 1; See also, Kyle R. Walker, "Katharine Smith Salisbury's Recollections of Joseph's Meetings with Moroni," *BYU Studies* 41, no. 3 (2002): 4–17.

21. "Awaiting a Revelation—Story of a Winter Journey," *Kansas City Daily Journal* 37, no. 304 (April 12, 1895): 3; see also, "The Saints Don't

Agree," *Kansas City Times* 50, no. 102 (April 12, 1895): 5. Katharine continued sharing her thoughts and spiritual impressions during the week-long conference. On April 13 she recounted the miraculous way the branch of Saints completed their journey from New York to Ohio in the year 1831 under the leadership of her mother Lucy. One of the issues that was debated during conference was a question regarding the authority of the Twelve Apostles and Joseph III. Katharine went so far as to publicly censure the Saints over this debate, claiming she was visited by an angel during the previous night, who told her the church was in the wrong, and that "unless the church shall follow the prophet [Joseph Smith III] in all things the Lord would certainly send His avenging angel and punish His undutiful and disobedient people. "No Prophecies This Year," *Kansas City Daily Journal* 37, no. 306 (April 14, 1895): 3.

22. Jennifer Reeder and Kate Holbrook, eds., *At the Pulpit: 185 Years of Discourses by Latter-Day Saint Women* (Salt Lake City: Church Historian's Press, 2017), 3–5.

23. "Awaiting a Revelation—Story of a Winter Journey," 3.

24. "Latter Day Saints—The Meeting at Montrose, Ia.—A Sister of Joseph Smith Speaks," *Sioux Valley News* 15, no. 16 (September 3, 1896): 1.

25. Standalone print of RLDS Leaders, William Crick, 1897. Thanks to Lachlan Mackay for sharing with me the details and date of this print.

26. Mary Salisbury Hancock, "The Three Sisters of the Prophet Joseph Smith, Part I," *Saints' Herald* 101, no. 2 (January 11, 1954): 10.

27. Jessie Salisbury, "Died," *True Latter Day Saints' Herald* 23, no. 19 (October 1, 1876), 607.

28. "Woolley," *Saints' Herald* 43, no. 47 (November 18, 1896), 768. Sophronia's only surviving daughter Mariah Stoddard Woolley, and her husband Nathaniel, had two daughters named Flora (1853–1881) and Ella (1857–1872). Ella died at the age of 17. Flora married Samuel Park, and died from complications due to childbirth two weeks after delivering her only daughter, Flora Isabelle Park. Flora Isabelle died at the age of three. See gravestones of Ella Woolley, Flora Park, and Flora Isabella Park, all in the Mount Auburn Cemetery, Colchester, IL.

29. S. J. Salisbury, "Died—Millikin [December 9, 1882]," *Saints' Herald* 30, no. 2 (January 13, 1883), 23; "Died—Millikin," *Saints' Herald* 29, no. 11 (June 1, 1882), 180; Nathan H. Williams, "Lucy Smith Millikin," in Kyle R. Walker, *United by Faith: The Joseph Sr. and Lucy Mack Smith Family* (American Fork, UT: Covenant Communications; Provo, UT: BYU Studies, 2006), 422–23. The Millikins were married for forty-two years and raised eight children.

30. Kyle R. Walker, *William B. Smith: In the Shadow of a Prophet* (Salt Lake City: Greg Kofford Books, 2015), 513–27.

31. Van Dine, "Catharine Smith Salisbury," 29; *The History of the Reorganized Church of Jesus Christ of Latter Day Saints*, vol. 4, *1873–1890*

(Independence, MO: Herald House, 1952), 719. Also see Joseph Smith III's account of preaching in these two schoolhouses when visiting William's sisters near the Hancock and McDonough County line, in Joseph Smith, "Hail the New Year," *True Latter Day Saints' Herald* 20, no. 1 (January 1, 1873): 17–18.

32. Richard P. Howard, ed., *The Memoirs of President Joseph Smith III (1832–1914)* (Independence, MO: Herald House Publishing, 1979), 186.

33. Catherine Salisbury (Fountain Green, IL) to Dear Sister Walker, February 27, 1888, *Saints' Herald* 35, no. 11 (March 17, 1888): 164; Alexander H. Smith (Lamoni, IA, and Blue Rapids, KS) to Fred Salisbury, June 2 and June 5, 1897, Community of Christ Library-Archives, Independence, MO.

34. Alex[ander] Hale Smith (Kewanee, Ill.) to Editors Herald, June 9, 1890, *Saints' Herald* 37, no. 25 (June 21, 1890): 407–8.

35. "Sister of a Prophet," reprinted from the *Chicago Record* in the *Saints' Herald* 40, no. 36 (September 9, 1893): 1.

36. Salisbury, "History of Salisburys, Part II," 4.

37. "Sister of a Prophet," 1.

38. Autobiography of Mary Salisbury Hancock, 2, holograph in possession of Mary Dennis, copy in author's possession.

39. Salisbury, "History of Salisburys, Part II," 4.

40. Van Dine, "Catharine Smith Salisbury," 34.

41. "Celebrated S. J. Salisbury's 89th Birthday, Sunday," *Carthage Republican* 71, no. 38 (September 17, 1924): 2.

42. Hancock, "Three Sisters, Part I," 11–12.

43. Ila Salisbury, "My Ancestors," *Carthage Republican* 75, no. 5 (February 1, 1928): 6.

44. Autobiography of Mary Salisbury Hancock, 2; Van Dine, "Catharine Smith Salisbury," 34. Warren L. Van Dine, "Information of the Smith and Salisbury Families, 1966–1975," unpublished typescript, 1966–1975, CHL.

45. "Aunt Katharine Salisbury Dead," *Saints' Herald* 47, no. 6 (February 7, 1900): 83; "Died. Salisbury," *Saints' Herald* 47, no. 7 (February 14, 1900): 112; Frederick V. Salisbury, "The Teachings and Testimonies of My Mother," unpublished typescript, 1926–1928, 18, Hancock County Historical Society, Carthage, Illinois; Van Dine, "Catharine Smith Salisbury," 35–36; Solomon J. Salisbury, "Old Nauvoo Days Recalled," *Autumn Leaves* 37, no. 4 (April 1924): 153.

46. This meetinghouse was built by members of the Ramus Stake and was one of the earliest church houses built by the Saints. LaMar C. Berrett, Keith W. Perkins, and Donald Q. Cannon, *Sacred Places: Ohio and Illinois* (Salt Lake City: Deseret Book, 2002), 202–3.

47. Solomon J. Salisbury, *Reminiscences of an Octogenarian* (self-pub., ca. 1926), 10; Salisbury, "Teachings and Testimonies of My Mother," 24.

48. Pilot Grove Branch Minute Book, 122, Community of Christ Library-Archives.
49. "Anniversary at Carthage," *Salt Lake Tribune* 44, no. 57 (June 24, 1894): 16.
50. Warren H. Orr (Carthage, IL) to Solomon J. Salisbury, September 15, 1922, in Salisbury, *Reminiscences of an Octogenarian*, 18.
51. Orville F. Berry, "The Mormon Settlement in Illinois," *Transactions of the Illinois State Historical Society, for the Year 1906* (Springfield: Illinois State Historical Society Library, 1906), 93.
52. Katherine Salisbury (Fountain Green, IL) to Dear Sister Walker, December 29, 1888, *Saints' Herald* 36, no. 4 (January 26, 1889): 53.

Bibliography

Aldrich, Lewis Cass, ed. *History of Yates County, N. Y.* Syracuse, NY: D. Mason, 1892.

"An Angel Told Him." *Kansas City Times* 1, no. 101 (April 11, 1895): 1.

Anderson, Devery S., and Gary James Bergera, eds. *The Nauvoo Endowment Companies, 1845–1846: A Documentary History*. Salt Lake City: Signature Books, 2005.

Anderson, Lavina Fielding, ed. *Lucy's Book: A Critical Edition of Lucy Mack Smith's Family Memoir*. Salt Lake City: Signature Books, 2001.

Anderson, Richard L. "Alvin Smith." In *United by Faith: The Joseph Sr. and Lucy Mack Smith Family*, edited by Kyle R. Walker, 82–121. American Fork, UT: Covenant Communications; Provo, UT: BYU Studies, 2006.

Anderson, Richard Lloyd. "Joseph Smith's Brothers: Nauvoo and After." *Ensign* 9, no. 9 (September 1979), 31.

Anderson, Richard Lloyd. "What Were Joseph Smith's Sisters Like, and What Happened to Them after the Martrydom?" *Ensign* 9, no. 3 (March 1979): 43.

Anderson, Richard Lloyd. "Who Were the Six Who Organized the Church on 6 April 1830?" *Ensign* 10, no. 6 (June 1980): 44–45.

"Anniversary of Carthage," *Salt Lake Tribune* 44, no. 57 (June 24, 1894): 16.

Arnold, Samantha. Samantha Arnold to Katharine Salisbury, January 1, 1853 [1854]. Copy of original in Katharine Smith Salisbury Correspondence, L. Tom Perry Special Collections, Harold B. Lee Library, Brigham Young University, Provo, UT.

Arnold, Samantha. Samantha Arnold to Katharine Salisbury, May 15, 1854. Photocopies of originals in Katharine Smith Salisbury Correspondence, 1853–1879, L. Tom Perry Special Collections, Harold B. Lee Library, Brigham Young University, Provo, UT.

Ashurst-McGee, Mark, et al., eds. *Documents, Volume 6: February 1838–August 1839*. Vol. 6 of the Documents series of *The Joseph Smith Papers*, edited by Ronald K. Esplin, Matthew J. Grow, and Matthew C. Godfrey. Salt Lake City: Church Historian's Press, 2017.

"Aunt Katharine Salisbury Dead." *Saints' Herald* 47, no. 6 (February 7, 1900): 83.

"Aunt Katharine Salisbury's Testimony." *Saints' Herald* 40, no. 18 (May 6, 1893): 275.

Avery, Valeen Tippetts, and Linda King Newell. "The Lion and the Lady: Brigham Young and Emma Smith." *Utah Historical Quarterly* 48, no. 1 (1980): 81–97.

Avery, Valeen Tippetts. *From Mission to Madness: Last Son of the Mormon Prophet*. Urbana: University of Illinois Press, 1998.

"Awaiting a Revelation—Story of a Winter Journey." *Kansas City Daily Journal* 37, no. 304 (April 12, 1895): 3.

Backman, Milton V., Jr., and James B. Allen. "Membership of Certain of Joseph Smith's Family in the Western Presbyterian Church of Palmyra." *BYU Studies* 1, no. 4 (Summer 1970), 482–84.

Backman, Milton V., Jr. *The Heavens Resound: A History of the Latter-day Saints in Ohio, 1830–1838*. Salt Lake City: Deseret Book, 1983.

Ball, Isaac Birkenhead. "The Prophet's Sister Testifies She Lifted the B. of M. Plates." Typescript interview with Herbert S. Salisbury, ca. 1954, 2. Church History Library (hereafter CHL).

Bateman, Newton, Paul Selby, and Charles J. Scofield, eds. *Historical Encyclopedia of Illinois and History of Hancock County*. Chicago: Munsell Publishing, 1921.

Bean, Victor E. Journals, 1884–1889. Vol. 2, 1885 January–October. CHL.

Beecher, Maureen Ursenbach, ed. *The Personal Writings of Eliza Roxey Snow*. Salt Lake City: University of Utah Press, 1995.

Bennett, Richard E., Susan Easton Black, and Donald Q. Cannon. *The Nauvoo Legion in Illinois: A History of the Mormon Militia, 1841–1846*. Norman, OK: Arthur H. Clark, 2010.

Bennett, Richard E. "'A Samaritan Had Passed By': George Miller—Mormon Bishop, Trailblazer, and Brigham Young Antagonist." *Journal of the Illinois State Historical Society* 82, no. 1 (Spring 1989): 2–16.

Bernauer, Barbara Hands. "Still 'Side by Side': The Final Burial of Joseph and Hyrum Smith." *John Whitmer Historical Association Journal* 11 (1991): 17–33.

Berry, Orville F. "The Mormon Settlement in Illinois." *Transactions of the Illinois State Historical Society for the Year 1906*, no. 11 (1906), 88–102.

Blair, W. W. Journal, March 4, 1859–January 14, 1860. Entry for July 20, 1859, P2, J1, Community of Christ Library-Archives, Independence, MO.

Bloch, Ruth R. "American Feminine Ideals in Transition: The Rise of the Moral Mother, 1785–1815." *Feminist Studies* 4, no. 2 (June 1978), 100–126.

Boyles, James C. "'Under a Spreading Chestnut-Tree': The Blacksmith and His Forge in Nineteenth-Century American Art." *Journal of the Society for Industrial Archeology* 34, nos. 1–2 (2008): 9–24.

Bradley, Martha Sonntag. "'Seizing Sacred Space': Women's Engagement in Early Mormonism." *Dialogue: A Journal of Mormon Thought* 27, no. 2 (1994): 57–70.

Bradshaw, M. Scott. "Joseph Smith's Performance of Marriages in Ohio." *BYU Studies* 39, no. 4 (2000): 23–69.

Bushman, Richard L. *Joseph Smith, Rough Stone Rolling*. New York: Alfred A. Knopf, 2005.

Case, Alice Montague. "A Missionary of the Church: The Life of Hubert Case." *Saints' Herald* 100, no. 1 (January 5, 1953): 10.

Case, Oscar. Reminiscence, ca. 1894. Tom and Carla Duke Papers, Burlington, IA. Typescript copy in author's possession.

Caton, Mary Anne. "The Aesthetics of Absence: Quaker Women's Plain Dress in the Delaware Valley, 1790–1900." In *Quaker Aesthetics: Reflections on a Quaker Ethic in American Design and Consumption*, edited by Emma Jones Lapsansky and Anne A. Verplanck. Philadelphia: University of Pennsylvania Press, 2003.

"Celebrated S. J. Salisbury's 89th Birthday, Sunday." *Carthage Republican* 71, no. 38 (September 17, 1924): 2.

Clayton, W. W. *History of Steuben County, New York, with Illustrations and Biographical Sketches of Some of Its Prominent Men and Pioneers*. Philadelphia: Lewis, Peck, 1879.

Cruea, Susan M. "Changing Ideals of Womanhood During the Nineteenth-Century Woman Movement." *ATQ: 19th Century American Literature and Culture* 19, no. 3 (2005): 187–204.

Clayton, Willliam, and Thomas Bullock. "Conference Minutes." *Times and Seasons* 6, no. 16 (November 1, 1845): 1013–14.

Cleveland Herald report reproduced in "General Conference." *Saints' Herald* 30, no. 16 (April 21, 1883): 242–43.

Cook, Thomas L. *Palmyra and Vicinity.* Palmyra, NY: Palmyra Courier Journal, 1930.

Cowles, George W., ed. *Landmarks of Wayne County New York.* Syracuse, NY: D. Mason, 1895.

Cross, Whitney R. *The Burned-Over District: The Social and Intellectual History of Enthusiastic Religion in Western New York, 1800–1850.* Ithaca, NY: Cornell University Press, 1950.

Dahl, Larry E., and Don Norton, comps. *Modern Perspectives on Nauvoo and the Mormons: Interviews with Long-Term Residents.* Provo, UT: Religious Studies Center, Brigham Young University, 2003.

Davidson, Gay. "Anniversary of Carthage." *Salt Lake Daily Tribune* 44, no. 57 (June 24, 1894): 16.

Davidson, Karen Lynn, et al., eds. *Histories, Volume 1: Joseph Smith Histories, 1832–1844.* Vol. 1 of the Histories series of *The Joseph Smith Papers,* edited by Dean C. Jessee, Ronald K. Esplin, and Richard Lyman Bushman. Salt Lake City: Church Historian's Press, 2012.

Davidson, Karen Lynn, Richard L. Jensen, and David J. Whittaker, eds. *Histories, Volume 2: Assigned Historical Writings, 1831–1847.* Vol. 2 of the Histories series of *The Joseph Smith Papers,* edited by Dean C. Jessee, Ronald K. Esplin, and Richard Lyman Bushman. Salt Lake City: Church Historian's Press, 2012.

Dean, Dorothy D. Handwritten family group sheet. Copy of original in author's possession.

"Death of General Don Carlos Smith." *Times and Seasons* 2, no. 20 (August 16, 1841): 503.

Deming, Arthur B. "C. M. Stafford's Statement." *Naked Truths About Mormonism* 1 (April 1888): 1.

Deming, Arthur B. "Mrs. M. C. R. Smith's Statement." *Naked Truths about Mormonism* (Oakland, CA), 1 (April 1888): 1.

Derr, Jill Mulvay, et al., eds. *The First Fifty Years of Relief Society: Key Documents in Latter-Day Saint History.* Salt Lake City: Church Historian's Press, 2016.

Dirkmaat, Gerrit J., et al., eds. *Documents, Volume 3: February 1833–March 1834*. Vol. 3 of the Documents series of *The Joseph Smith Papers*, edited by Ronald K. Esplin and Matthew C. Grow. Salt Lake City: Church Historian's Press, 2014.

Dowdle, Brett D., et al., eds. *The Joseph Smith Papers, Documents, Volume 15: 16 May—28 June 1844*. Vol. 15 of the Documents series of *The Joseph Smith Papers*, edited by Matthew C. Godfrey, R. Eric Smith, and Ronald K. Esplin. Salt Lake City: Church Historian's Press, 2023.

Dowdle, Brett D. "'What Means This Carnage?': The Civil War in Mormon Thought." In *Civil War Saints*, edited by Kenneth L. Alford, 107–25. Provo, UT: Religious Studies Center, Brigham Young University, 2012.

Eliason, Eric A. "Seer Stones, Salamanders, and Early Mormon 'Folk Magic' in the Light of Folklore Studies and Bible Scholarship." *BYU Studies* 55, no. 1 (2016): 73–93.

Enders, Donald L. "The Joseph Smith, Sr., Family: Farmers of the Genesee." In *Joseph Smith: The Prophet, the Man*, edited by Susan Easton Black and Charles D. Tate Jr., 213–25. Provo, UT: Religious Studies Center, Brigham Young University, 1993.

Enders, Donald L., and Mark L. Staker. *A Visionary House: The First Visions of Joseph Smith's Family in Context*. Provo, UT: Religious Studies Center, Brigham Young University, forthcoming.

Ferris, Benjamin G. *Utah and the Mormons: The History, Government, Doctrines, Customs and Prospects of the Latter-day Saints*. New York: Harper & Brothers, 1854.

Fountain Green Rifle Company Roll, January 25, 1849. Hancock County Historical Society, Carthage, IL.

Fox, Norman. "George Fox and the Early Friends." *Baptist Quarterly* 11, no. 4 (October 1877): 433.

"Further Particulars of the Affair." *Carthage Gazette* 16, no. 13 (September 4, 1880), 3.

Geddes, Thomas. Certificate, January 25, 1849. Fountain Green Vertical File, Hancock County Historical Society, Carthage, IL.

Godfrey, Kenneth W. "The Battle of Nauvoo Revisited." *John Whitmer Historical Association Journal*, Nauvoo Conference Special Edition (2002): 133–46.

Godfrey, Matthew C., et al., eds. *Documents, Volume 4: April 1834–September 1835*. Vol. 4 of the Documents series of *The Joseph Smith Papers*, edited by Ronald K. Esplin and Matthew J. Grow. Salt Lake City: Church Historian's Press, 2016.

Granger, Oliver, and William Smith. Bond, Kirtland Township, Geauga County, Ohio, to James Hall, assignee of Keeler, McNeil & Co., NY, January 20, 1843. Hiram Kimball Collection, CHL.

Gregg, Thomas. *The Prophet of Palmyra*. New York: John B. Alden, 1890.

Gregg, Thomas. *History of Hancock County, Illinois*. Chicago: Chas. C. Chapman, 1880.

Gallup, Joseph A. *Sketches of Epidemic Diseases in the State of Vermont, from Its Settlement to 1815*. Boston: T. B. Wait and Sons, 1815.

Gillespie, Michele. "Artisan Accommodation to the Slave South: The Case of William Talmage, a Blacksmith, 1834–1847." *Georgia Historical Quarterly* 81, no. 2 (Summer 1997): 265–286.

Grow, Matthew J., et al., eds. *Administrative Records, Council of Fifty Minutes, March 1844–January 1846*. First volume of the Administrative Records series of *The Joseph Smith Papers*, edited by Ronald K. Esplin, Matthew J. Grow, and Matthew C. Godfrey. Salt Lake City: Church Historian's Press, 2016.

Haight, David Francis, ed. "Biography of John Lyman Smith." CHL.

Hancock, Mary Salisbury. Autobiography, 1963, 2. L. Tom Perry Special Collections, Harold B. Lee Library, Brigham Young University, Provo, UT.

Hancock, Mary Salisbury. "The Three Sisters of the Prophet Joseph Smith, Part 1." *Saints' Herald* 101, no. 2 (January 11, 1954): 10–12.

Hancock, Mary Salisbury. "The Three Sisters of the Prophet Joseph Smith, Part II." *Saints' Herald* 101, no. 3 (January 18, 1954): 10–11.

Hancock, Mary Salisbury. "The Three Sisters of the Prophet Joseph Smith, Part III." *Saints' Herald* 101, no. 4 (January 25, 1954): 10–11, 23.

Harper, Steven C. *First Vision: Memory and Mormon Origins*. New York: Oxford University Press, 2019.

Hartley, William G. "Missouri's 1838 Extermination Order and the Mormons' Forced Removal to Illinois." In *A City of Refuge: Quincy, Illinois*, edited by Susan Easton Black and Richard E. Bennett, 1–30. Salt Lake City: Millennial Press, 2000.

Hedges, Andrew H., Alex D. Smith, and Brent M. Rogers, eds. *Journals, Volume 3: May 1843–June 1844*. Vol. 3 of the Journals series of *The Joseph Smith Papers*, edited by Ronald K. Esplin and Matthew J. Grow. Salt Lake City: Church Historian's Press, 2015.

Hedges, Andrew H., Alex D. Smith, and Richard Lloyd Anderson, eds. *Journals, Volume 2: December 1841–April 1843*. Vol. 2 of the Journals series of *The Joseph Smith Papers*, edited by Dean C. Jessee, Ronald K.

Esplin, and Richard Lyman Bushman. Salt Lake City: Church Historian's Press, 2011.

Hicks, Michael. *Mormonism and Music: A History*. Urbana: University of Illinois Press, 1989.

"History of Orson Pratt," *Millennial Star* 27 (1865): 23–25, 39–40, 55–57, 71–71, 86–89.

History of the Reorganized Church of Jesus Christ of Latter Day Saints, 8 vols. Independence, MO: Herald House, 1973.

Holt, Cyrus. *History of McDonough County, Illinois*. Springfield, IL: Continental Historical Co., 1885.

Hotchkin, James H. *A History of the Purchase and Settlement of Western New York, and of the Rise, Progress, and Present State of the Presbyterian Church in that Section*. New York: M. W. Dodd, 1848.

Howard, Richard P. "The Changing RLDS Response to Mormon Polygamy: A Preliminary Analysis." In *Restoration Studies III: A Collection of Essays about the History, Beliefs, and Practices of the Reorganized Church of Jesus Christ of Latter Day Saints*, edited by Maurice L. Draper and Debra Combs, 145–62. Independence, MO: Herald Publishing House, 1986.

Howard, Richard P., ed. *The Memoirs of President Joseph Smith III (1832–1914)*. Independence, MO: Herald Publishing House, 1979.

Howe, Eber D. *Mormonism Unvailed*. Painesville, OH: Eber D. Howe, 1834.

Huff, Roy B., and Kyle R. Walker. "Don Carlos Smith." In *United by Faith: The Joseph Sr. and Lucy Mack Smith Family*, edited by Kyle R. Walker, 354–97. American Fork, UT: Covenant Communications; Provo, UT: BYU Studies, 2006.

Hyde, Orson. Orson Hyde to Dear Brethren, March 27, 1846. Brigham Young Office Files, 1832–78, General Correspondence, Incoming, 1840–77, Letters from Church Leaders and Others, 1840–77, Orson Hyde, 1846. CHL.

Hyde, Orson. "The History of Orson Hyde," *Millennial Star* 26, no. 49 (December 3, 1864): 774–776.

Interview with Catherine Salisbury. As reported in Gay Davidson. "Anniversary of Carthage." *Salt Lake Tribune* 44, no. 57 (June 24, 1894): 16.

Ireland, Robert M. "The Problem of Concealed Weapons in Nineteenth-Century Kentucky." *Register of the Kentucky Historical Society* 91, no. 4 (Autumn 1993): 370–85.

Jarman, Dean L., and Kyle R. Walker. "Samuel Harrison Smith." In *United by Faith: The Joseph Sr. and Lucy Mack Smith Family*, edited by Kyle R.

Walker, 205–45. American Fork, UT: Covenant Communications; Provo, UT: BYU Studies, 2006.

Jeffrey, Julie Roy. *Converting the West: A Biography of Narcissa Whitman* (Norman: University of Oklahoma Press, 1991).

Jessee, Dean C., Mark Ashurst-McGee, and Richard L. Jensen, eds. *Journals, Volume 1: 1832–1839*. Vol. 1 of the Journals series of *The Joseph Smith Papers*, edited by Dean C. Jessee, Ronald K. Esplin, and Richard Lyman Bushman. Salt Lake City: Church Historian's Press, 2008.

Jessee, Dean C., ed. *John Taylor Nauvoo Journal*. Provo, UT: Grandin Book, 1996.

Jessee, Dean C. "Joseph Knight's Recollection of Early Mormon History." *BYU Studies Quarterly* 17, no. 1 (1976): 29–39.

Jones, Gracia N. "Sophronia Smith McCleary." In *United by Faith: The Joseph Sr. and Lucy Mack Smith Family*, edited by Kyle R. Walker, 164–203. American Fork, UT: Covenant Communications; Provo, UT: BYU Studies, 2006.

Joseph Smith's Store Daybook B. Entry for Joseph Smith. Nauvoo, Hancock County, Illinois, 18 July 1842—A, 34[b], note, https://www.josephsmithpapers.org.

"Jubilee Notes." *Deseret Evening News* 30, no. 117 (April 10, 1897): 1.

Kelley, William H. "The Hill Cumorah, and the Book of Mormon." *Saints' Herald* 28, no. 11 (June 1, 1881):161–68.

Kelteaux, Mary Bailey Smith. Mary Bailey Smith Kelteaux to Dear Aunt Catharine Younger. Katharine Smith Salisbury Correspondence, 1853–1879, L. Tom Perry Special Collections, Harold B. Lee Library, Brigham Young University, Provo, UT.

Kimball, Sarah M. Sarah M. Kimball to Mrs. Serepta Heywood. In *Joseph L. Heywood Letters*, 1841–47. CHL.

Kimball, Vilate. Vilate Kimball to Heber C. Kimball, June 30, 1844. CHL.

Kirtland high council, minutes, May 16, 1836. In Minute Book 1. CHL.

Kirtland Safety Society Bank Stock Ledger, Kirtland Township, Geauga County, Ohio, October 18, 1836–June 12, 1837, 193–96. Chicago History Museum, https://www.josephsmithpapers.org.

Kriebel, Karen J. "From Bloomers to Flappers: The American Women's Dress Reform Movement." PhD diss., Ohio State University, 1998.

Land transactions of Saints, Kirtland, Ohio 1830s & 1840s. CHL.

Laub, George. Reminiscences and journal, 1845–46, 49–52. CHL.

"Latter Day Saints—The Meeting at Montrose, Ia.—A Sister of Joseph Smith Speaks." *Sioux Valley News* 15, no. 16 (September 3, 1896): 1.

Leonard, Glen M. *Nauvoo: A Place of Peace, A People of Promise*. Salt Lake City: Deseret Book, 2002.

Lyman, Edward Leo, Susan Ward Payne, and S. George Ellsworth, eds. *No Place to Call Home: The 1807–1857 Life Writings of Caroline Barnes Crosby, Chronicler of Outlying Mormon Communities*. Logan: Utah State University Press, 2005.

Macedonia Branch Record, 1839–1850. CHL.

Mack, Solomon. *Narraitve [sic] of the Life of Solomon Mack*. Windsor, VT: self-published, 1811.

MacKay, Michael Hubbard, et al., eds. *Documents, Volume 1: July 1828–June 1831*. Vol. 1 of the Documents series of *The Joseph Smith Papers*, edited by Dean C. Jessee et al. Salt Lake City: Church Historian's Press, 2013.

MacKay, Michael Hubbard. *Sacred Space: Exploring the Birthplace of Mormonism*. Provo, UT: Religious Studies Center, Brigham Young University; Salt Lake City: Deseret Book, 2016.

Madsen, Carol Cornwall. *Emmeline B. Wells: An Intimate History*. Salt Lake City: University of Utah Press, 2017.

Marquardt, H. Michael, comp. *Early Patriarchal Blessings of The Church of Jesus Christ of Latter-day Saints*. Salt Lake City: Smith-Pettit Foundation, 2007.

McBride, Spencer W., and Jennifer Hill Dorsey, eds. *New York's Burned-Over District: A Documentary History*. Ithaca, NY: Cornell University Press, 2023.

McBride, Spencer W., et al., eds. *Documents, Volume 11: September 1842–February 1843*. Vol. 11 of the Documents series of *The Joseph Smith Papers*, edited by Matthew C. Godfrey et al. Salt Lake City: Church Historian's Press, 2020.

McCleary, Sophronia. Sophronia McCleary to Naomi Seaver, November 2, 1840. Copy of original in author's possession, courtesy of Richard L. Anderson.

McGavin, E. Cecil. *The Family of Joseph Smith*. Salt Lake City: Bookcraft, 1963.

McKenzie, D. D. McKenzie to Mrs. Katharine Salisbury, November 13, 1871. Brigham Young Office Files, box 8, vol. 12. CHL.

Millikin, Arthur. Arthur Millikin to Dear Nephew [John Smith], July 25, 1863. L. Tom Perry Special Collections, Harold B. Lee Library, Brigham Young University. Provo, UT.

Minute Book 1, [ca. 3 December 1832–30 November 1837], March 12, 1833. CHL.

Moon, June. *"Multum in Parvo," A History of Colchester, Illinois*. Colchester, IL: Colchester Chronicle, 1956.

Murdock, John. Diary, 1832 February–September. Entry for March 15, 1832. In John Murdock Journal and Autobiography, 1830–1867. CHL.

Murdock, S. Reed. *Joseph and Emma's Julia: The Other Twin*. Salt Lake City: Eborn Books, 2004.

Nauvoo Temple Endowment Register, 1845–46. CHL.

Neff, Estel G. Interview by the author, May 17, 2002, Nauvoo, IL.

Newell, Linda King, and Valeen Tippetts Avery, *Mormon Enigma: Emma Hale Smith*. 2nd ed. Chicago: University of Illinois Press, 1994.

Newell, Linda King, and Valeen Tippetts Avery, "Sweet Counsel and Seas of Tribulation: The Religious Life of the Women in Kirtland." *BYU Studies* 20, no. 2 (Winter 1980): 151–62.

Newell, Quincy D. *Your Sister in the Gospel: The Life of Jane Manning James, A Nineteenth-Century Black Mormon*. New York: Oxford University Press, 2019.

Noel, Patricia Lewis. "Reviving His Work: Social Isolation, Religious Fervor and Reform in the Burned Over District of Western New York, 1790–1860." Master's thesis, Virginia Commonwealth University, 2006.

Norman, Mary Bailey Smith. "Samuel Harrison Smith." Reminiscence, typescript, June 24, 1914. CHL.

Norman, Mary Bailey Smith. Mary Bailey Smith Norman to Ina Coolbrith, April 24, 1908. Community of Christ Library-Archives, Independence, MO.

Norman, Mary Bailey Smith. Mary Bailey Smith Norman to My Dear Ina (Coolbrith), n.d. Community of Christ Library-Archives, Independence, MO.

Oaks, Dallin H., and Marvin S. Hill. *Carthage Conspiracy: The Trial of the Accused Assassins of Joseph Smith*. Chicago: University of Illinois Press, 1975.

O'Donovan, Connell. "The Mormon Priesthood Ban and Elder Q. Walker Lewis: 'An Example for His More Whiter Brethren to Follow.'" *John Whitmer Historical Association Journal* 26 (2006): 66–71.

O'Donovan, Connell. "Joseph T. Ball, 1804–1861: Mormonism's First African American High Priest." Unpublished manuscript, 2011, 6. Copy in author's possession, courtesy of O'Donovan.

"Opening of Navigation." *Buffalo Journal & General Advertiser* 16, no. 48 (May 11, 1831), 2.

"Opinions of the Smith Family." *Voree Herald* 1, no. 6 (June 1846): 1.

"Oscar Case Preaches at Campus—He's Only 96." *Saints' Herald* 115, no. 17 (September 1, 1968): 606.

Osterud, Nancy Grey. *Bonds of Community: The Lives of Farm Women in Nineteenth-Century New York.* Ithaca, NY: Cornell University Press, 1991.

Owens, Megan. "Divorce and Family Life in Nineteenth-Century Vanderburgh County." *Grand Valley Journal of History* 7, no. 1 (October 2019): 3–4.

Parrin, William Henry, ed. *History of Cass County, Illinois.* Chicago: O. L. Baskin, 1882.

Partridge, Scott H., ed. *Eliza Maria Partridge Journal.* Provo, UT: Grandin Book, 2003.

Peterson, John W. "Wm. B. Smith's Last Statement." *Zion's Ensign* 5 (January 1894): 6.

Phelps, William W. W. W. Phelps to Reuben Miller, May 30, 1847. CHL.

Phillips, Emma M. *Dedicated to Serve: Biographies of 31 Women of the Restoration.* Independence, MO: Herald House, 1970.

Pilot Grove Reorganized Branch Minutes. Holograph. Community of Christ Library-Archives, Independence, MO.

Porter, Larry C. *A Study of the Origins of The Church of Jesus Christ of Latter-day Saints in the States of New York and Pennsylvania.* Provo, UT: BYU Studies, 2000.

Porter, Larry C. "Organizational Origins of the Church of Jesus Christ, 6 April 1830." In *Regional Studies in Latter-day Saint Church History: New York and Pennsylvania,* edited by Larry C. Porter, Milton V. Backman Jr., and Susan Easton Black, 149–64. Provo, UT: BYU Department of Church History and Doctrine, 1992.

Porter, Larry C. "'Ye Shall Go to the Ohio': Exodus of the New York Saints to Ohio, 1831." In *Regional Studies in Latter-day Saint Church History: Ohio,* edited by Milton V. Backman Jr., 1–25. Provo, UT: Brigham Young University Department of Church History and Doctrine, 1990.

Pratt, Parley P. P. P. Pratt to Brigham Young, May 7, 1845. Brigham Young Office files 1832–1878, Letters from Church Leaders and Others, 1840–1877. CHL.

"Records of Early Church Families." *Utah Genealogical Magazine* 26 (1935): 101–53.

Reeder, Jennifer. *First: The Life and Faith of Emma Smith.* Salt Lake City: Deseret Book, 2021.

Reeder, Jennifer, and Kate Holbrook, eds. *At the Pulpit: 185 Years of Discourses by Latter-day Saint Women*. Salt Lake City: Church Historian's Press, 2017.

Reeve, W. Paul. *Religion of a Different Color: Race and the Mormon Struggle for Whiteness*. New York: Oxford University Press, 2015.

"Reminiscences of Joseph Smith, as Told by His Sister, Catherine Smith-Salisbury, to Her Grandson, Herbert S. Salisbury." *Saints' Herald* 60 (October 8, 1913): 984.

Robbins, Lewis. Autobiographical Sketch, circa 1845, 4, MS 18637. CHL.

Rogers, Brent M., et al., eds. *Documents, Volume 8: February–November 1841*. Vol. 8 of the Documents series of *The Joseph Smith Papers*, edited by Ronald K. Esplin et al. Salt Lake City: Church Historian's Press, 2019.

Rogers, Brent M., et al., eds. *Documents, Volume 5: October 1835–January 1838*. Vol. 5 of the Documents series of *The Joseph Smith Papers*, edited by Ronald K. Esplin and Matthew J. Grow, and Matthew C. Godfrey. Salt Lake City: Church Historian's Press, 2017.

Rorabaugh, W. J. *The Alcoholic Republic: An American Tradition*. New York: Oxford Press, 1979.

Rugh, Susan Sessions. *Our Common Country: Family Farming, Culture, and Community in Nineteenth-Century Midwest*. Bloomington: Indiana University Press, 2001.

Rumball, Miss Hannah Frances. "The Relinquishment of Plain Dress: British Quaker Women's Abandonment of Plain Quaker Attire, 1860–1914." PhD thesis, University of Brighton, 2016.

Russell, William D. "A Priestly Role for a Prophetic Church: The RLDS Church and Black Americans." *Dialogue: A Journal of Mormon Thought* 12, no. 2 (Summer 1979): 37–49.

Saints: The Story of the Church of Jesus Christ in the Latter Days. Vol. 1, *The Standard of Truth, 1815–1846*. Salt Lake City: The Church of Jesus Christ of Latter-day Saints, 2018.

Salisbury, Catherine. Catherine Salisbury to Dear Sister Walker, February 27, 1888. *Saints' Herald* 35, no. 11 (March 17, 1888): 164.

Salisbury, Don Carlos. Don Carlos Salisbury to Mother, Brothers, and Sister, May 8, 1861. L. Tom Perry Special Collections, Harold B. Lee Library, Brigham Young University, Provo, UT.

Salisbury, Don Carlos. Don Carlson Salisbury to Dear Brother Alvin [Salisbury], August 28, 1862. L. Tom Perry Special Collections, Harold B. Lee Library, Brigham Young University, Provo, UT.

Salisbury, D.[on] C.[arlos]. D. C. Salisbury to Mariah Woolley, August 28, 1862. L. Tom Perry Special Collections, Harold B. Lee Library, Brigham Young University, Provo, UT.

Salisbury, Frederick V. "The Teachings and Testimonies of My Mother." Unpublished typescript, ca. 1926–28, 2. Warren L. Van Dine Papers, Hancock County Historical Society, Carthage, IL.

Salisbury, Fred. Fred Salisbury to Editors Herald, November 7, 1891. *Saints' Herald* 38, no. 48 (November 28, 1891): 763.

Salisbury, Frederick. Frederick Salisbury to Audentia Anderson, June 2, 1930. Audentia Anderson Genealogy Research Letters, Miscellaneous, P78-4, folder 37. Community of Christ Library-Archives, Independence, MO.

Salisbury, Gideon. Family Bible. Photocopy of original in Gideon Salisbury Revolutionary War Pension File, US Revolutionary War Pension and Bounty-Land Warrant Application Files, 1800–1900, ancestry.com.

Salisbury, Herbert S. "History of Salisburys, Part II, Life of Don Carlos [Salisbury] after His Return to Illinois [1866], Including Herbert's Description of His Own Life (1870 up to 1945)." Unpublished typescript, ca. 1945. Copy in author's possession.

Salisbury, Herbert S. Herbert S. Salisbury to Catherine Groom, February 24, 1944. Community of Christ Library-Archives, Independence, MO.

Salisbury, Herbert S. "The Prophet's Sister Testifies She Lifted the B. of M. Plates." *Messenger*, October 1954, 1, 4.

Salisbury, Herbert S. "Reminiscences of Joseph Smith, as Told by His Sister, Catherine Smith–Salisbury, to Her Grandson, Herbert S. Salisbury." *Saints' Herald* 60, no. 41 (October 8, 1913): 984.

Salisbury, Herbert S. "Things the Prophet's Sister Told Me." Typescript, San Rafael, CA, June 30, 1945. CHL.

Salisbury, H.[erbert] S. "The Western Adventures of Don Carlos Salisbury." Typescript, San Rafael, CA, ca. 1945.

Salisbury, Ila. "My Ancestors." *Carthage Republican* 75, no. 5 (February 1, 1928): 6.

Salisbury, Jessie. "Died." *True Latter Day Saints' Herald* 23, no. 19 (October 1, 1876), 607.

Salisbury, W[ilkins] J[enkins]. W J Salisbury to Brigham Young, July 28, 1845. Brigham Young Office Files 1832–1878, General Correspondence, Incoming, 1844–1877, box 20, folder 15. CHL.

Salisbury, W[ilkins] J[enkins]. W J Salisbury to Brigham Young, May 9, 1845. Brigham Young Office Files 1832–1878, General Correspondence, Incoming, 1844–1877, box 20, folder 15. CHL.

Salisbury, W. J. W. J. Salisbury to Mr. Editor. *Nauvoo Neighbor* 3, no. 7 (June 18, 1845): 3.

Salisbury, W. J. W. J. Salisbury to Mr. [Thomas] Sharp for the *Warsaw Signal, Warsaw Signal* 3, no. 2 (April 8, 1846): 2.

Salisbury, Katharine Smith. Affidavit, April 15, 1881. Holograph. Community of Christ Library-Archives.

Salisbury, Katharine. Katharine Salisbury to Dear Nephews [Joseph F. Smith, John Smith], September 11, 1865. L. Tom Perry Special Collections, Harold B. Lee Library, Brigham Young University, Provo, UT.

Salisbury, Katharine. Katharine Salisbury to Brigham Young, May 28, 1871. Brigham Young Office Files, 1832–1878, General Correspondence, Incoming, 1840–1877, Re–Sn. CHL.

Salisbury, Katharine. Katharine Salisbury to Dear Cousin [George A. Smith] and Brigham Young, January 14, 1872. Brigham Young Office Files, 1832–1877, box 34, folder 15. CHL.

Salisbury, Katharine. Katharine Salisbury to Brigham Young, October 20, 1872. Brigham Young Office Files, 1832–1878, General Correspondence, Incoming, 1840–1877, General Letters, N–Sn, 1872. CHL.

Salisbury, Katharine. Katherine Salisbury to George A. Smith and Brigham Young, July 25, 1873. George A. Smith Papers 1834–1875, Incoming Letters, folder 13. CHL.

Salisbury, Katharine. Katharine Salisbury to John Taylor, August 15, 1879. First Presidency (John Taylor) correspondence, 1877–1887. CHL.

Salisbury, Katharine. Katharine Salisbury to Orson Pratt, January 23, 1878. Historian's Office correspondence files, 1856–1926. CHL.

Salisbury, Katharine. Katharine Salisbury to Orson Pratt, December 20, 1877. Historian's Office correspondence files, 1856–1926. CHL.

Salisbury, Katharine. Katharine Salisbury to Dear Sisters, Illinois, March 10, 1886. *Saints' Herald* 33, no. 17 (May 1, 1886): 260.

Salisbury, Katharine. Katharine Salisbury to Dear Sisters of the "Home Column," Illinois, May 16, 1886. *Saints' Herald* 33, no. 26 (July 3, 1886): 405.

Salisbury, Katherine. Katharine Salisbury to Sister Frances, December 24, 1886. *Saints' Herald* 34, no. 6 (February 5, 1887): 84.

Salisbury, Katharine. Katharine Salisbury to Dear Sister Walker, February 27, 1888. *Saints' Herald* 35, no. 11 (March 17, 1888): 164.

Salisbury, Katherine. Katharine Salisbury to Dear Sister Walker, December 29, 1888. *Saints' Herald* 36, no. 4 (January 26, 1889): 53.

Salisbury, Katharine. Katharine Salisbury to Dear Friend [unknown], February 26, 1889. Community of Christ Library-Archives.

Salisbury, Katharine. Katharine Salisbury to Dear Sisters, July 2, 1895. *Saints' Herald* 42, no. 30 (July 24, 1895): 473.

Salisbury, Katharine. Katharine Salisbury to unnamed granddaughter, February 11 [no year]. Original in possession of Estel Neff, Nauvoo, IL, copy in author's possession.

Salisbury, Katharine. Katharine Salisbury to Editors Herald, March 26, 1899. Reproduced as "Testimony of Katharine Salisbury." *Saints' Herald* 46, no. 17 (April 26, 1899): 261.

Salisbury, S. J. "Died—Millikin [December 9, 1882]." *Saints' Herald* 30, no. 2 (January 13, 1883), 23.

Salisbury, Solomon J. *Reminiscences of an Octogenarian*. Self-published, 1922.

Saunders, Lorenzo. Interview by William H. Kelley, September 17, 1884, 1–18. E. L. Kelley Papers, Community of Christ Library-Archives, Independence, MO.

"Says He Saw Christ." *Kansas City Times* 50, no. 99 (April 9, 1895): 1.

Scherer, Mark. *Journal of a People: The Era of Reorganization, 1844 to 1946*. Independence, MO: Community of Christ Seminary Press, 2013.

Schindler, Harold. *Orrin Porter Rockwell: Man of God Son of Thunder*. 2nd rev. ed. Salt Lake City: University of Utah Press, 1983.

Scofield, Charles J., ed. *History of Hancock County Illinois*. Chicago: Munsell Publishing, 1921.

"Sermon by Elder Wm. B. Smith. Delivered at the Saints' Church at Independence, Mo." *Zion's Ensign* 3, no. 35 (August 27, 1892): 2.

Sessions, Perrigrine. Reminiscences and Diaries, 1839–1886. Vol. 4. CHL.

"Shooting Affair Near Fountain Green." *Carthage Gazette* 8, no. 52 (June 11, 1873): 3.

Simpson, Matthew. *Cyclopedia of Methodism*. Philadelphia: Everts & Stewart, 1878.

"Sister of a Prophet." *Saints' Herald* 40, no. 36 (September 9, 1893): 565.

Small, William. William Small to Benjamin Winchester, November 24, 1845. *Messenger and Advocate of the Church of Christ* 2, no. 2 (December 1845): 407–8.

Smith, Alexander H. Alexander H. Smith to Fred Salisbury, June 2 and June 5, 1897. Community of Christ Library-Archives, Independence, MO.

Smith, Alex[ander] Hale. Alex Hale to Editors Herald, June 9, 1890. In *Saints' Herald* 37, no. 25 (June 21, 1890): 407.

Smith, Alex D. "The Day Joseph Smith Was Killed: A Carthage Woman's Perspective." *BYU Studies* 58, no. 2 (2019): 105–12.

Smith, Don C[arlos]. Don C Smith to Bro. Joseph [Smith], ca. May 1838. CHL.

Smith, Emma, comp. *A Collection of Sacred Hymns for the Church of the Latter Day Saints*. Kirtland, OH: F. G. Williams & Co., 1835.

Smith, George A. Diary, 1872 May–November, files 1–20. Entry for September 18, 1872, unpaginated. CHL.

Smith, George A. "History of George Albert Smith: Zion's Camp." May 16–May 22, 1844. Typescript. L. Tom Perry Special Collections, Harold B. Lee Library, Brigham Young University, Provo, UT.

Smith, George A. George A. Smith to Cousin Catherine [Salisbury], Salt Lake City, August 17, 1865. Historian's Office letterpress copybooks, 1854–79. Vol. 2, 1859–69. CHL.

Smith, George A. George A. Smith to Brigham Young, November 1, 1872. Brigham Young Office Files, 1832–1878, General Correspondence, Incoming, 1840–1877, Letters from Church Leaders and Others, George A. Smith, 1872–1873. CHL.

Smith, George A. George A. Smith to Catherine Smith Salisbury, August 6, 1873. Historian's Office letterpress copybooks, 1854–1879. Vol. 3. CHL.

Smith, George A. Papers, 1834–1877. Autobiographical Writings, Journal, 1856 April–1857 May. CHL.

Smith, George D., ed. *An Intimate Chronicle: The Journals of William Clayton*. Salt Lake City: Signature Books, 1995.

Smith, Hyrum. Diary, 18 November 1831–21 February 1835. Joseph Smith Sr. Family Collection, L. Tom Perry Special Collections, Harold B. Lee Library, Brigham Young University, Provo, UT.

Smith, Hyrum. Family Bible. L. Tom Perry Special Collections, Harold B. Lee Library, Brigham Young University, Provo, UT.

Smith, Hyrum. Hyrum Smith to the Saints Scattered Abroad. In *Times and Seasons* 1, no. 2 (December 1839): 21.

Smith, J. Winter. Taped interview by Dean Jacobs, transcription by Tom Duke, Smith Family Reunion, August 18–19, 1972, Nauvoo, IL.

Smith, John. Papers, 1833–54. Journal, 1846 February–1854 May. CHL.

Smith, John Henry. *Church, State, and Politics: The Diaries of John Henry Smith*. Edited by Jean Bickmore White. Salt Lake City: Signature Books, 1990.

Smith, Joseph. History, 1838–1856, volume F-1 [1 May 1844–8 August 1844, June 18, 1844]. CHL.

Smith, Joseph. Joseph Smith to Emma Smith, May 18, 1834. CHL.

Smith, Joseph. Joseph Smith to Jenkins Salisbury, ca. 1841–44. Letter cut and most content removed, original in possession of Greg T. Walker, Mesquite, NV.

Smith, Joseph F. Joseph F. Smith to George A. Smith, August 22, 1860. George A. Smith Papers, 1834–1877, General Correspondence, Incoming Letters, R–Y, 1860. CHL.

Smith, Joseph F. Joseph F. Smith to Catherine Salisbury, August 29, 1879. Joseph F. Smith Letterpress Copybooks, 1875–1917. CHL.

Smith, Joseph F. Joseph F. Smith (Salt Lake City) to Catherine Salisbury, September 7, 1879. Joseph F. Smith Letterpress Copybooks, 1875–1917. CHL.

Smith, Joseph F. Joseph F. Smith to Arthur Millkin, September 7, 1879. Joseph F. Smith Letterpress Copybooks, 1875–1917. CHL.

Smith, Joseph, III. Joseph Smith III to John M. Bernhisel, August 6, 1856. John M. Bernhisel Papers, 1818–1872. CHL.

Smith, Joseph, III. "Last Testimony of Sister Emma," *Saints' Herald* 26, no. 19 (October 1, 1879): 289–90.

Smith, Joseph F. Joseph F. Smith to Levira Smith, June 28, 1860. Joseph F. Smith Papers, 1854–1918. Family Correspondence. CHL.

Smith, Lucy Mack. Lucy Mack Smith to Wiliam Smith, January 23, 1845. CHL.

Smith, Lucy Mack. General conference, October 8, 1845, Nauvoo, Illinois. Historian's Office, General Church Minutes, 1839–1877, October 6–8, 1845, 7–13. CHL.

Smith, Lucy Mack. *Biographical Sketches of Joseph Smith the Prophet and his Progenitors for Many Generations*. Liverpool: S. W. Richards, 1853.

Smith, Ruby K. *Mary Bailey*. Salt Lake City: Deseret Book, 1954.

Smith, Samuel Harrison. Diary, 1832 February–1833 May. Entries for June 26, 1832, and July 30, 1832. CHL.

Smith, Samuel H. B. Samuel H. B. Smith to George A. Smith, June 2, 1857. George A. Smith Papers, 1834–1877, General Correspondence, Incoming Letters, 1857. CHL.

Smith, Samuel H. B. Reminiscences and Diary, 1856 April–1863. CHL.

Smith, William. "A Proclamation," *Warsaw Signal* 2, no. 32 (October 29, 1845): 1.

Smith, William. William Smith to Brigham Young, August 24, 1844. CHL.

Smith, William. William Smith to Dear Brethren, May 10, 1845. *Nauvoo Neighbor* 3, no. 2 (May 14, 1845): 2–3.

Smith, William. William Smith to Jesse C. Little, August 20, 1845, Jesse C. Little correspondence, 1845–1846. CHL.

Smith, William. William Smith to Emma Smith, October 21, 1845. CHL.

Smith, William. William Smith to Orson Hyde, November 12, 1845. In *Warsaw Signal* 2, no. 36 (November 26, 1845): 2.

Smith, William. William Smith to Brother [James] Strang, March 17, 1846. James Jesse Strang Collection, 1832–1947. Beinecke Rare Book and Manuscript Library, Yale University, New Haven, CT.

Smith, William. *A Revelation Given to William Smith, in 1847, On the Apostacy of the Church and the Pruning of the Vineyard of the Lord* (n.p., 1848), 1–2, M293.1. CHL.

Smith, William. William Smith to Brigham Young, May 7, 1855. Brigham Young Office Files, 1832–1878, Letters from Church Leaders and Others, 1840–1877. CHL.

Smith, William. William Smith to the editor, *New York Tribune* 17, no. 5025 (May 28, 1857): 5.

Smith, William. William Smith to D[on] C[arlos] Smith, December 1, 1840. In "Communications." *Times and Seasons* 2 (December 15, 1840): 252–53.

Smith, William. William Smith to Joshua Grant Jr. "Married." *Nauvoo Neighbor* 3, no. 9 (July 2, 1845): 3.

Smith, William. William Smith to Joshua Grant Jr., August 12, 1845. *Nauvoo Neighbor* 3, no. 16 (August 20, 1845): 3.

Smith, William. William Smith to Brother [Edmund L. Kelley], ca. 1893, Suplaiment [*sic*], Miscellaneous Letters, P19, folder 49. Community of Christ Library-Archives.

Smith, William. "Notes Written on 'Chambers' Life of Joseph Smith." Ca. 1875, 29. CHL.

Smith, William. *William Smith on Mormonism*. Lamoni, IA: Herald Steam Book and Job Office, 1883.

Smith, William. Testimony, Temple Lot Case Testimonies, 186. US Eighth Circuit Court, 1892, MS 1160. CHL.

Sprague, William B. *Annals of the American Pulpit*. New York: Robert Carter & Brothers, 1858.

Staker, Mark Lyman. *Hearken, O Ye People: The Historical Setting for Joseph Smith's Ohio Revelations*. Salt Lake City: Greg Kofford Books, 2009.

Stanley, Harvey. Journal. In Jedediah M. Grant, Journal, 1836 April–1839 August, 9. CHL.

Stapley, Jonathan A. *The Power of Godliness: Mormon Liturgy and Cosmology*. New York: Oxford University Press, 2018.

Stevenson, Edward. Journal. CHL.

Stoddard Family Bible. Original in possession of Reid Moon, Provo, UT.

Talmage, Jeremy. "'Effusions of an Enthusiastic Brain', Joseph Smith's First Vision and the Limits of Experiential Religion." *BYU Studies* 59, no. 1 (2020): 25–48.

"Tells of Solomon Salisburys' Life." *Saints' Herald* 74, no. 5 (February 2, 1927): 136.

"Testimony of Katherine Salisbury." Sworn Affidavit, April 15, 1881. Copy of holograph, Community of Christ Library-Archives, Independence, MO. Also printed in *Saints' Herald* 28, no. 11 (June 1, 1881): 169.

"Testimony of Katherine Salisbury." *Saints' Herald* 28, no. 11 (June 1, 1881): 169.

"Terrible Tragedy." *Carthage Gazette* 16, no. 12 (August 28, 1880): 3.

"The Duff Trial Concluded, Verdict of the Jury." *Carthage Gazette* 16, no. 42 (March 26, 1881): 3.

"The Tragedy at Fountain Green Last Friday Night—Duff Held to Answer, Without Bail." *Quincy Daily Whig* 29 (August 27, 1880): 2.

Tracy, Nancy A. Reminiscences and Diary, 1896 May–1899 July. Typescript, 9. CHL.

Tucker, Pomeroy. *Origin, Rise, and Progress of Mormonism*. New York: D. Appleton, 1867.

Tullidge, Edward. *The Women of Mormondom*. New York: Tullidge & Crandall, 1877.

Ulrich, Laurel Thatcher. *A House Full of Females: Plural Marriage and Women's Rights in Early Mormonism, 1835–1870*. New York: Alfred A. Knopf, 2017.

Van Dine, Warren L. "Biographical Sketch of Catherine Smith Salisbury." Unpublished typescript, 1971. CHL.

Van Dine, Warren L. "Catharine Smith Salisbury." Unpublished typescript, paper presented at the Smith Family Reunion, 1973. CHL.

Van Dine, Warren L. "Catharine Smith Salisbury." Unpublished manuscript, 1972. Typescript copy in the Community of Christ Library-Archives, Independence, MO.

Van Dine, Warren L. "Information on the Smith and Salisbury Families, 1966–1975." Typescript from a taped interview conducted by Norma Hiles, Burnside, IL, 1975, 33. CHL.

Van Dine, Warren L. "Statement About His Salisbury Family." Unpublished typescript, ca. 1975, 7. Hancock County Historical Society, Carthage, IL.

Van Dine, Warren. "Statement by Warren L. Van Dine about certain points sometimes brought up in connection with Mrs. Salisbury after his [her] death." Unpublished typescript, n.d., n.p., Hancock County Historical Society, Carthage, IL.

Ventilla, Andrea. "'Death Had Lost All Terrors': Eliza Dana Gibbs (1813–1900)." In *Women of Faith in the Latter Days*. Vol. 1, *1775–1820*. Edited by Richard E. Turley Jr. and Brittany A. Chapman, 29–40. Salt Lake City: Deseret Book, 2011.

Vogel, Dan., ed. *Early Mormon Documents*. Vol. 2. Salt Lake City: Signature Books, 1998.

Vogel, Dan., ed. *Early Mormon Documents*. Vol. 3. Salt Lake City: Signature Books, 2000.

Walker, Kyle R. "'As Fire Shut Up in My Bones': Ebenezer Robinson, Don Carlos Smith, and the 1840 Edition of the Book of Mormon." *Journal of Mormon History* 36, no. 1 (Winter 2010): 1–40.

Walker, Kyle R. *The Joseph Sr. and Lucy Mack Smith Family: A Family Process Analysis of a Nineteenth-Century Household*. Provo, UT: BYU Studies, 2008.

Walker, Kyle R. "Katharine Smith Salisbury: Purveyor of Women's Values in the Early Restoration." *John Whitmer Historical Association Journal* 40, no. 2 (Fall/Winter 2020): 81–97.

Walker, Kyle R. "Katharine Smith Salisbury's Recollections of Joseph's Meeting with Moroni." *BYU Studies* 41, no. 3 (2002): 4–17.

Walker, Kyle R. "Looking After the First Family of Mormonism: LDS Church Leaders' Support of the Smiths after the Murders of Joseph and Hyrum." *John Whitmer Historical Association Journal* 32, no. 1 (Spring/Summer 2012): 17–32.

Walker, Kyle R. "Smith Family Recollections of Joseph Smith's First Vision." *Journal of Mormon History* 47, no. 2 (April 2021): 1–22.

Walker, Kyle R. *William B. Smith: In the Shadow of a Prophet*. Salt Lake City: Greg Kofford Books, 2015.

Walker, Kyle R. "William B. Smith and the 'The Josephites.'" *Journal of Mormon History* 40, no. 4 (Fall 2014): 82–103.

Waller, Altina L. *Feud: Hatfields, McCoys and Social Change in Appalachia, 1860–1900*. Chapel Hill: University of North Carolina Press, 1988.

Waite, Truman. Report, 1833, 1. Missionary Reports, 1831–1900. CHL.

West, Mary Ann [Covington Sheffield]. Testimony, in United States Testimony 1892, Court of Appeals (Eighth Circuit), 495–96, MS 1160. CHL.

"William B. Smith Experience and Testimony." *Saints' Herald* 30, no. 16 (June 16, 1883): 388.

"Wm. B. Smith's Last Statement" [John W. Peterson to Editor]. *Zion's Ensign* 5 (January 13, 1894): 6.

Williams, Nathan H. "Lucy Smith Millikin." In *United by Faith: The Joseph Sr. and Lucy Mack Smith Family*, edited by Kyle R. Walker, 399–431. American Fork, UT: Covenant Communications; Provo, UT: BYU Studies, 2006.

Woloch, Nancy. *Women and the American Experience: A Concise History*. 2nd ed. New York: McGraw, 1994.

Woodruff, Wilford. Wilford Woodruff to Brigham Young, October 9, 1844. CHL. https://wilfordwoodruffpapers.org.

Woodruff, Wilford. Wilford Woodruff to Brigham Young, November 16, 1844. CHL. https://wilfordwoodruffpapers.org.

Woods, Fred E. "Mormon Migration on Lake Erie and Through Fairport Harbor." *Inland Seas* 60 (Winter 2004): 291–305.

Wright, Kristine. "'We Baked a Lot of Bread': Reconceptualizing Mormon Women and Ritual Objects." In *Women and Mormonism: Historical and Contemporary Perspectives*, edited by Kate Holbrook and Matthew Bowman, 84–85. Salt Lake City: University of Utah Press, 2016).

Young, Brigham. Brigham Young to Katharine Salisbury, May 17, 1871. Brigham Young Office Files, box 8, Letterpress Copybook, vol. 12, 684–85. CHL.

Young, Brigham, and George A. Smith. Brigham Young and George A. Smith (Salt Lake City) to Daniel H. Wells, October 26, 1871. Brigham Young Office Files, box 73, folder 34. CHL.

Young, Brigham. In "Conference Minutes." *Times and Seasons* 6, no. 16 (November 1, 1845): 1014.

Young, Brigham. Office Files 1832–1878. Brigham Young Journals, 1832–1846. CHL.

Young, E. H. *A History of Round Prairie and Plymouth, 1831–1875*. Chicago: Geo. J. Titus, Book and Job Printer, 1876.

Youngreen, Buddy. "The Death Date of Lucy Mack Smith: 8 July 1775–14 May 1856." *BYU Studies* 12, no. 3 (Spring 1972): 318.

Index

L

Lambert, Joseph R., 205–6
Laub, George, 129n11
Lewis, Q. Walker, 218

M

Mack, Lovina, 90n46
Mack, Lovisa, 90n46
Mack, Solomon, 20, 26n14,
        90n46, 213n17
malaria, 157
Mansion House, 120, 124, 134,
        167, 183, 234n5
Marks, William, 134, 145n11
Masonry, 124–25
McCleary, William, 94, 97, 100,
        142, 143, 148n50
McCurley, Susan, 174, 178n30
McKiernan, James, 259
Methodism, 218
Methodist minister, and First
        Vision, 22, 27n23, 258
Miller, George, 99–100
Millikin, Arthur, 108, 140,
        166–67, 200–201, 206, 252
missionary work
    of Jenkins Salisbury, 71–75
    Katharine's contributions to,
        62–63, 71–72
Missouri. *See also* Alexandria,
        Missouri; Far West,
        Missouri; Jackson County,
        Missouri; Utica, Missouri
    church migration to, 95–98,
        101n12
    Salisburys move to, 154–58,
        162n22
modesty, 61–62, 68n16, 203,
        243–46
Morley, Isaac, 57

Mormon Hotel, 104–5, 107, 133,
        145n3
Moroni, 24, 248
mountain Saints. *See also* western
        migration
    financial support from, 186–94
    visits and correspondence with,
        181–86
Mull, Jack, 228–29
Murdock, John, 58, 174
music, 10–11, 84, 90n46

N

Nauvoo, Illinois
    anti-Mormon sentiment in,
        117–21, 127
    following martyrdom, 138–42
    Katharine's life in, 150–51
    Katharine's visits to, 108–12
    and martyrdom of Joseph and
        Hyrum, 124–25
    Salisburys move to, 134–37
    Salt Lake Valley Saints visit
        relatives in, 181–83
    William Smith and Jenkins
        Salisbury vie for property in,
        151–52
Nauvoo House, 112, 116n36,
        125–26
Nauvoo Legion, 110–12
Nauvoo's Female Relief Society,
        112, 116n38
Nauvoo Temple, 142–44
Niagara, 50–52
Norman, John, 195n4

O

Orr, Warren H., 261
Osterud, Nancy Grey, 173

P

Q

R

About the Author

KYLE R. WALKER is an administrator in the Counseling Center at Brigham Young University–Idaho, where he also teaches part-time in Religious Education. He received his PhD in marriage and family therapy from Brigham Young University. His doctoral dissertation focused on the family dynamics of the Joseph Sr. and Lucy Mack Smith family. He is the editor of *United by Faith: The Joseph Sr. and Lucy Mack Smith Family*. He is also the author of the award-winning biography *William B. Smith: In the Shadow of the Prophet*. He serves as president of the John Whitmer Historical Association.